D0936624

THE MESOZOIC ERA
AGE OF DINOSAURS

THE GEOLOGIC HISTORY OF EARTH

THE MESOZOIC ERA
AGE OF DINOSAURS

EDITED BY JOHN P. RAFFERTY, ASSOCIATE EDITOR, EARTH SCIENCES

IN ASSOCIATION WITH

Published in 2011 by Britannica Educational Publishing
(a trademark of Encyclopædia Britannica, Inc.)
in association with Rosen Educational Services, LLC
29 East 21st Street, New York, NY 10010.

Distributed exclusively by Rosen Educational Services.
For a listing of additional Britannica Educational Publishing titles, call toll free (800) 237-9932.

First Edition

Britannica Educational Publishing
Michael I. Levy: Executive Editor
J.E. Luebering: Senior Manager
Marilyn L. Barton: Senior Coordinator, Production Control
Steven Bosco: Director, Editorial Technologies
Lisa S. Braucher: Senior Producer and Data Editor
Yvette Charboneau: Senior Copy Editor
Kathy Nakamura: Manager, Media Acquisition
John P. Rafferty: Associate Editor, Earth Sciences

Rosen Educational Services
Hope Lourie Killcoyne: Senior Editor and Project Manager
Joanne Randolph: Editor
Nelson Sá: Art Director
Cindy Reiman: Photography Manager
Matthew Cauli: Designer, Cover Design
Introduction by David Nagle

Library of Congress Cataloging-in-Publication Data

The Mesozoic era: age of dinosaurs/edited by John P. Rafferty.
p. cm.—(The geologic history of Earth)
"In association with Britannica Educational Publishing, Rosen Educational Services."
Includes index.
ISBN 978-1-61530-103-4 (lib. bdg.)
1. Geology, Stratigraphic—Mesozoic. I. Rafferty, John P.
QE675.M367 2010
560'.176—dc22

2009043136

Manufactured in the United States of America

On the cover: *Tyrannosaurus rex*, "king of the tyrant lizards," reigned during the Jurassic period, which occurred midway through the Mesozoic era. This model of *T. rex* is part of the collection at the Museum of Natural History, Santa Barbara, Calif. *Charles C. Place/ Photographer's Choice/Getty Images*

p. 12 © www.istockphoto.com / Robert King; pp. 23, 102, 140, 209, 275, 277, 279 © www.istockphoto.com / Colton Stiffler

Contents

Introduction 12

Chapter 1: Overview of the Mesozoic Era 23
Mesozoic Geology 24
The Tethys Sea 27
Mesozoic Life 29
Life in the Oceans 30
Life on Land 31
Mass Extinction at the end of the Mesozoic 32
The Dinoaurs 34
The Search for Dinosaurs 36
Natural History of Dinosaurs 47
Dinosaur Classification 60
The End of the Dinosaurs 93

Chapter 2: The Triassic Period 102
The Triassic Environment 104
Paleogeography 104
Paleoclimate 106
Triassic Life 109
Mass Extinction of the Triassic 109
The Permian-Triassic Extinctions 110
The End-Triassic Extinctions 111
Invertebrates 112
Vertebrates 114
Fishes and Marine Reptiles 114
Terrestrial Reptiles and the First Mammals 115
From Reptiles to Dinosaurs 116

35

41

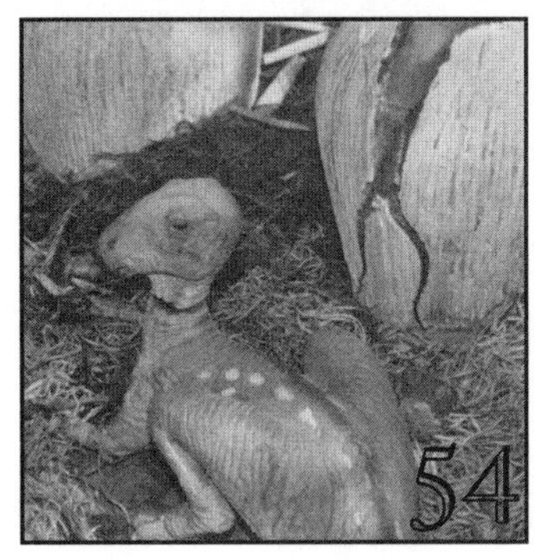
54

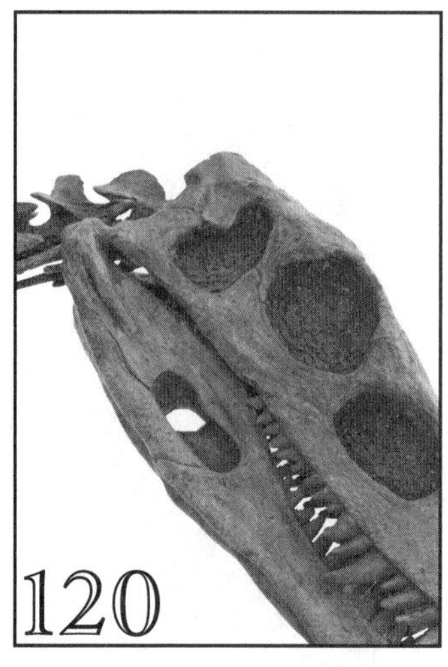

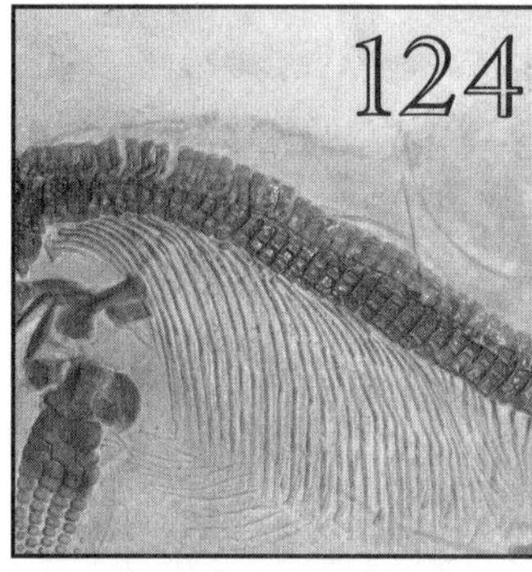

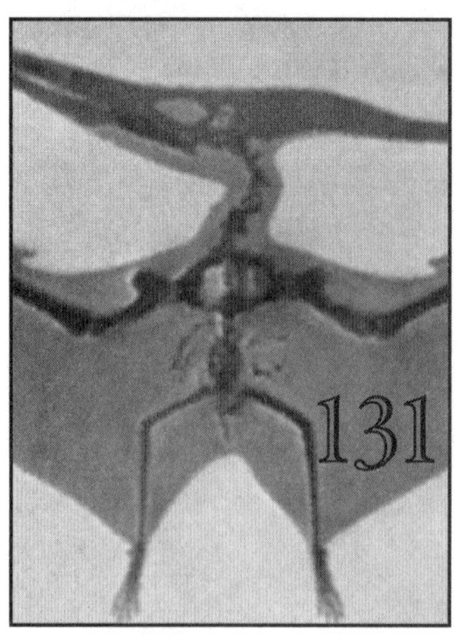

Flying Reptiles 117
Plants 117
Significant Dinosaurs of the Triassic Period 118
Coelophysis 119
Herrerasaurus 119
Plateosaurus 120
Other Significant Life-Forms of the Triassic Period 121
Bauria 121
Chondrosteiformes 122
Cynognathus 122
Daonella 123
Euparkeria 123
Ichthyosaurs 124
Leptolepis 126
Marasuchus 126
Myophoria 127
Nothosaurus 127
Phytosaurs 128
Pleuromeia 128
Pterosaurs 129
Tetractinella 131
Thrinaxodon 132
Tritylodon 132
Tropites 133
Voltzia 133
Triassic Geology 133
Continental Rifting in the Triassic 134
Mountain-Building Activity in the Triassic 134
The Stages of the Triassic Period 134
Induan Stage 135
Olenekian Stage 135
Anisian Stage 136

Ladinian Stage 136
Carnian Stage 137
Noria Stage 137
Rhaetian Stage 138

Chapter 3: The Jurassic Period 140
The Jurassic Environment 141
Paleogeography 141
Paleoclimate 144
Jurassic Life 145
Marine Life 146
Protists and Invertebrates 148
Vertebrates 150
Terrestrial Life 151
Invertebrates 151
Vertebrates 151
Plants 154
Significant Dinosaurs of the Jurassic Period 155
Allosaurus 155
Apatosaurus 156
Archaeopteryx 158
Brachiosaurs 159
Camarasaurus 160
Camptosaurus 161
Carnosaurs 162
Ceratosaurus 162
Compsognathus 163
Confuciusornis 163
Dimorphodon 165
Diplodocus 166
Docodon 167
Iguanodon 167
Ornitholestes 169
Pterodactyls 169
Rhamphorhynchus 170

138

153

159

Scutellosaurus 170
Stegosaurus 172
Steneosaurus 174
Tyrannosaurs 174
Yinlong 181
Other Significant Life-Forms of the Jurassic Period 182
Aucella 182
Cardioceras 182
Diarthrognathus 183
Gryphaea 183
Holectypus 184
Inoceramus 184
Multituberculate 184
Pliosaurs 185
Pycnodontiformes 186
Spalacotherium 187
Triconodon 187
Trigonia 187
Jurassic Geology 188
The Economic Significance of Jurassic Depoits 188
The Occurrence and Distribution of Jurassic Rocks 189
North America 190
Eurasia and Gondwana 192
Ocean Basins 194
The Major Subdivisions of the Jurassic System 195
The Stages of the Jurassic Period 195
Hettangian Stage 196
Sinemurian Stage 196
Pliensbachian Stage 197
Toarcian Stage 198
Aalenian Stage 198

Bajocian stage 199
Bathonian Stage 199
Callovian Stage 200
Oxfordian Stage 201
Kimmeridgian Stage 202
Tithonian Stage 203
Significant Jurassic Formations and Discoveries 204
Corpolites 204
The Morrison Formation 205
The Purbeck Beds 206
The Solnhofen Limestone 207

Chapter 4: The Cretaceous Period 209
The Cretaceous Environment 211
Paleogeographic 211
Paleoclimate 215
Cretaceous Life 216
Marine Life 217
Terrestrial Life 219
The End-Cretaceous Mass Extinction 220
Significant Dinosaurs of the Cretaceous Period 222
Albertosaurus 222
Anatosaurus 223
Ankylosaurus 224
Caudipteryx 225
Deinonychus 226
Dilong 227
Dromaeosaurs 229
Euoplocephalus 230
Hesperornis 231
Hypsilophodon 231

218

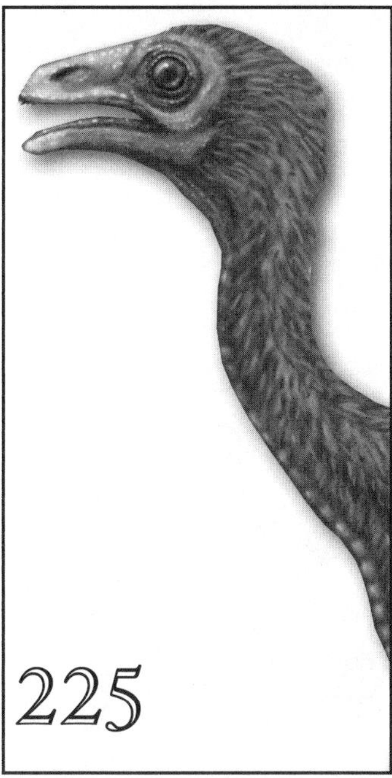
225

Ichthyornis 232
Lambeosaurus 233
Maiasaura 234
Nodosaurus 235
Ornithomimus 236
Oviraptor 236
Pachycephalosaurus 238
Pachyrhinosaurus 238
Pentaceratops 239
Protoceratops 240
Psittacosaurus 241
Spinosaurus 241
Struthiomimus 243
Therizinosaurs 243
Triceratops 244
Velociraptor 245
Other Significant Life-Forms of the Cretaceous Period 246
Anchura 246
Archelon 246
Baculites 246
Clidastes 247
Condylarthra 248
Dawn Redwood 249
Deltatheridium 250
Exogyra 250
Monopleura 251
Mosasaurs 251
Plesiosaus 252
Pteranodon 253
Scaphites 254
Turritellids 254
Cretaceous Geology 255
The Economic Significance of Cretaceous Deposits 255
The Occurence and Distribution of Cretaceous Rocks 256

Types of Cretaceous Rocks 258
The Correlation of Cretaceous Strata 260
The Major Subdivisions of the Cretaceous System 262
The Stages of the Cretaceous Period 264
Berriasian Stage 264
Valanginian Stage 265
Hauterivian Stage 265
Barremian Stage 266
Aptian Stage 267
Albian Stage 267
Cenomanian Stage 268
Turonian Stage 268
Coniacian Stage 269
Santonian Stage 269
Campanian Stage 270
Maastrichtian Stage 270
Significant Cretaceous Formations and Discoveries 271
The Hell Creek Formation 271
The Lance Formation 273
The Niobrara Limestone 273
Earth at the End of the Mesozoic 274

Glossary 275
For Further Reading 277
Index 279

INTRODUCTION

It was a time of huge "thunder lizards" roaming steamy fern jungles; of "mammal-reptiles" walking the land of Laurasia; of continental movements, mountain building, and massive volcanoes; and a time of the most horrific, earth-shattering extinctions that ever occurred on this planet. It was the middle times of what is called the Phanerozoic Eon, a geologic interval lasting almost a half billion years. It was the time of the dinosaurs...and much, much more. We call this time the Mesozoic Era.

Dinosaurs. The word itself immediately calls to mind large, predatory reptiles stalking the Earth. As young and old alike experience such visual, visceral responses to the word, it is difficult to believe that a mere 200 years ago, no one had any idea that these creatures had ever existed. This book takes readers back to that point of discovery and classification, when English anatomist Sir Richard Owen first attempted to classify strange bones found in his country. And discoveries continue. Readers will learn about new and contradictory ideas of what the dinosaurs were—and were not. Were they cold-blooded? Did they all vanish in an extinction? The answers might surprise you.

Dinosaurs were the dominant life form of the Mesozoic Era. Each period within that era had a different variety of these amazing creatures, but all can generally be assigned to one of two major groups: Saurischia ("lizard hips") or Ornithischia ("bird hips"). Those in the Saurischia group belong to either the Sauropodomorpha subgroup, which consist of herbivores, or the Theropoda subgroup, the carnivores. Examples of the first subgroup would include the Brontosaurs, an out-of-date term, but one which many people can identify as the massive long-necked leaf-eater of cartoons. These animals could reach 30 metres (100 feet) in length and weigh in excess of 70 metric tons. Probably the most recognizable theropod would be the mighty *Tyrannosaurus rex*, 15 metres (50 feet) and 5 metric tons of mean, hungry lizard machine. Ornithischia include such dinosaurs as the *Stegosaurus* and *Triceratops*, both herbivores and, again, immediately recognizable.

Readers will also learn about the flora and geology of this era. As one might imagine, many events can take place over the course of 185 million years; having the luxury of peering back and reading a condensed yet thorough distillation of this massive period of time in easily decipherable segments provides readers the opportunity to review the whole era in sequences and overlays that make sense to the modern mind.

Mesozoic is a Greek term meaning "Middle Life," and is so-called due to the fact that it comes after the Paleozoic Era ("Old" or "Ancient Life") and before the Cenozoic Era ("New" or "Recent Life"), all three comprising the Phanerozoic Eon. It was just before the Mesozoic Era that the Earth's greatest mass extinction ever—the Permian extinction—occurred. At that time, approximately 251 million years ago, over 90 percent of marine invertebrates and 70 percent of land vertebrates inexplicably disappeared. This life change resulted in a great diversification of vertebrate life, which, along with tremendous geologic changes, caused the start of ecosystems on Earth that resembled those of modern times.

So, what was it like at the start of the Mesozoic Era? First, we have to realize that in speaking of these times and circumstances, a few hundred thousand years seems to pass in the blink of an eye. Knowing that many important changes can actually occur such a large timeframe, scientists subdivide larger time periods into smaller sequences so as to keep a perspective of the larger time interval while focusing on more specific time developments. In the case of the Mesozoic Era, it is further split into three periods: the Triassic (251 million–200 million years ago), the Jurassic (200 million–145 million years ago), and the Cretaceous (145 million–65.5 million years ago). The book will further refine these periods (e.g., upper, middle, lower, and so on), but we will focus on the bigger picture for now.

The Triassic Period begins with the Earth appearing far different than it does today. If one could look at the ancient world from outer space, the surface of our planet would appear to be all blue liquid except for one huge land mass. We call this mass Pangea, and as we fast-forward toward the Jurassic period, we see that the land starts to break up from the middle along the equator to form two separate continents: Laurasia in the north and Gondwana in the south. This continental rift was caused by numerous geologic forces, most importantly the shifting of subsurface rock plates. The expanding water mass that would eventually separated these continents from one another was the Tethys Sea, a massive salt-water ocean that flowed from east to west.

Plant life on Pangea was dominated by seed ferns at lower levels of the forest, gymnosperms (with outer seeds) at middle levels, and conifers higher up. There forests were different than present-day forest ecosystems. The warm, relatively dry climate did not allow for much growth. This would change during the latter part of the Triassic period.

And what was swimming—or crawling—around in the ocean during the Triassic? As previously mentioned, most marine invertebrates became extinct with the Permian extinction: Ammonoids, early mollusk predecessors of octopus and squid, had almost died out in the early Triassic, but were revitalized much later on. Many species of fishes faded away after the huge extinction, replaced by others that thrived and filled the sea, among them shellfish-eating hybodont sharks and various varieties of ray-finned fishes. Marine reptiles were represented by nothosaurs

Geologic Time Scale

Cenozoic Era
Mesozoic Era
Paleozoic Era
present
1,000[1]
2,000[1]
3,000[1]
4,000[1]
4,600[1]
Precambrian time

Eonothem/ Eon	Erathem/ Era	System/ Period	Series/ Epoch	Stage/ Age	mya[1]
Phanerozoic	Cenozoic	Quaternary	Holocene		0.0117
			Pleistocene	Tarantian	0.126
				"Ionian"	0.781
				Calabrian	1.806
				Gelasian	2.588
		Neogene	Pliocene	Piacenzian	3.600
				Zanclean	5.332
			Miocene	Messinian	7.246
				Tortonian	11.608
				Serravallian	13.82
				Langhian	15.97
				Burdigalian	20.43
				Aquitanian	23.03
		Paleogene	Oligocene	Chattian	28.4 ± 0.1
				Rupelian	33.9 ± 0.1
			Eocene	Priabonian	37.2 ± 0.1
				Bartonian	40.4 ± 0.2
				Lutetian	48.6 ± 0.2
				Ypresian	55.8 ± 0.2
			Paleocene	Thanetian	58.7 ± 0.2
				Selandian	~61.1
				Danian	65.5 ± 0.3
	Mesozoic	Cretaceous	Upper	Maastrichtian	70.6 ± 0.6
				Campanian	83.5 ± 0.7
				Santonian	85.8 ± 0.7
				Coniacian	~88.6
				Turonian	93.6 ± 0.8
				Cenomanian	99.6 ± 0.9
			Lower	Albian	112.0 ± 1.0
				Aptian	125.0 ± 1.0
				Barremian	130.0 ± 1.5
				Hauterivian	~133.9
				Valanginian	140.2 ± 3.0
				Berriasian	145.5 ± 4.0

Eonothem/ Eon	Erathem/ Era	System/ Period	Series/ Epoch	Stage/ Age	mya[1]
					145.5 ± 4.0
Phanerozoic	Mesozoic	Jurassic	Upper	Tithonian	150.8 ± 4.0
				Kimmeridgian	~155.6
				Oxfordian	161.2 ± 4.0
			Middle	Callovian	164.7 ± 4.0
				Bathonian	167.7 ± 3.5
				Bajocian	171.6 ± 3.0
				Aalenian	175.6 ± 2.0
			Lower	Toarcian	183.0 ± 1.5
				Pliensbachian	189.6 ± 1.5
				Sinemurian	196.5 ± 1.0
				Hettangian	199.6 ± 0.6
		Triassic	Upper	Rhaetian	203.6 ± 1.5
				Norian	216.5 ± 2.0
				Carnian	~228.7
			Middle	Ladinian	237.0 ± 2.0
				Anisian	~245.9
			Lower	Olenekian	~249.5
				Induan	251.0 ± 0.4
	Paleozoic	Permian	Lopingian	Changhsingian	253.8 ± 0.7
				Wuchiapingian	260.4 ± 0.7
			Guadalupian	Capitanian	265.8 ± 0.7
				Wordian	268.0 ± 0.7
				Roadian	270.6 ± 0.7
			Cisuralian	Kungurian	275.6 ± 0.7
				Artinskian	284.4 ± 0.7
				Sakmarian	294.6 ± 0.8
				Asselian	299.0 ± 0.8
		Carboniferous — Pennsylvanian[2]	Upper	Gzhelian	303.4 ± 0.9
				Kasimovian	307.2 ± 1.0
			Middle	Moscovian	311.7 ± 1.1
			Lower	Bashkirian	318.1 ± 1.3
		Carboniferous — Mississippian[2]	Upper	Serpukhovian	328.3 ± 1.6
			Middle	Visean	345.3 ± 2.1
			Lower	Tournaisian	359.2 ± 2.5

[1] Millions of years ago.
[2] Both the Mississippian and Pennsylvanian time units are formally designated as sub-periods within the Carboniferous Period.
[3] Several Cambrian unit age boundaries are informal and are awaiting ratified definitions.

Encyclopædia Britannica, Inc. *Source*: International Commission on Stratigraphy (ICS)

Eonothem/ Eon	Erathem/ Era	System/ Period	Series/ Epoch	Stage/ Age	mya[1]
Phanerozoic	Paleozoic	Devonian	Upper	Famennian	359.2 ± 2.5
				Frasnian	374.5 ± 2.6
			Middle	Givetian	385.3 ± 2.6
				Eifelian	391.8 ± 2.7
			Lower	Emsian	397.5 ± 2.7
				Pragian	407.0 ± 2.8
				Lochkovian	411.2 ± 2.8
		Silurian	Pridoli		416.0 ± 2.8
			Ludlow	Ludfordian	418.7 ± 2.7
				Gorstian	421.3 ± 2.6
			Wenlock	Homerian	422.9 ± 2.5
				Sheinwoodian	426.2 ± 2.4
			Llandovery	Telychian	428.2 ± 2.3
				Aeronian	436.0 ± 1.9
				Rhuddanian	439.0 ± 1.8
		Ordovician	Upper	Hirnantian	443.7 ± 1.5
				Katian	445.6 ± 1.5
				Sandbian	455.8 ± 1.6
			Middle	Darriwilian	460.9 ± 1.6
				Dapingian	468.1 ± 1.6
			Lower	Floian	471.8 ± 1.6
				Tremadocian	478.6 ± 1.7
		Cambrian[3]	Furongian	Stage 10	488.3 ± 1.7
				Stage 9	~492.0
				Paibian	~496.0
			Series 3	Guzhangian	~499.0
				Drumian	~503.0
				Stage 5	~506.5
			Series 2	Stage 4	~510.0
				Stage 3	~515.0
			Terreneuvian	Stage 2	~521.0
				Fortunian	~528.0
					542.0 ± 1.0

	Eonothem/ Eon	Erathem/ Era	System/ Period	mya[1]
Precambrian	Proterozoic	Neoproterozoic	Ediacaran	542
			Cryogenian	~635
			Tonian	850
		Mesoproterozoic	Stenian	1,000
			Ectasian	1,200
			Calymmian	1,400
		Paleoproterozoic	Statherian	1,600
			Orosirian	1,800
			Rhyacian	2,050
			Siderian	2,300
	Archean	Neoarchean		2,500
		Mesoarchean		2,800
		Paleoarchean		3,200
		Eoarchean		3,600
	Hadean (informal)			4,000
				4,600

Published with permission from the International Commission on Stratigraphy (ICS). International chronostratigraphic units, ranks, names, and formal status are approved by the ICS and ratified by the International Union of Geological Sciences (IUGS).
Source: 2009 International Stratigraphic Chart produced by the ICS.

(from which would come the plesiosaurs in the Jurassic) as well as ichthyosaurs, animals that resembled streamlined dolphins and may have preyed upon early squid-like creatures called belemnites.

Pangea was home to the earliest ancestors of today's lizards, turtles, and crocodiles. Although very small, mammal-like creatures existed during this time, they would never dominate any area. Such mammal-like creatures would eventually fade away as more efficient predators consistently won the best food and shelter. Thecodonts, ancestors of dinosaurs and crocodiles, were represented by Lagosuchus, small, swift bipedal lizards; the small gliding *Icarosaurus*; and the somewhat larger *Sharovipteryx*, the first true pterosaur (flying lizard). All of these animals would become extinct by the latter stages of the Triassic, as their niches were assumed by the larger pterosaurs and earliest dinosaurs.

As for what types of dinosaurs were around in the Triassic period, generally, they were smaller and lighter than what we might normally assume a dinosaur should be. *Coelophysis* and Herrerasaurus are two examples of such dinosaurs, approximately 2 metres (6.5 feet), 20 kg (45 pounds) and 3 metres (10 feet), 181 kg (400 pounds), respectively. The largest dinosaur during the Triassic period was probably *Plateosaurus*; at about 8 metres (26 feet) long; it was actually larger than many dinosaurs that would follow, and it was the first real large herbivorous dinosaur.

It was during the Triassic period that *Cynognathus*, a wolf-sized predator that was a forerunner to present-day mammals, appeared. *Leptolepis*, an ancient herring type of fish, generally assumed to be the progenitor of almost all modern-day fishes, also made its entrance during this period.

The Jurassic Period was as geologically active as the Triassic was tame. It was during this period that increased plate tectonic movement caused Pangea to split apart, creating massive mountains and producing extreme volcanic activity. As continents collided, the upthrusts were responsible for creating what would become the Rocky mountain range, the Andes mountain range, and a large assortment of smaller mountain groupings. Geologists can ascertain much of what occurred by comparing formations of rock from different places and seeing rocks and fossils between them. It is this type of research methodology that helps us understand that the modern-day continent of Africa was once joined with modern-day South America and that huge igneous and metamorphic rock formations found from Alaska to Baja, California were the result of one common event.

From the middle to the late Jurassic Period both sea and air temperatures increased, most likely the result of increased volcanic activity and a moving seafloor, which in turn released large amounts of carbon dioxide (CO_2). Being a "greenhouse gas," increased CO_2 concentrations would have contributed to higher overall temperatures around the globe and consequently to more tropical, sluggish waters and decreased wind activity.

And what of marine life at this time? In these warm oceans there had occurred a major extinction at the beginning of the Jurassic, and a number of smaller extinction events throughout the first half of the period. Great diversification of marine species, from giant to microscopic, resulted. In addition, different types of plankton emerged that would form the deep-sea sediments we find today, and the largest bony fish that ever existed, *Leedsichthys*, swam in the same waters as some of the largest pliosaurs (carnivorous reptiles) ever recorded. Also, the first true lobsters and crabs appeared, and the mollusks and shrimp were varied and plentiful. Jurassic seas could have provided a number of huge seafood dinners—and they did. The impact of extensive predatory activity led to the "Mesozoic Marine Revolution," a continual battle between prey and predators that led to increased diversification of marine animals and their behaviours.

On land the story was much the. The most abundant terrestrial life forms were insects, including dragonflies, beetles, flies, ants and bees, the last providing an intriguing clue as to when the first flowering plants appeared on Earth. Dinosaurs multiplied and flourished; it was during the early Jurassic that Sauropods first appeared, reaching their peak size, number, and diversity during the later Jurassic. If we were able to observe the dinosaur inhabitants of the later Jurassic period, what we would see? *Allosaurus*, a relatively large carnivore at 11 metres (35 feet) and nearly 2 metric tons might be stealthily walking upright, sneaking toward a spike-tailed, armour-plated *Stegosaurus* munching on ferns, as a *Steneosaurus*, an extinct crocodilian, swam by the shore.

There were numerous plant-eaters and meat-eaters, the most impressive and probably most recognized being the *Tyrannosaurus rex*. Topping out at about 6.5 metres (21 feet) tall and weighing up to 7,000 kg (about 9,000 to 15,000 pounds), these dinosaurs were voracious predators, proven by study of both bite marks shown on various prey animals and coprolite (fossilized feces) of the giant predator. The first bird, *Archaeopteryx*, also dates back to the late Jurassic.

The last period of the Mesozoic Era is the Cretaceous Period, spanning a total of 80 million years. It was by the end of this period that most of Pangea had evolved into present-daycontinents. (The exceptions were India, which was surrounded by ocean, and Australia, which was still connected to Antarctica.) The Cretaceous climate was warmer than today, with the polar regions covered with forest rather than ice. Both ocean circulation and wind activity were depressed during the Cretaceous due to this warm climate.

This was the period when different groups of plants and animals developed modern characteristics that were shaped before the mass extinction that marks the end of this period. Almost all flowering plants and placental mammals appeared during the Cretaceous, and many other groups (plankton, clams, snails, snakes, lizards, fishes) had developed into modern varieties by this time. Pterosaurs (flying reptiles) were abundant in the skies, and dinosaurs, including those with feathers, horns, or armour, evolved throughout the period. Albertosaurs, slightly smaller versions of, and probable ancestors to, T. *rex,* were common, as were *Triceratops*, a type of large plant-eater with a thick bony collar and three horns for defence. Triceratops was most likely one of the last dinosaurs to have evolved, with fossils dating only to the last 5 million years of this period.

Numerous plant-eaters (*Pentaceratops, Psittacosaurus*, Pachyrhinosaurus, Maiasaura, etc.) existed during the Cretaceous, as did almost as many meat-eaters (*Dromaeosaurus*, Caudipteryx, *Deinonychus, Velociraptor*), including the largest carnivorous dinosaur discovered to date: Spinosaurus, maxing out at 59 feet and 22 tons. Its skull alone was nearly 1.75 metres (6 feet) long. Other significant life forms included mammals related to modern rats and ungulates (e.g., deer).

The term "Cretaceous" comes from the French word "chalk," and was used to describe this period due to its massive chalk deposits created from certain plankton types. Chalk was far from the most significant geologic feature, however. It was during the Cretaceous that the majority of the world's petroleum and coal deposits were formed, and massive ore deposits containing gold, silver, copper, and many more metals were formed during igneous activity also.

The Cretaceous Period—and the Mesozoic Era—came to a sudden end roughly 65.5 million years ago. Many scientists contend that this transition is somehow related to the strike of a 9.5 km (6-mile) diameter asteroid in what is today called the Yucatan Peninsula of Mexico Although it has been discovered that numerous organisms had gone extinct some millions of years prior to the impact, the asteroid may have been responsible for the disappearance of a massive number of species, either directly or through attrition because of colder temperatures caused by huge ash plumes. As the Cretaceous period ended, the Cenozoic or modern era began, a time that has taken the remnant flora and fauna of the Cretaceous—living groups that were already present at the Cretaceous end—and further transformed the Earth and its organisms into what we see about us today.

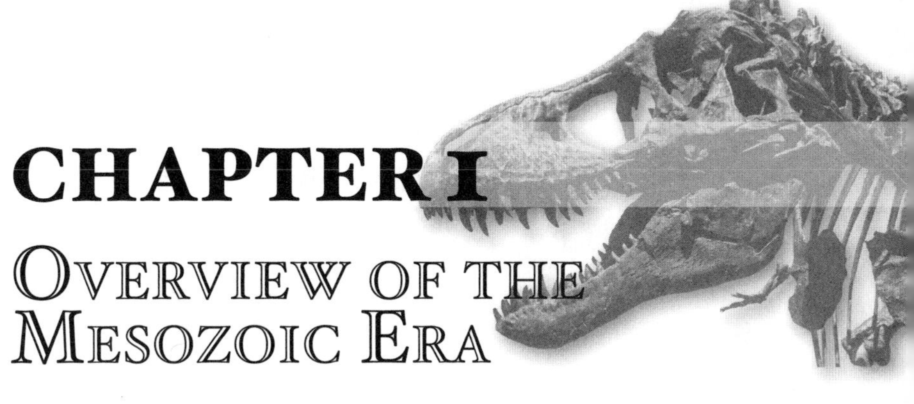

CHAPTER 1

Overview of the Mesozoic Era

Some of the most popular exhibits in museums are those that display animals of the Mesozoic Era. Undeniably, the most prominent animals of this time were a group of large reptiles called dinosaurs. For over 100 years, dinosaur fossils and scientific interpretations of how they lived have captured the imagination of the public. Although the Mesozoic is best known as the time of the dinosaurs, it is also the time in which the ancestors of several plant and animal groups that exist today first appeared.

The Mesozoic is the second of the Earth's three major geologic eras of Phanerozoic time, an interval spanning the most recent 542 million years. Its name is derived from the Greek term for "middle life." The Mesozoic Era began 251 million years ago, following the Paleozoic Era, and ended 65.5 million years ago, at the dawn of the Cenozoic Era. The major divisions of the Mesozoic Era are, from oldest to youngest, the Triassic Period, the Jurassic Period, and the Cretaceous Period.

The Earth's climate during the Mesozoic Era was generally warm, and there was less difference in temperature between equatorial and polar latitudes than there is today. The Mesozoic was a time of geologic and biological transition. During this era the continents began to move into their present-day configurations. A distinct modernization of life-forms occurred, partly because of the demise of many earlier types of organisms. Three of the five largest mass extinctions in Earth history are associated with the Mesozoic. A mass extinction occurred at the boundary between the Mesozoic and the preceding Paleozoic; another occurred within the Mesozoic at the end of the Triassic Period; and a third occurred at the boundary between the Mesozoic and subsequent Cenozoic, resulting in the demise of the dinosaurs.

MESOZOIC GEOLOGY

At the outset of the Mesozoic, all of the Earth's continents were joined together into the supercontinent of Pangea. By the close of the era, Pangea had fragmented into multiple landmasses. The fragmentation began with continental rifting during the Late Triassic. This separated Pangea into the continents of Laurasia and Gondwana. By the Middle Jurassic these landmasses had begun further fragmentation. At that time much of Pangea lay between 60° N and 60° S, and at the Equator the widening Tethys Sea cut between Gondwana and Laurasia. When rifting had sufficiently progressed, oceanic spreading centres formed between the landmasses. During the Middle Jurassic, North America began pulling apart from Eurasia and Gondwana. By the Late Jurassic, Africa had started to split off from South America, and Australia and Antarctica had separated from India. Near the close of the Cretaceous, Madagascar separated from Africa, and South America drifted northwestward.

As the continents rifted and ruptured, thick sequences of marine sediments accumulated in large linear troughs along their margins. Ocean basin deposits of Jurassic age are found today in the circum-Pacific region, along the coasts of eastern North America and the Gulf of Mexico, and on the margins of Eurasia and Gondwana (that is, along the northern and southern boundaries of the Tethys Sea).

Major mountain building (orogeny) began on the western margins of both North and South America and between the separating fragments of Gondwana. For example, the northwesterly movement of North America resulted in a collision of the western edge of the North American continental plate with a complex of island arcs during the Late Jurassic. So-called exotic terranes, geologic fragments that differ markedly in stratigraphy, paleomagnetism, and paleontology from adjoining continental crust, were accreted to the margin of the North American plate. As thrusting occurred in an eastward direction, huge granitic batholiths formed in what is now the Sierra Nevada range along the California-Nevada border. Other notable episodes of mountain building during the Mesozoic include the Sevier and Laramide orogenies, which took place in western North America during Cretaceous time. These events created the Rocky Mountains.

Mesozoic rocks are widely distributed, appearing in various parts of the world. A large percentage of these rocks are sedimentary. At various times during the Mesozoic, shallow seas invaded continental interiors and then drained away. During Middle Triassic time, a marine incursion—the Muschelkalk Sea—covered the continental interior of Europe. Seas again transgressed upon the continents between the Early and Late Jurassic and in the Early Cretaceous, leaving extensive beds of sandstone, ironstone, clays, and limestone. A last major transgression of marine waters flooded large segments of all the continents later in the Cretaceous. These sharp rises in sea level and resultant worldwide flooding are thought to have had two causes. The first was warm global temperatures, which prevented large volumes of water from being sequestered on land in the form of ice sheets. The second was related to accelerated seafloor spreading; the attendant enlargement of ocean ridges displaced enormous amounts of ocean water onto the landmasses. Marine transgression was so extensive that in North America, for example, a seaway spread all the way from the Arctic to the Gulf of Mexico in the Cretaceous Period. Widespread deposition of chalk, clay, black shales, and marl occurred. In parts of North America, lake and river sediments rich in dinosaur fossils were deposited alongside marine sediments.

A substantial amount of igneous rock also formed during the Mesozoic. The orogenies of the Jurassic and Cretaceous periods involved volcanism and plutonic intrusion such as occurred during the emplacement of granites and andesites in the Andes of South America during the Late Jurassic. Two of the largest volcanic events in Earth's history occurred during the Mesozoic. The Central Atlantic Magmatic Province, a huge volume of basalt, was created at the end of the Triassic during the initial rifting of Pangea. The surface area of this igneous province originally covered more than 7 million square km (about 3 million square miles), and its rocks can be found today from Brazil to France. Despite such a massive volume of basaltic material extruded, volcanic activity was probably short-lived, spanning only a few million year. At the end of the Cretaceous, another igneous province, the flood basalts of the Deccan Traps, formed on what is now the Indian subcontinent. Some scientists have suggested that both of these large igneous events may have injected significant amounts of carbon dioxide and aerosols into the atmosphere, triggering a change in global climate. The timing of these volcanic events appears to overlap the Triassic-Jurassic and Cretaceous-Tertiary (or Cretaceous-Paleogene) mass extinctions, and they may have played a role in them.

THE TETHYS SEA

The supercontinents of Laurasia in the north and Gondwana in the south were separated from one another by a large tropical body of salt water called the Tethys Sea during much of the Mesozoic Era. Laurasia consisted of what are now North America and the portion of Eurasia north of the Alpine-Himalayan mountain ranges, while Gondwana consisted of present-day South America, Africa, peninsular India, Australia, Antarctica, and those Eurasian regions south of the Alpine-Himalayan chain. These mountains were created by continental collisions that eventually eliminated the sea. Tethys was named in 1893, by the Austrian geologist Eduard Suess, after the sister and consort of Oceanus, the ancient Greek god of the ocean.

At least two Tethyan seas successively occupied the area between Laurasia and Gondwana during the Mesozoic Era. The first, called the Paleo (Old) Tethys Sea, was created when all landmasses converged to form the supercontinent of Pangea about 320 million years ago, late in the Paleozoic Era. During the Permian and Triassic periods (approximately 300 to 200 million years ago), Paleo Tethys formed an eastward-opening oceanic embayment of Pangea in what is now the Mediterranean region. This ocean was eliminated when a strip of continental material (known as the Cimmerian continent) detached from northern Gondwana and rotated northward, eventually colliding with the southern margin of Laurasia during the Early Jurassic Epoch (some 176 million years ago). Evidence of the Paleo Tethys Sea is preserved in marine sediments now incorporated into mountain ranges that stretch from northern Turkey through Transcaucasia (the Caucasus and the Pamirs), northern Iran and Afghanistan, northern Tibet (Kunlun Mountains), and China and Indochina.

The Neo (New, or Younger) Tethys Sea, commonly referred to simply as Tethys or the Tethys Sea, began forming in the wake of the rotating Cimmerian continent during the earliest part of the Mesozoic Era. During the Jurassic the breakup of Pangea into Laurasia to the north and Gondwana to the south resulted in a gradual opening of Tethys into a dominant marine seaway of the Mesozoic. A large volume of warm water flowed westward between the continents and connected the major oceans, most likely playing a large role in the Earth's heat transport and climate control. During times of major increases in sea level, the Tethyan seaway expanded and merged with seaways that flowed to the north, as indicated by fossil evidence of mixed Tethyan tropical faunas and more-temperate northern faunas.

Tethyan deposits can be found in North America and Eurasia (especially in the Alpine and Himalayan regions) and in southern Asia (Myanmar and Indonesia). Limestones are a dominant sedimentary facies of Tethys. These sediments are often very rich in fossils, indicating an abundant and diverse tropical marine fauna. Reefs are common within Tethyan deposits, including ones constructed by rudist bivalves. Turbidites (deposits created by a gravity-driven flow of fluidized sediments), shales, and siliciclastic rocks (sedimentary rocks made of fragments with a high silica content) can also be found in Tethyan deposits.

Initial compressional forces resulting from the subduction of Africa under Europe caused block faulting (elevation of isolated rock masses relative to adjacent ones) during the Jurassic. By Cretaceous time the collision between the African and Eurasian plates resulted in more deformation of the Tethyan deposits, as shown by the contemporaneous generation of many faults and rock folds. Volcanic activity was common, and some oceanic volcanoes grew tall enough for their peaks to emerge above the surface of the sea, creating new islands. The presence of ophiolite sequences—packages of deep-sea sediments and sections of ocean crust thrust up onto continental crust—is further evidence that compressional forces in this area became intense. East of the Alpine region, the Indian Plate was moving northward approaching the Asian Plate. Tethys closed during the Cenozoic Era about 50 million years ago when continental fragments of Gondwana—India, Arabia, and Apulia (consisting of parts of Italy, the Balkan states, Greece, and Turkey)—finally collided with the rest of Eurasia. The result was the creation of the modern Alpine-Himalayan ranges, which extend from Spain (the Pyrenees) and northwest Africa (the Atlas) along the northern margin of the Mediterranean Sea (the Alps and Carpathians) into southern Asia (the Himalayas) and then to Indonesia. Remnants of the Tethys Sea remain today as the Mediterranean, Black, Caspian, and Aral seas.

The final closure of the Tethys Sea so severely defaced evidence of earlier closures that the prior existence of the Paleo Tethys Sea was not generally recognized until the 1980s. An important effect of the evolution of the Tethys Sea was the formation of the giant petroleum basins of North Africa and the Middle East, first by providing basins in which organic material could accumulate and then by providing structural and thermal conditions that allowed hydrocarbons to mature.

MESOZOIC LIFE

Amidst this geologic shifting, plants and animals also experienced major changes. The fauna and flora of the

Mesozoic were distinctly different from those of the Paleozoic. The Permian extinction, the largest mass extinction in Earth history, occurred at the boundary of the two eras, and some 90 percent of all marine invertebrate species and 70 percent of terrestrial vertebrate genera disappeared. At the start of the Mesozoic, the remaining biota began a prolonged recovery of diversity and total population numbers, and ecosystems began to resemble those of modern days. Vertebrates, less severely affected by the extinction than invertebrates, diversified progressively throughout the Triassic. The Triassic terrestrial environment was dominated by the therapsids, sometimes referred to as "mammal-like reptiles," and the thecodonts, ancestors of dinosaurs and crocodiles, both of which appeared during the Late Triassic. The first true mammals, which were small, shrewlike omnivores, also appeared in the Late Triassic, as did the lizards, turtles, and flying pterosaurs. In the oceans, mollusks—including ammonites, bivalves, and gastropods—became a dominant group. Fishes, sharks, and marine reptiles such as plesiosaurs, nothosaurs, and ichthyosaurs also swam the Mesozoic seas.

Another major extinction event struck at the close of the Triassic, one that wiped out as much as 20 percent of marine families and many terrestrial vertebrates, including therapsids. The cause of this mass extinction is not yet known but may be related to climatic and oceanographic changes. In all, 35 percent of the existing animal groups suffered extinction.

Life in the Oceans

In the oceans the ammonites and brachiopods recovered from the Late Triassic crisis, thriving in the warm continental seas. Ammonites rapidly became very common invertebrates in the marine realm and are now important index fossils for worldwide correlation of Jurassic rock strata. Many other animal forms, including mollusks (notably the bivalves), sharks, and bony fishes, flourished during the Jurassic. During the Jurassic and Cretaceous, the ecology of marine ecosystems began to change, as shown by a rapid increase in diversity of marine organisms. It is believed that increasing predation pressures caused many marine organisms to develop better defenses and burrow more deeply into the seafloor. In response, predators also evolved more-effective ways to catch their prey. These changes are so significant that they are called the "Mesozoic Marine Revolution."

Life on Land

The dominant terrestrial vertebrates were dinosaurs, which exhibited great diversity during the Jurassic and Cretaceous. Birds are believed to have evolved from dinosaur ancestors during the Late Jurassic. Ancestors of living vertebrates, such as frogs, toads, and salamanders, appeared on land along with the two important modern mammal groups, the placentals and the marsupials. Plant life also exhibited a gradual change toward more-modern forms during the course of the Mesozoic. Whereas seed ferns had predominated in the Triassic, forests of palmlike gymnosperms known as cycads and conifers proliferated under the tropical and temperate conditions that prevailed during the Jurassic. The first flowering plants, or angiosperms, had appeared by the Cretaceous. They radiated rapidly and supplanted many of the primitive plant groups to become the dominant form of vegetation by the end of the Mesozoic.

Mass Extinction at the End of the Mesozoic

The Mesozoic closed with an extinction event that devastated many forms of life. In the oceans all the ammonites, reef-building rudist bivalves, and marine reptiles died off, as did 90 percent of the coccolithophores (single-celled plantlike plankton) and foraminifera (single-celled

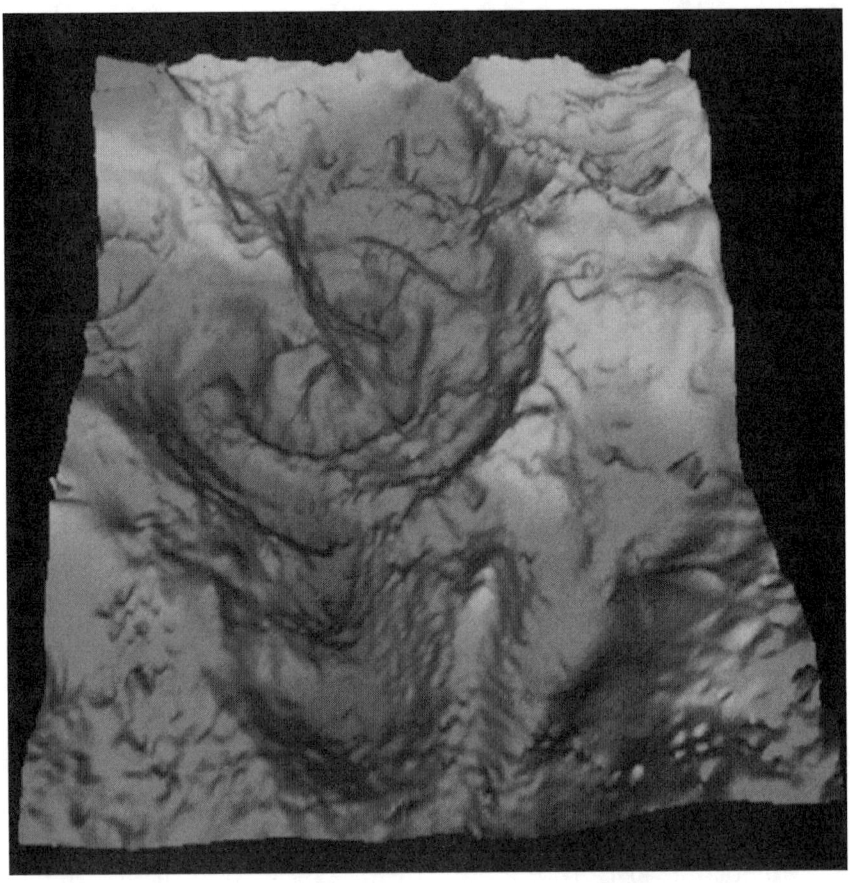

Chicxulub crater on the northern coast of the Yucatán Peninsuala in Mexico, image synthesized from gravity and magnetic-field data. The buried structure measures at least 180m (6 miles). The coastline bisects across the crater almost horizontally through its centre. V.L. Sharpton, University of Alaska, Fairbanks; NASA

animal-like plankton). On land the overwhelming majority of dinosaurs and flying reptiles became extinct. The Late Cretaceous extinctions have been variously attributed to such phenomena as global tectonics, draining of the continental seas, northward migration of the continents into different and much cooler climatic zones, intensified volcanic activity, and a catastrophic meteorite or asteroid impact. The Cretaceous extinction may very well have had multiple causes. As the landmasses were uplifted by plate tectonism and migrated poleward, the climate of the Late Cretaceous began to deteriorate In fact, some of the extinctions were not sudden but rather spanned millions of years, suggesting that a gradual decline of some organisms had already begun before the end of the Cretaceous. However, strong evidence supports the contention that a large-scale impact played a significant role in the mass extinctions at the end of the Mesozoic, including the sudden disappearance of many groups (such as ammonite and microfossil species), the presence of geochemical and mineralogical signatures that most likely came from extraterrestrial sources, and the discovery of the Chicxulub crater in the Yucatán Peninsula. It is believed that an asteroid with a diameter of about 10 km (6 miles) hit the Earth and caused wildfires, acid rain, months of darkness (because of the large amount of ash injected into the atmosphere), and cold temperatures (caused by increased reflection of solar energy back into space by airborne particles). An intense warming may have followed, heat being trapped by atmospheric aerosols. Whatever the cause, this major mass extinction marks the end of the Mesozoic Era. The end of the dinosaurs (except birds) and many other forms of life allowed the development of modern biota in the Cenozoic Era.

The Dinosaurs

Before the demise of nearly all of their kind at the end of the Cretaceous Period some 66 million years ago, dinosaurs, the common name given to a group of often very large reptiles, were the dominant players in terrestrial environments. They first appeared in the Late Triassic Period about 215 million years ago and thrived worldwide for some 150 million years. Historically, it was thought that all dinosaurs died out at the end of the Cretaceous. However, many lines of evidence now show that one lineage evolved into birds about 150 million years ago.

The name dinosaur comes from the Greek words *deinos* ("terrible" or "fearfully great") and *sauros* ("reptile" or "lizard"). The English anatomist Richard Owen proposed the formal term *Dinosauria* in 1842 to include three giant extinct animals (*Megalosaurus*, *Iguanodon*, and *Hylaeosaurus*) represented by large fossilized bones that had been unearthed at several locations in southern England during the early part of the 19th century. Owen recognized that these reptiles were far different from other known reptiles of the present and the past for three reasons: they were large yet obviously terrestrial, unlike the aquatic ichthyosaurs and plesiosaurs that were already known; they had five vertebrae in their hips, whereas most known reptiles have only two; and, rather than holding their limbs sprawled out to the side in the manner of lizards, dinosaurs held their limbs under the body in columnar fashion, like elephants and other large mammals.

Originally applied to just a handful of incomplete specimens, the category Dinosauria now encompasses more than 800 generic names and at least 1,000 species, with new names being added to the roster every year as the result of scientific explorations around the world. Not all of these names are valid taxa, however. A great many of

Scientists excavating dinosaur fossils from a quarry wall in Dinosaur National Monument, Colorado. National Park Service

them have been based on fragmentary or incomplete material that may actually have come from two or more different dinosaurs. In addition, bones have sometimes been misidentified as dinosaurian when they are not from dinosaurs at all. Nevertheless, dinosaurs are well documented by abundant fossil remains recovered from every continent on Earth, and the number of known dinosaurian taxa is estimated to be 10–25 percent of actual past diversity.

The extensive fossil record of genera and species is testimony that dinosaurs were diverse animals, with widely varying lifestyles and adaptations. Their remains are found in sedimentary rock layers (strata) dating to the Late Triassic Period (about 229 million to 200 million years ago). The abundance of their fossilized bones is substantive proof that dinosaurs were the dominant form of terrestrial animal life during the Mesozoic Era. It is likely that the known remains represent a very small fraction (probably less than 00001 percent) of all the individual dinosaurs that once lived.

The Search for Dinosaurs

Dinosaurs are still relatively new to science. Despite their initial discoveries over 2,000 years ago, most of the progress made in their reconstruction and classification has occurred only within the last 200 years. During the 19th century, as more and more fossils were discovered, described, reconstructed, and displayed, the public's fascination with dinosaurs rose. Significant discoveries made during the second half of the late 19th century accelerated the scientific community's interest in these animals, leading to advances in classification as well as the drive to discover and describe new types. More recently, the focus has shifted from description of individual specimens and types to the study of the anatomical relationships and other links between various groups.

The First Finds

Before Richard Owen introduced the term *Dinosauria* in 1842, there was no concept of anything even like a dinosaur. Large fossilized bones quite probably had been observed long before that time, but there is little record—and no existing specimens—of such findings much before 1818. In any case, people could not have been expected to understand what dinosaurs were even if they found their remains. For example, some classical scholars now conclude that the Greco-Roman legends of griffins from the 7th century BC were inspired by discoveries of protoceratopsian dinosaurs in the Altai region of Mongolia. In 1676

Robert Plot of the University of Oxford included, in a work of natural history, a drawing of what was apparently the knee-end of the thigh bone of a dinosaur, which he thought might have come from an elephant taken to Britain in Roman times. Fossil bones of what were undoubtedly dinosaurs were discovered in New Jersey in the late 1700s and were probably discussed at the meetings of the American Philosophical Society in Philadelphia. Soon thereafter, Lewis and Clark's expedition encountered dinosaur fossils in the western United States.

The earliest verifiable published record of dinosaur remains that still exists is a note in the 1820 American Journal of Science and Arts by Nathan Smith. The bones described had been found in 1818 by Solomon Ellsworth, Jr., while he was digging a well at his homestead in Windsor, Connecticut. At the time, the bones were thought to be human, but much later they were identified as *Anchisaurus.* Even earlier (1800), large birdlike footprints had been noticed on sandstone slabs in Massachusetts. Pliny Moody, who discovered these tracks, attributed them to "Noah's raven," and Edward Hitchcock of Amherst College, who began collecting them in 1835, considered them to be those of some giant extinct bird. The tracks are now recognized as having been made by several different kinds of dinosaurs, and such tracks are still commonplace in the Connecticut River Valley today.

Better known are the finds in southern England during the early 1820s by William Buckland (a clergyman) and Gideon Mantell (a physician), who described *Megalosaurus* and *Iguanodon* , respectively. In 1824 Buckland published a description of *Megalosaurus*, fossils of which consisted mainly of a lower jawbone with a few teeth. The following year Mantell published his "Notice on the *Iguanodon*, a Newly Discovered Fossil Reptile, from the Sandstone of Tilgate Forest, in Sussex," on the basis of several teeth and some leg bones. Both men collected fossils as an avocation and are credited with the earliest published announcements in England of what later would be recognized as dinosaurs. In both cases their finds were too fragmentary to permit a clear image of either animal. In 1834 a partial skeleton was found near Brighton that corresponded with Mantell's fragments from Tilgate Forest. It became known as the Maidstone *Iguanodon*, after the village where it was discovered. The Maidstone skeleton provided the first glimpse of what these creatures might have looked like.

Two years before the Maidstone *Iguanodon* came to light, a different kind of skeleton was found in the Weald of southern England. It was described and named *Hylaeosaurus* by Mantell in 1832 and later proved to be one of the armoured dinosaurs. Other fossil bones began turning up in Europe: fragments described and named as *Thecodontosaurus* and *Palaeosaurus* by two English students, Henry Riley and Samuel Stutchbury, and the first of many skeletons named *Plateosaurus* by the naturalist Hermann von Meyer in 1837. Richard Owen identified two additional dinosaurs, albeit from fragmentary evidence: *Cladeiodon*, which was based on a single large tooth, and *Cetiosaurus*, which he named from an incomplete skeleton composed of very large bones. Having carefully studied most of these fossil specimens, Owen recognized that all of these bones represented a group of large reptiles that were unlike any living varieties. In a report to the British Association for the Advancement of Science in 1841, he described these animals, and the word *Dinosauria* was first published in the association's proceedings in 1842.

Dinosaur Reconstruction and Classification

During the decades that followed Owen's announcement, many other kinds of dinosaurs were discovered and named in England and Europe: *Massospondylus* in 1854, *Scelidosaurus* in 1859, *Bothriospondylus* in 1875, and *Omosaurus* in 1877. Popular fascination with the giant reptiles grew, reaching a peak in the 1850s with the first attempts to reconstruct the three animals on which Owen based Dinosauria—*Iguanodon*, *Megalosaurus*, and *Hylaeosaurus*—for the first world exposition, the Great Exhibition of 1851 in London's Crystal Palace. A sculptor under Owen's direction (Waterhouse Hawkins) created life-size models of these two genera, and in 1854 they were displayed together with models of other extinct and living reptiles, such as plesiosaurs, ichthyosaurs, and crocodiles.

By the 1850s it had become evident that the reptile fauna of the Mesozoic Era was far more diverse and complex than it is today. The first important attempt to establish an informative classification of the dinosaurs was made by the English biologist T.H. Huxley as early as 1868. Because he observed that these animals had legs similar to birds as well as other birdlike features, he established a new order called Ornithoscelida. He divided the order into two suborders. Dinosauria was the first and included the iguanodonts, the large carnivores (or megalosaurids), and the armoured forms (including *Scelidosaurus*) Compsognatha was the second order, named for the very small birdlike carnivore *Compsognathus.*

Huxley's classification was replaced by a radically new scheme proposed in 1887 by his fellow Englishman H.G. Seeley, who noticed that all dinosaurs possessed one of two distinctive pelvic designs, one like that of birds and the other like that of reptiles. Accordingly, he divided the dinosaurs into the orders Ornithischia (having a birdlike pelvis) and Saurischia (having a reptilian pelvis) Ornithischia included four suborders: Ornithopoda (*Iguanodon* and similar herbivores), Stegosauria (plated forms), Ankylosauria (*Hylaeosaurus* and other armoured forms), and Ceratopsia (horned dinosaurs, just then being discovered in North America). Seeley's second order, the Saurischia, included all the carnivorous dinosaurs, such as *Megalosaurus* and *Compsognathus*, as well as the giant herbivorous sauropods, including *Cetiosaurus* and several immense "brontosaur" types that were turning up in North America. In erecting Saurischia and Ornithischia, Seeley cast doubt on the idea that Dinosauria was a natural grouping of these animals. This uncertainty persisted for a century thereafter, but it is now understood that the two groups share unique features that indeed make the Dinosauria a natural group.

In 1878 a spectacular discovery was made in the town of Bernissart, Belgium, where several dozen complete articulated skeletons of *Iguanodon* were accidentally uncovered in a coal mine during the course of mining operations. Under the direction of the Royal Institute of Natural Science of Belgium, thousands of bones were retrieved and carefully restored over a period of many years. The first skeleton was placed on exhibit in 1883, and today the public can view an impressive herd of *Iguanodon*. The discovery of these multiple remains gave the first hint that at least some dinosaurs may have traveled in groups and showed clearly that some dinosaurs were bipedal (walking on two legs). The supervisor of this extraordinary project was Louis Dollo, a zoologist who was to spend most of his life studying *Iguanodon*, working out its structure, and speculating on its living habits.

American Hunting Expeditions

England and Europe produced most of the early discoveries and students of dinosaurs, but North America soon began to contribute a large share of both. One leading student of fossils was Joseph Leidy of the Academy of Natural Sciences in Philadelphia, who named some of the earliest dinosaurs found in America, including *Palaeoscincus*,

Trachodon, *Troodon*, and *Deinodon*. Unfortunately, some names given by Leidy are no longer used, because they were based on such fragmentary and undiagnostic material. Leidy is perhaps best known for his study and description of the first dinosaur skeleton to be recognized in North America, that of a duckbill, or hadrosaur, found at Haddonfield, New Jersey, in 1858, which he named *Hadrosaurus foulkii*. Leidy's inference that this animal was probably amphibious influenced views of dinosaur life for the next century.

Othniel Charles Marsh (1831-1899), a professor of Paleontology at Yale, discovered a number of major dinosaur fossils, primarily through his work in the Rockies. Hulton Archive/Getty Images

Two Americans whose work during the second half of the 19th century had worldwide impact on the science of paleontology in general, and the growing knowledge of dinosaurs in particular, were O.C. Marsh of Yale College and E.D. Cope of Haverford College, the University of Pennsylvania, and the Academy of Natural Sciences in Philadelphia. All previous dinosaur remains had been discovered by accident in well-populated regions with temperate, moist climates, but Cope and Marsh astutely focused their attention on the wide arid expanses of bare exposed rock in western North America. In their intense quest to find and name new dinosaurs, these scientific pioneers became fierce and unfriendly rivals.

Marsh's field parties explored widely, exploiting dozens of now famous areas, among them Yale's sites at Morrison and Canon City, Colorado, and, most important, Como Bluff in southeastern Wyoming. The discovery of Como Bluff in 1877 was a momentous event in the history of paleontology that generated a burst of exploration and study as well as widespread public enthusiasm for dinosaurs. Como Bluff brought to light one of the greatest assemblages of dinosaurs, both small and gigantic, ever found. For decades the site went on producing the first known specimens of Late Jurassic Period (about 161 million to 145.5 million years ago) dinosaurs such as *Stegosaurus*, *Camptosaurus*, *Camarasaurus*, *Laosaurus*, *Coelurus*, and others. From the Morrison site came the original specimens of *Allosaurus*, *Diplodocus*, *Atlantosaurus*, and *Brontosaurus* (later renamed *Apatosaurus*). Canon City provided bones of a host of dinosaurs, including *Stegosaurus*, *Brachiosaurus*, *Allosaurus*, and *Camptosaurus*.

Another major historic site was the Lance Creek area of northeastern Wyoming, where J.B. Hatcher discovered and collected dozens of Late Cretaceous horned dinosaur remains for Marsh and for Yale College, among them the first specimens of *Triceratops* and *Torosaurus*. Marsh was aided in his work at these and other localities by the skills and efforts of many other collaborators like Hatcher—William Reed, Benjamin Mudge, Arthur Lakes, William Phelps, and Samuel Wendell Williston, to name a few. Marsh's specimens now form the core of the Mesozoic collections at the National Museum of Natural History of the Smithsonian Institution and the Peabody Museum of Natural History at Yale University.

Cope's dinosaur explorations ranged as far as, or farther than, Marsh's, and his interests encompassed a wider variety of fossils. Owing to a number of circumstances, however, Cope's dinosaur discoveries were fewer and his collections far less complete than those of Marsh. Perhaps his most notable achievement was finding and proposing the names for *Coelophysis* and *Monoclonius*. Cope's dinosaur explorations began in the eastern badlands of Montana, where he discovered *Monoclonius* in the Judith River Formation of the Late Cretaceous Period (about 100 million to 65.5 million years ago). Accompanying him there was a talented young assistant, Charles H. Sternberg. Later Sternberg and his three sons went on to recover countless dinosaur skeletons from the Oldman and Edmonton formations of the Late Cretaceous along the Red Deer River of Alberta, Canada.

Dinosaur Ancestors

During the early decades of dinosaur discoveries, little thought was given to their evolutionary ancestry. Not only were the few specimens known unlike any living animal, but they were so different from any other reptiles that it was difficult to discern much about their relationships. Early on it was recognized that, as a group, dinosaurs appear to be most closely allied to crocodilians, though T.H. Huxley had proposed in the 1860s that dinosaurs and birds must have had a very close common ancestor in the distant past. Three anatomic features—socketed teeth, a skull with two large holes (diapsid), and another hole in the lower jaw—are present in both crocodiles and dinosaurs. The earliest crocodilians occurred nearly simultaneously with the first known dinosaurs, so neither could have given rise to the other. It was long thought that the most likely ancestry of dinosaurs could be found within a poorly understood group of Triassic reptiles termed thecodontians ("socket-toothed reptiles"). Today it is recognized that "thecodontian" is simply a name for the basal, or most primitive, members of the archosaurs ("ruling reptiles"), a group that is distinguished by the three anatomic features mentioned above and that includes dinosaurs, pterosaurs (flying reptiles), crocodiles, and their extinct relatives. An early candidate for the ancestor of dinosaurs was a small basal archosaur from the Early Triassic Period (251 million to 246 million years ago) of South Africa called *Euparkeria*. New discoveries suggest creatures that are even more dinosaur-like from the Middle Triassic (about 246 million to 229 million years ago) and from an early portion of the Late Triassic (about 229 million to 200 million years ago) of South America; these include *Lagerpeton*, *Lagosuchus*, *Pseudolagosuchus*, and *Lewisuchus*. Other South American forms such as *Eoraptor* and *Herrerasaurus* are particularly dinosaurian in appearance and are sometimes considered dinosaurs.

The earliest appearance of "true dinosaurs" is almost impossible to pinpoint, since it can never be known with certainty whether the very first (or last) specimen of any kind of organism has been found. The succession of deposits containing fossils is discontinuous and contains many gaps. Even within these deposits, the fossil record of dinosaurs and other creatures contained within is far from complete. Further complicating matters is that evolution from ancestral to descendant form is usually a stepwise process. Consequently, as more and more gaps are filled between the first dinosaurs and other archosaurs, the number of features distinguishing them becomes smaller and smaller. Currently, paleontologists define dinosaurs as *Triceratops* (representing Ornithischia), birds (the most recent representatives of the Saurischia), and all the descendants of their most recent common ancestor. That common ancestor apparently had a suite of features not present in other dinosaur relatives, including the loss of the prefrontal bone above the eye, a long deltopectoral crest on the humerus, three or fewer joints on the fourth finger of the hand, three or more hip vertebrae, a fully open hip socket, and a cnemial crest on the shin bone (tibia). These features were passed on and modified in the descendants of the first dinosaurs. Compared with most of their contemporaries, dinosaurs had an improved stance and posture with a resulting improved gait and, in several independent lineages, an overall increase in size. They also were more efficient at gathering food and processing it and apparently had higher metabolic rates and cardiovascular nourishment. All these trends, individually or in concert, probably contributed to the collective success of dinosaurs, which resulted in their dominance among the terrestrial animals of the Mesozoic.

Modern Studies of Dinosaurs

During the first century or more of dinosaur awareness, workers in the field more or less concentrated on the search for new specimens and new types. Their discoveries then required detailed description and analysis, followed by comparisons with other known dinosaurs in order to classify the new finds and develop hypotheses about evolutionary relationships. These pursuits continue, but newer methods of exploration and analysis have been adopted. Emphasis has shifted from purely descriptive procedures to analyses of relationships by using the methods of cladistics, which dispenses with the traditional taxonomic hierarchy in favour of "phylogenetic trees" that are more explicit about evolutionary relationships. Phylogenetic analyses also help us to understand how certain features evolved in groups of dinosaurs and give us insight into their possible functions. For example, in the evolution of horned dinosaurs (ceratopsians), it can be seen that the beak evolved first, followed by the frill, and finally the nose and eye horns, which were differently developed in different groups. The hypothesis that the frill was widely used in defense by ceratopsians such as *Protoceratops* can thus be tested phylogenetically. On this basis, the idea is now generally rejected because the frill was basically just an open rim of bone in nearly all ceratopsians except *Triceratops*, which is often pictured charging like a rhinoceros.

Functional anatomic studies extensively use analogous traits of present-day animals that, along with both mechanical and theoretical models, make it possible to visualize certain aspects of extinct animals. For example, estimates of normal walking and maximum running speeds can be calculated on the basis of the analysis of trackways, which can then be combined with biomechanical examination of the legs and joints and reconstruction of limb musculature. Similar methods have been applied to jaw mechanisms and tooth wear patterns to obtain a better understanding of feeding habits and capabilities.

The soft parts of dinosaurs are only imperfectly known. Original colours and patterns cannot be known, but skin textures have occasionally been preserved. Most show a knobby or pebbly surface rather than a scaly texture as in most living reptiles. Impressions of internal organs are rarely preserved, but, increasingly, records of filaments and even feathers have been found on some dinosaurs. Gastroliths ("stomach stones") used for processing food in the gizzard have been recovered from a variety of dinosaurs.

Natural History of Dinosaurs

Dinosaurs owe their great diversity in part to the breakup of Pangea during the Mesozoic. Changing regional climates forced these animals to adapt to local conditions; the groups that could not adapt were quickly replaced. As plant communities changed, some types developed adaptations that made them more efficient at digesting certain types of food. Other types learned to group together for increased protection against predators or for increased hunting success. Some scientists suggest that certain groups of dinosaurs evolved to become warm-blooded, giving them the ability to sustain greater levels of physical activity. Such increased metabolism might have helped these groups to exploit harsh habitats or become more efficient in their activities in milder ones.

Dinosaur Habitats

Dinosaurs lived in many kinds of terrestrial environments, and although some remains, such as footprints, indicate where dinosaurs actually lived, their bones tell us only where they died (assuming that they have not been scattered or washed far from their place of death). Not all environments are equally well preserved in the fossil record. Upland environments, forests, and plains tend to experience erosion or decomposition of organic remains, so remains from these environments are rarely preserved in the geologic record. As a result, most dinosaur fossils are known from lowland environments, usually floodplains, deltas, lake beds, stream bottoms, and even some marine environments, where their bones apparently washed in after death. Much about the environments dinosaurs lived in can be learned from studying the pollen and plant remains preserved with them and from geochemical isotopes that indicate temperature and precipitation levels. These climates, although free from the extensive ice caps of today and generally more equable, suffered extreme monsoon seasons and made much of the globe arid.

Only a few specimens represent the meagre beginning of the dinosaurian reign. This is probably because of a highly incomplete fossil record. Just before dinosaurs appeared, the world's continents were joined into one large landmass called Pangea. Movements of the Earth's great crustal plates then began changing Earth's geography. By the Early Triassic Period, as dinosaurs were beginning to gain a foothold, Pangea had started to split apart at a rate averaging a few centimetres a year.

As the dinosaur line arose and experienced its initial diversification during the Late Triassic Period, the land areas of the world were in motion and drifting apart. Their respective inhabitants were consequently isolated from each other. Throughout the remainder of the Mesozoic Era, ocean barriers grew wider and the separate faunas became increasingly different. As the continents drifted apart, successive assemblages arose on each landmass and then diversified, waned, and disappeared, to be replaced by new fauna. By the Late Cretaceous Period, each continent occupied its own unique geographic position and climatic zone, and its fauna reflected that separation.

Food and Feeding

The Plant Eaters

From the Triassic through the Jurassic and into the Cretaceous, the Earth's vegetation changed slowly but fundamentally from forests rich in gymnosperms (cycadeoids, cycads, and conifers) to angiosperm-dominated forests of palmlike trees and magnolia-like hardwoods. Although conifers continued to flourish at high latitudes, palms were increasingly confined to subtropical and tropical regions. These forms of plant life, the vast majority of them low in calories and proteins and made largely of hard-to-digest cellulose, became the foods of changing dinosaur communities. Accordingly, certain groups of dinosaurs, such as the ornithopods, included a succession of types that were increasingly adapted for efficient food processing. At the peak of the ornithopod lineage, the hadrosaurs (duck-billed dinosaurs of the Late Cretaceous) featured large dental batteries in both the upper and lower jaws, which consisted of many tightly compressed teeth that formed a long crushing or grinding surface. The preferred food of the duckbills cannot be certified, but at least one specimen found in Wyoming offers an intriguing clue: fossil plant remains in the stomach region have been identified as pine needles.

The hadrosaurs' Late Cretaceous contemporaries, the ceratopsians (horned dinosaurs), had similar dental batteries that consisted of dozens of teeth. In this group the upper and lower batteries came together and acted as serrated shearing blades rather than crushing or grinding surfaces. Ordinarily, slicing teeth are found only in flesh-eating animals, but the bulky bodies and the unclawed, hooflike feet of dinosaurs such as *Triceratops* clearly are those of plant eaters. The sharp beaks and specialized shearing dentition of the ceratopsians suggest that they probably fed on tough, fibrous plant tissues, perhaps palm or cycad fronds.

The giant sauropods such as *Diplodocus* and *Apatosaurus* must have required large quantities of plant food, but there is no direct evidence as to the particular plants they preferred. Because angiosperms rich in calories and proteins did not exist during most of the Mesozoic Era, it must be assumed that these sauropods fed on the abundant conifers and palm trees. Such a cellulose-heavy diet would have required an unusual bacterial population in the intestines to break down the fibre. A digestive tract with one or more crop chambers containing stones might have aided in the food-pulverizing process, but such gastroliths, or "stomach stones," are only rarely found in association with dinosaur skeletons. (A *Seismosaurus* specimen found with several hundred such stones is an important exception.)

The food preference of herbivorous dinosaurs can be inferred to some extent from their general body plan and from their teeth. It is probable, for example, that low-built animals such as the ankylosaurs, stegosaurs, and ceratopsians fed on low shrubbery. The tall ornithopods, especially the duckbills, and the long-necked sauropods probably browsed on high branches and treetops. No dinosaurs could have fed on grasses (family Poaceae), as these plants had not yet evolved.

The Flesh Eaters

The flesh-eating dinosaurs came in all shapes and sizes and account for about 40 percent of the diversity of Mesozoic dinosaurs. They must have eaten anything they could catch, because predation is a highly opportunistic lifestyle. In several instances the prey victim of a particular carnivore has been established beyond much doubt. Remains were found of the small predator *Compsognathus* containing a tiny skeleton of the lizard *Bavarisaurus* in its stomach region. In Mongolia two different dinosaur skeletons were found together, a nearly adult-size *Protoceratops* in the clutches of its predator *Velociraptor*. Two of the many skeletons of *Coelophysis* discovered at Ghost Ranch in New

Mexico, U.S., contained bones of several half-grown *Coelophysis*, apparently an early Mesozoic example of cannibalism. Fossilized feces (coprolites) from a large tyrannosaur contained crushed bone of another dinosaur. Skeletons of *Deinonychus* unearthed in Montana, U.S., were mixed with fragmentary bones of a much larger victim, the herbivore *Tenontosaurus*. This last example is significant because the multiple remains of the predator *Deinonychus* , associated with the bones of a single large prey animal, *Tenontosaurus*, strongly suggest that *Deinonychus* hunted in packs.

Dinosaur Herding Behaviour

It should not come as a surprise that *Deinonychus* was a social animal, because many animals today are gregarious and form groups. Fossil evidence documents similar herding behaviour in a variety of dinosaurs. The mass assemblage in Bernissart, Belgium, for example, held at least three groups of *Iguanodon*. Group association and activity is also indicated by the dozens of *Coelophysis* skeletons of all ages recovered in New Mexico, U.S. The many specimens of *Allosaurus* at the Cleveland-Lloyd Quarry in Utah, U.S., may denote a herd of animals attracted to the site for the common purpose of scavenging. In the last two decades, several assemblages of ceratopsians and duckbills containing thousands of individuals have been found. Even *Tyrannosaurus rex* is now known from sites where a group has been preserved together.

These rare occurrences of multiple skeletal remains have repeatedly been reinforced by dinosaur footprints as evidence of herding. Trackways were first noted by Roland T. Bird in the early 1940s along the Paluxy riverbed in central Texas, U.S., where numerous washbasin-size depressions proved to be a series of giant sauropod footsteps preserved in limestone of the Early Cretaceous

Period. Because the tracks are nearly parallel and all progress in the same direction, Bird concluded that "all were headed toward a common objective" and suggested that the sauropod trackmakers "passed in a single herd." Large trackway sites also exist in the eastern and western United States, Canada, Australia, England, Argentina, South Africa, and China, among other places These sites, dating from the Late Triassic Period to the latest Cretaceous, document herding as common behaviour among a variety of dinosaur types.

Some dinosaur trackways record hundreds, perhaps even thousands, of animals, possibly indicating mass migrations. The existence of so many trackways suggests the presence of great populations of sauropods, prosauropods, ornithopods, and probably most other kinds of dinosaurs. The majority must have been herbivores, and many of them were huge, weighing several tons or more. The impact of such large herds on the plant life of the time must have been great, suggesting constant migration in search of food.

Nesting sites discovered in the late 20th century also establish herding among dinosaurs. Nests and eggs numbering from dozens to thousands are preserved at sites that were possibly used for thousands of years by the same evolving populations of dinosaurs.

Growth and Life Span

Much attention has been devoted to dinosaurs as living animals—moving, eating, growing, reproducing biological machines. But how fast did they grow? How long did they live? How did they reproduce? The evidence concerning growth and life expectancy is sparse but growing. In the 1990s histological studies of fossilized bone by Armand de Ricqlès in Paris and R.E.H. Reid in Ireland showed that dinosaur skeletons grew quite rapidly. The time required for full growth has not been quantified for most dinosaurs, but de Ricqlès and his colleagues have shown that duckbills (hadrosaurs) such as *Hypacrosaurus* and *Maiasaura* reached adult size in seven or eight years and that the giant sauropods reached nearly full size in as little as 12 years. How long dinosaurs lived after reaching adult size is difficult to determine, but it is thought that the majority of known skeletons are not fully grown, because their bone ends and arches are very often not fused. In mature individuals these features would be fused.

Dinosaur Reproduction

The idea that dinosaurs, like most living reptiles and birds, built nests and laid eggs had been widely debated even before the 1920s, when a team of scientists from the American Museum of Natural History, New York, made an expedition to Mongolia. Their discovery of dinosaur eggs in the Gobi Desert proved conclusively that at least one kind of dinosaur had been an egg layer and nest builder. These eggs were at first attributed to *Protoceratops*, but they are now known to have been those of *Oviraptor*. In 1978 John R. Horner and his field crews from Princeton University discovered dinosaur nests in western Montana. A few other finds, mostly of eggshell fragments from a number of sites, established oviparity as the only known mode of reproduction. In recent years an increasing number of dinosaur eggshells have been found and identified with the dinosaurs that laid them, and embryos have been found inside some eggs.

The almost complete absence of juvenile dinosaur remains was puzzling until the 1980s. Horner, having moved to Montana State University, demonstrated that most paleontologists simply had not been exploring the right territory. After a series of intensive searches for the remains of immature dinosaurs, he succeeded beyond all

Rendering of Late Cretaceous parasaurolophus (crested duck-bill dinosaur) nest, eggs, and newborns. Ken Lucas/Visuals Unlimited/Getty Images

expectations. The first such bones were unearthed near Choteau, Montana, and thereafter Horner and his crews discovered hundreds of nests, eggs, and newly hatched dinosaurs (mostly duckbills). Horner observed that previous explorations had usually concentrated on lowland areas, where sediments were commonly deposited and where most fossil remains were preserved. He recognized that such regions were not likely to produce dinosaur nests and young because they would have been hazardous places for nesting and raising the hatchlings. Upland regions would have been safer, but they were subject to erosion rather than deposition and were therefore less likely to preserve nests and eggs. However, it was exactly in such upland areas, close to the young and still-rising Rocky Mountains, that Horner made his discoveries.

Egg Mountain, as the area was named, produced some of the most important clues to dinosaurian habits yet found. For example, the sites show that a number of different dinosaur species made annual treks to this same nesting ground (though perhaps not all at the same time). Because of the succession of similar nests and eggs lying one on top of the other, it is thought that particular species returned to the same site year after year to lay their clutches. As Horner concluded, "site fidelity" was an instinctive part of dinosaurian reproductive strategy. This was confirmed more recently with the discovery of sauropod nests and eggs spread over many square kilometres in Patagonia, Argentina.

Body Temperature

Beyond eating, digestion, assimilation, reproduction, and nesting, many other processes and activities went into making the dinosaur a successful biological machine. Breathing, fluid balance, temperature regulation, and other such capabilities are also required. Dinosaurian body temperature regulation, or lack thereof, has been a hotly debated topic among students of dinosaur biology. Because it is obviously not possible to take an extinct dinosaur's temperature, all aspects of their metabolism and thermophysiology can be assessed only indirectly.

Ectothermy and Endothermy

All animals thermoregulate. The internal environment of the body is under the influence of both external and internal conditions. Land animals thermoregulate in several ways. They do so behaviorally, by moving to a colder or warmer place, by exercising to generate body heat, or by panting or sweating to lose it. They also thermoregulate physiologically, by activating internal metabolic processes that warm or cool the blood. But these efforts have limits, and, as a result, external temperatures and climatic conditions are among the most important factors controlling the geographic distribution of animals.

Today's so-called warm-blooded animals are the mammals and birds. Reptiles, amphibians, and most fishes are called cold-blooded. These two terms, however, are imprecise and misleading. Some "cold-blooded" lizards have higher normal body temperatures than do some mammals, for instance. Another pair of terms, *ectothermy* and *endothermy*, describes whether most of an animal's heat is absorbed from the environment ("ecto-") or generated by internal processes ("endo-"). A third pair of terms, *poikilothermy* and *homeothermy*, describes whether the body temperature tends to vary with that of the immediate environment or remains relatively constant.

Today's mammals and birds have a high metabolism and are considered endotherms, which produce body heat internally. They possess biological temperature sensors that control heat production and switch on heat-loss mechanisms such as perspiration. Today's reptiles and amphibians, on the other hand, are ectotherms that mostly gain heat energy from sunlight, a heated rock surface, or some other external source. The endothermic state is effective but metabolically expensive, as the body must produce heat continuously, which requires correspondingly high quantities of fuel in the form of food. On the other hand, endotherms can be more active and survive lower external temperatures. Ectotherms do not require as much fuel, but most cannot deal as well with cold surroundings.

From the time of the earliest discoveries in the 19th century, dinosaur remains were classified as reptilian because their anatomic features are typical of living reptiles such as turtles, crocodiles, and lizards. Because dinosaurs all have lower jaws constructed of several bones, a reptilian jaw joint, and a number of other nonmammalian, nonbirdlike characteristics, it was assumed that living dinosaurs were similar to living reptiles—scaly, cold-blooded, ectothermic egg layers (predominantly), not furry, warm-blooded live-bearers. A chauvinistic attitude seems to prevail that the warm-bloodedness of mammals is better than the cold-blooded reptilian state, even though turtles, snakes, and other reptiles do very well regulating their body temperature in a different way. Moreover, both birds and mammals evolved from ectothermic, poikilothermic ancestors. At what point did metabolism heat up?

Clues to Dinosaurian Metabolism

The question of whether any extinct dinosaur was a true endotherm or homeotherm cannot be answered, but some interesting anatomic facts suggest these "warmer" possibilities. Probably the most direct evidence of dinosaurian physiology comes from bones themselves, particularly in regard to how they grew. The long bones (such as arm and leg bones) of most dinosaurs are composed almost exclusively of a well-vascularized type of bone matrix (fibro-lamellar) also found in most mammals and large birds. This type of bone tissue always indicates rapid growth, and it is very different from the more compact, poorly vascularized, parallel-fibred bone found in crocodiles and other reptiles and amphibians. It is generally thought that well-vascularized, rapidly growing bone can be sustained only by high metabolic rates that bring a continual source of nutrients and minerals to the growing tissues. It is difficult to explain these histological features in any other metabolic terms. On the other hand, most dinosaurs retain lines of arrested growth (LAGs) in most of their long bones. LAGs are found in other reptiles, amphibians, and fishes, and they often reflect a seasonal period during which metabolism slows, usually because of environmental stresses. This slowdown produces "rest lines" as LAGs in the bones. The presence of these lines in dinosaur bones has been taken as an indication that they were metabolically incapable of growing throughout the year. However, LAGs in dinosaurs are less pronounced than in other reptiles. LAGs can also appear in different numbers in different bones of the same skeleton, and they are sometimes even completely absent. Finally, some living birds and mammals, which are clearly endotherms, have LAGs very much like those of dinosaurs, so LAGs are probably not strong indicators of metabolism in any of these animals.

Other, less direct lines of evidence may reveal other clues about dinosaurian metabolism. Two dinosaurian groups, the hadrosaurs and the ceratopsians, had highly specialized sets of teeth that were obviously effective at processing food. Both groups were herbivorous, but unlike living reptiles they chopped and ground foliage thoroughly. Such highly efficient dentitions may suggest a highly effective digestive process that would allow more energy to be extracted from the food. This feature by itself, however, may not be crucial. Pandas, for example, are not very efficient in digesting plant material, but they survive quite well on a diet of almost nothing but bamboo.

Another line of evidence is that dinosaurs had anatomic features reflecting a high capacity for activity. The first dinosaurs walked upright, holding their legs under their bodies; they could not sprawl. This indicates that, by standing and walking all day, they probably expended more energy than reptiles, which typically sit and wait for prey. As some lineages of dinosaurs grew larger, they reverted to four-legged (quadrupedal) locomotion, but their stance was still upright. They also put one foot directly in front of the other when they walked (parasagittal gait), instead of swinging the limbs to the side Such posture and gait are present in all nonaquatic endotherms (mammals and birds) today, whereas a sprawling or semierect posture is typical of all ectotherms (reptiles and amphibians). Bipedal stance and parasagittal gait are not sustained in any living ectotherm, perhaps because they require a relatively higher level of sustained energy.

The high speeds at which some dinosaurs must have traveled have also been invoked as evidence of high metabolic levels. For example, the ostrichlike dinosaurs, such as *Struthiomimus*, *Ornithomimus*, *Gallimimus*, and *Dromiceiomimus*, had long hind legs and must have been very fleet. The dromaeosaurs, such as *Deinonychus*, *Velociraptor*, and *Dromaeosaurus*, also were obligatory bipeds. They killed prey with talons on their feet, and one can argue that it must have taken a high level of metabolism to generate the degree of activity and agility required of such a skill. However, most ectotherms can move very rapidly in bursts of activity such as running and fighting, so this feature may not provide conclusive evidence either.

Related to the upright posture of many dinosaurs is the fact that the head was often positioned well above the level of the heart. In some sauropods (*Apatosaurus*, *Diplodocus*, *Brachiosaurus*, and *Barosaurus*, for instance), the brain must have been several metres above the heart. The physiological importance of this is that a four-chambered heart would be required for pumping freshly oxygenated blood to the brain. Brain death follows very quickly when nerve cells are deprived of oxygen, and to prevent it most dinosaurs must have required two ventricles. In a four-chambered heart, one ventricle pumps oxygen-poor venous blood at low pressure to the lungs to absorb fresh oxygen (high pressure would rupture capillaries of the lungs). A powerful second ventricle pumps freshly oxygenated blood to all other parts of the body at high pressure. To overcome the weight of the column of blood that must be moved from the heart to the elevated brain, high pressure is certainly needed. In short, like birds and mammals, many dinosaurs apparently had the required four-chambered heart necessary for an animal with a high metabolism.

The significance of thermoregulation can be seen by comparing today's reptiles with mammals. The rate of metabolism is usually measured in terms of oxygen consumed per unit of body weight per unit of time. The resting metabolic rate for most mammals is about 10 times that of modern reptiles, and the range of metabolic rates among living mammals is about double that seen among reptiles. These differences mean that endothermic mammals have much more endurance than their cold-blooded counterparts. Some dinosaurs may have been so endowed, and although they seem to have possessed the cardiovascular system necessary for endothermy, that capacity does not conclusively prove that they were endothermic. There exists the possibility that dinosaurs were neither complete ectotherms nor complete endotherms. Rather, they may have evolved a range of metabolic strategies, much as mammals have (as is illustrated by the differences between sloths and cheetahs, bats and whales, for example).

Dinosaur Classification

The chief difference between the two major groups of dinosaurs is in the configuration of the pelvis. It was primarily on this distinction that the English biologist H.G. Seeley established the two dinosaurian orders and named them Saurischia ("lizard hips") and Ornithischia ("bird hips") in 1887. This differentiation is still maintained.

As in all four-legged animals, the dinosaurian pelvis was a paired structure consisting of three separate bones on each side that attached to the sacrum of the backbone. The ilium was attached to the spine, and the pubis and ischium were below, forming a robust bony plate. At the centre of each plate was a deep cup—the hip socket (acetabulum). The hip socket faced outward and was open at its centre for the articulation of the thighbone. The combined saurischian pelvic bones presented a triangular outline as seen from the side, with the pubis extending down and forward and the ischium projecting down and backward from the hip socket. The massive ilium formed a deep vertical plate of bone to which the muscles of the pelvis, hind leg, and tail were attached. The pubis had a stout shaft, commonly terminating in a pronounced expansion or bootlike structure (presumably for muscle attachment) that solidly joined its opposite mate. The ischium was slightly less robust than the pubis, but it too joined its mate along a midline. There were minor variations in this structure between the various saurischians.

The ornithischian pelvis was constructed of the same three bones on each side of the sacral vertebrae, to which they were attached. The lateral profile of the pelvis was quite different from that of the saurischians, which had a long but low iliac blade above the hip socket and a modified ischium-pubis structure below. Here the long, thin ischium extended backward and slightly downward from the hip socket. In the most primitive, or basal, ornithischians, the pubis had a moderately long anterior blade, but this was reduced in later ornithischians. Posteriorly it stretched out into a long, thin postpubic process lying beneath and closely parallel to the ischium. The resulting configuration superficially resembled that of birds, whose pubis is a thin process extending backward beneath the larger ischium. These anatomic dissimilarities are thought to reflect important differences in muscle arrangements in the hips and hind legs of these two orders. However, the soft parts of these dinosaurs are not well enough understood to reveal any functional or physiological basis for the differences. Other marked dissimilarities between saurischians and ornithischians are found in their jaws and teeth, their limbs, and especially their skulls. Details regarding these differences are given in the following discussions of the major dinosaur groups.

The classification shows how the groups are subdivided. This classification is based on their relationships to each other, as far as they are known. Fossil remains are often difficult to interpret, especially when only a few fragmentary specimens of a type have been found. No universally accepted classification of dinosaurs exists. Occasionally, for example, the Sauropodomorpha have been divided into more or fewer lower-rank categories (e.g., families, subfamilies), and the suborder Theropoda has been divided into two infraorders, the Carnosauria and the Coelurosauria. Increasingly, taxonomists have abandoned the traditional Linnaean ranks of family, order, and so on because they are cumbersome and not comparable among different kinds of organisms. Instead, the names of the groups alone are used without denoting a category. Generally, a phylogeny such as the accompanying diagram clearly shows which groups are subsumed under others. Additionally, words with similar roots but different endings may indicate more or less inclusive groups. Ornithomimosauria, for example, denotes a more inclusive group than Ornithomimidae. Because the results of different phylogenetic analyses vary among researchers, and will continue to change as new specimens and taxa are discovered, the classification can be expected to change accordingly. This is a normal part of scientific activity and reflects continuing growth of knowledge and reappraisal of current understanding.

Saurischia

Saurischians are known from specimens ranging from the Late Triassic to the present day, because, as will be seen, birds are highly derived saurischian dinosaurs. Two distinctly different groups are traditionally included in the saurischians—the Sauropodomorpha (herbivorous sauropods and prosauropods) and the Theropoda (carnivorous dinosaurs). These groups are placed together on the basis of a suite of features that they share uniquely. These include elongated posterior neck vertebrae, accessory articulations on the trunk vertebrae, and a hand that is nearly half as long as the rest of the arm (or longer). In addition, the second finger of the hand (not the third, as in other animals) is invariably the longest. The thumb is borne on a short metacarpal bone that is offset at its far end, so that the thumb diverges somewhat from the other fingers. The first joint of the thumb, which bears a robust claw, is longer than any other joint in the hand.

Sauropodomorpha

Included in this group are the well-known sauropods, or "brontosaur" types, and their probable ancestral group, the prosauropods. All were plant eaters, though their relationship to theropods, along with the fact that the closest relatives of dinosaurs were evidently carnivorous, suggests that they evolved from meat eaters. Sauropodomorpha are distinguished by leaf-shaped tooth crowns, a small head, and a neck that is at least as long as the trunk of the body and longer than the limbs.

Prosauropoda

Most generalized of the Sauropodomorpha were the so-called prosauropods. Found from the Late Triassic to Early Jurassic periods (229 million to 176 million years ago), their remains are probably the most ubiquitous of all Triassic dinosaurs. They have been found in Europe (Germany), North America (New England, Arizona, and New Mexico), South America (Argentina), Africa (South Africa, Lesotho, Zimbabwe), China (Yunnan), and Antarctica. The best-known examples include *Plateosaurus* of Germany and *Massospondylus* of South Africa. Prosauropods were not especially large. They ranged from less than 2 metres (7 feet) in length up to about 8 metres (26 feet) and up to several tons in maximum weight. Many of these animals are known from very complete skeletons (especially the smaller, more lightly built forms). Because their forelimbs are conspicuously shorter than their hind limbs, they have often been reconstructed poised on their hind legs in a bipedal stance. Their anatomy, however, clearly indicates that some of them could assume a quadrupedal (four-footed) position. Footprints generally attributed to prosauropods appear to substantiate both forms of locomotion.

Prosauropods have long been seen as including the first direct ancestors of the giant sauropods, probably among the melanorosaurids. That view has long prevailed largely because of their distinctly primitive sauropod-like appearance and also because of their Late Triassic–Early Jurassic occurrence. No better candidate has been discovered, and the first true sauropods are not found until the Early Jurassic, so the transition between prosauropods and sauropods has been generally accepted. In the 1990s, however, several studies have suggested that prosauropods may be a distinct group that shared common ancestors with sauropods earlier in the Triassic. If this view is correct, scientists have yet to uncover why the smaller prosauropods are so widespread throughout the Late Triassic, yet none of the larger and more conspicuous sauropods have been found from that period.

In general body form, prosauropods were mostly rather stocky, with a long, moderately flexible neck containing surprisingly long and flexible cervical ribs. The head was small in comparison with the body. The jaw was long and contained rows of thin, leaflike teeth suited for chopping up (but not grinding or crushing) plant tissues, although there is an indication of direct tooth-on-tooth occlusion.

Prosauropod forelimbs were stout, with five complete digits. The hind limbs were about 50 percent longer than the forelimbs and even more heavily built. The foot was of primitive design, and its five-toed configuration could be interpreted as a forerunner of the sauropod foot. Walking apparently was done partly on the toes (semidigitigrade), with the metatarsus held well off the ground. The vertebral column was unspecialized and bore little indication of the cavernous excavations that were to come in later sauropod vertebrae, nor did it show projections that were to buttress the sauropod vertebral column. The long tail probably served as a counterweight or stabilizer whenever the animal assumed a bipedal position.

Sauropoda

The more widely known sauropods—the huge "brontosaurs" and their relatives—varied in length from 6 or 7 metres (about 20 feet) in the primitive ancestral sauropod *Vulcanodon* of Africa, *Barapasaurus* of India, and *Ohmdenosaurus* of Germany, up to 28 to 30 metres (90 to 100 feet) or more in Late Jurassic North American forms such as *Apatosaurus* (formerly known as *Brontosaurus*), *Diplodocus*, *Seismosaurus*, and *Sauroposeidon*. Weights ranged from about 20 tons or less in *Barapasaurus* to 80 tons or more for the gigantic *Brachiosaurus* of Africa and North America. Sauropods were worldwide in distribution but have not as yet been found in Antarctica. In geologic time they ranged from the Late Triassic *Riojasaurus* to the Late Cretaceous *Alamosaurus* of North America and *Laplatasaurus* of South America. Their greatest diversity and abundance took place 120 million–150 million years ago, during the Late Jurassic and Early Cretaceous periods.

Sauropods are notable for their body form as well as their enormous size. Their large bodies were heart-shaped in cross section, like elephants, with long (sometimes extremely long) necks and tails. Their columnar legs, again like those of elephants, had little freedom to bend at the knee and elbow. The legs were maintained in a nearly vertical position beneath the shoulder and hip sockets. Because of their great bulk, sauropods unquestionably were obligate quadrupeds.

The sauropod limb bones were heavy and solid. The feet were broad, close to plantigrade (adapted for walking on the soles), and graviportal (adapted for bearing great weight). The toes were generally short, blunt, and broad, but some sauropods had a large straight claw on the first digit of the forefoot and the first and second toes of the hind foot. These animals must have moved relatively slowly and with only short steps because of the comparative inflexibility of the limbs. Running must have been stiff-legged at no better than an elephantine pace of 16 km (10 miles) per hour, if that. Their tremendous bulk placed them out of the reach of predators and eliminated any need for speed. Evidently their fast growth was adaptive to predator avoidance.

The vertebrae of the backbone were highly modified, with numerous excavations and struts to reduce bone weight. Complex spines and projections for muscle and ligament attachment compensated for any loss of skeletal strength that resulted from reductions in bone density and mass. The long and sometimes massive tail, characteristic of so many sauropods, would appear to have been carried well off the ground. Tail drag marks associated with sauropod trackways are not known, and damaged (stepped-on) tails are also not known, even though these animals apparently traveled in herds (albeit of undetermined density). Another possible use of the tail, like the neck, may have been thermal regulation, as improved heat loss through its large surface area could have been a result. The tail was also the critical anchor of the large, powerful hind leg muscles that produced most of the walking force required for moving the many tons of sauropod weight. The muscle arrangement of the tail was precisely that of modern alligators and lizards.

The most important part of any skeleton is the skull because it provides the most information about an animal's mode of life and general biology. Sauropod skulls were of several main types, including the high, boxy *Camarasaurus* type (often incorrectly associated with *Apatosaurus*); the shoe-shaped *Brachiosaurus* type, with its large, delicately arched nasal bones; and the low, narrow, streamlined, almost horselike *Diplodocus* type. The first had broad, spatulate teeth, while the latter two had narrow, pencil-shaped teeth largely confined to the front parts of the jaws, especially in diplodocids.

Until recently, sauropods were visualized as swamp or lake dwellers because their legs were thought to be incapable of supporting their great weights or because such huge creatures would naturally prefer the buoyancy of watery surroundings. The 19th-century English biologist Richard Owen, in fact, identified the first known sauropods as giant aquatic crocodiles and called them cetiosaurs (whale lizards) because they were so large and because they were found in aquatic sediments. Eventually enough skeletal remains were discovered to show that these animals were neither crocodiles nor aquatic. However, the image of amphibious habits, thought necessary to support the great weights of sauropods, persisted for a long time, however incorrectly. Experiments with fresh bone samples have shown that bone of the type that composed the sauropods' limb bones could easily have supported their estimated weights. Moreover, there is no feature in their skeletons that suggests an aquatic, or even amphibious, existence. In addition, numerous trackway sites clearly prove that sauropods could navigate on land, or at least where the water was too shallow to buoy up their weight. Accordingly, newer interpretations see these animals as floodplain and forest inhabitants.

Still another blow has been dealt to the old swamp image by the physical laws of hydrostatic pressure, which prohibit the explanation that the long neck enabled a submerged animal to raise its head to the surface for a breath of fresh air. The depth at which the lungs would be submerged would not allow them to be expanded by normal atmospheric pressure, the only force that fills the lungs. Consequently, the long necks of sauropods must be explained in terms of terrestrial functions such as elevating the feeding apparatus or the eyes. On all counts, sauropods are best seen as successful giraffelike browsers and only occasional waders.

Theropoda

This group includes all the known carnivorous dinosaurs as well as the birds. No obviously adapted herbivores are recognized in the group, but some theropods, notably the toothless oviraptorids and ornithomimids, may well have been relatively omnivorous like today's ostriches. Mesozoic Era theropods ranged in size from the smallest known adult

Mesozoic nonavian dinosaur, the crow-sized *Microraptor*, up to the great *Tyrannosaurus* and *Giganotosaurus*, which were 15 or more metres (50 feet) long, more than 5 metres (16 to 18 feet) tall, and weighed 6 tons or more. Theropods have been recovered from deposits of the Late Triassic through the latest Cretaceous and from all continents.

Theropods may be defined as birds and all saurischians more closely related to birds than to sauropods. They have a carnivorous dentition and large, recurved claws on the fingers. They also share many other characteristics, such as a distinctive joint in the lower jaw, epipophyses on the neck vertebrae, and a unique "transition point" in the tail where the vertebrae become longer and more lightly built. Other similarities include the reduction or loss of the outer two fingers, long end joints of the fingers, and a straplike fibula attached to a crest on the side of the tibia.

Herrerasaurus and several fragmentary taxa from South America, including *Staurikosaurus* and *Ischisaurus*, from the Middle to Late Triassic of Argentina are carnivores that have often been included in the Dinosauria, specifically in Theropoda. Whereas these animals closely resemble dinosaurs and have many carnivorous features, they also lack a number of features present in dinosaurs, saurischians, and theropods. For example, they have only two sacral vertebrae, unlike dinosaurs; their hips are more primitive than those of saurischians, as are their wrists; and the second finger is not the longest, unlike those of all saurischians. It remains probable that the features they seem to share with theropod dinosaurs are simply primitive and related to carnivory, the general habit of archosaurs. Future discoveries and analyses may help to resolve these questions.

In all theropods the hind leg bones were hollow to varying degrees—extremely hollow and lightly built in small to medium-size members (*Compsognathus*, *Coelurus*, and *Ornitholestes*, among others) and more solid in the larger forms (such as *Allosaurus*, *Daspletosaurus*, and *Tarbosaurus*.

In stance and gait, theropods were obligatory bipeds. Their bodies conformed to a common shape in which the hind legs were dominant and designed for support and locomotion. The forelimbs, on the other hand, had been modified from the primitive design and entirely divested of the functions of locomotion and body support. Hind limbs were either very robust and of graviportal (weight-bearing) proportions, as in *Allosaurus*, *Megalosaurus*, and the tyrannosaurids, or very slender, elongated, and of cursorial (adapted for running) proportions, as in *Coelurus*, *Coelophysis*, *Ornitholestes*, and the ornithomimids. Theropod feet, despite the group's name, which means "beast (i.e., mammal) foot," usually looked much like those of birds, which is not surprising, because birds inherited their foot structure from these dinosaurs. Three main toes were directed forward and splayed in a V-shaped arrangement. An additional inside toe was directed medially or backward. The whole foot was supported by the toes (digitigrade), with the "heel" elevated well above the ground. Toes usually bore sharp, somewhat curved claws.

The forelimbs varied widely from the slender, elongated ones of *Struthiomimus*, for example, to shorter, more massively constructed grasping appendages like those of *Allosaurus*, to the greatly abbreviated arms and hands of *Tyrannosaurus*, to the abbreviated, stout limb and single finger of *Mononykus*, to the range of wings now seen in birds. The hands typically featured long, flexible fingers with pronounced, often strongly curved claws, which bore sharp piercing talons. Early theropods such as *Coelophysis* had four fingers, with the fifth reduced to a nubbin of the metacarpal and the fourth greatly reduced. Most theropods were three-fingered, having lost all remnants of the fourth and fifth fingers. Tyrannosaurids (including *Albertosaurus*, *Daspletosaurus*, *Tarbosaurus*, and *Tyrannosaurus*) were notable for their two-fingered hands and unusually short arms. They had lost the third finger. The odd *Mononykus* lost even its second finger, retaining only a bizarre thumb. This separation of function between fore and hind limbs was a feature of the first dinosaurs. Although the first theropods, sauropodomorphs, and ornithischians were all bipedal, only theropods remained exclusively so.

The jaws of theropods are noted for their complement of sharp, bladelike teeth. In nearly all theropods these laterally compressed blades had serrations along the rear edge and often along the front edge as well. Tyrannosaur teeth differed in having a rounder, less-compressed cross section, better adapted to puncture flesh and tear it from bone. Troodontid teeth had recurved serrations slightly larger than those typical of theropods. *Archaeopteryx* and other basal birds had narrow-waisted teeth with greatly reduced serrations or none at all. Some theropods, such as most ornithomimids and oviraptorids, had lost most or all of their teeth.

In recent years a series of unusually well-preserved theropod dinosaurs have been discovered in deposits from the Early Cretaceous Period in Liaoning province, China. These theropods have filamentous integumentary structures of several kinds that resemble feathers. Such structures indicate that today's birds very likely evolved from theropod dinosaurs. See Dinosaur descendants.

Ceratosauria

Ceratosauria includes *Ceratosaurus* and all theropods more closely related to it than to birds. This group includes basal theropods such as *Dilophosaurus* and *Coelophysis*. It may also include the abelisaurids of South America and elsewhere, but this is not certain. Originally thought to be a natural group, Ceratosauria, as traditionally constituted, may represent a more general grouping of basal theropods, including the ancestral stock of most later theropods. The Late Triassic *Coelophysis*, about 1.5 meters long (5 feet), is generally regarded as an archetypal primitive theropod. It has a long neck and a long, low head with numerous small, sharp, recurved teeth. The legs were long, the arms relatively short, and the tail very long. *Dilophosaurus*, from the Early Jurassic Period, is considerably larger (about 4 metres [13 feet] in total length) and is distinguished by a pair of thin bony crests running along the top of the skull. Because no other theropod had such structures, these were apparently not necessary for any physiological function and so are thought to have been for display or species recognition. There is no evidence that *Dilophosaurus* spat venom.

Tetanurae

These comprise birds and all the theropods closer to birds than to *Ceratosaurus*. They would include the true carnosaurs and coelurosaurs described below as well as a few relatively large carnivorous basal forms (such as *Torvosaurus*, *Spinosaurus*, *Baryonyx*, *Afrovenator*, and *Megalosaurus*). The tetanuran theropods are distinguished by several features, including the complete loss of digits four and five of the hand, an upper tooth row extending backward only to the eye, and a fibula that is reduced and clasped by the tibia. The name Tetanurae, or "stiff tails," refers to another unusual feature, a transition point in the tail sequence where the vertebrae change form in a distinctive way.

Carnosauria includes *Allosaurus* and all theropods more closely related to it than to birds, including forms such as *Acrocanthosaurus*, *Sinraptor*, and *Giganotosaurus*. The first known members appear in the Late Jurassic and persist into the Cretaceous. Originally, this group was designed to include all the big predatory dinosaurs, but it was recently recognized that only size, not their relationships, was the trait unifying this group. Some, such as *Dilophosaurus* and *Carnotaurus*, were probably more closely related to basal ceratosaurs. Others, such as *Baryonyx* and *Spinosaurus*, represented an unusual diversification of fish-eating forms that were almost crocodilian in some of their habits. Still others, such as *Tyrannosaurus* and its relatives, the albertosaurs and daspletosaurs, were probably just giant coelurosaurs, as had been hypothesized by German paleontologist Friedrich von Huene early in the 20th century. As these groups were removed from the original Carnosauria, only *Allosaurus* and its relatives of the great Late Jurassic and Early Cretaceous diversification were left. Along with *Torvosaurus* and the megalosaurs, they must have been among the most deadly and rapacious large predators of their time. They are distinguished by relatively few characteristics. It is commonly thought that carnosaurs had very short limbs, but this is not particularly true—they were proportionally much shorter in tyrannosaurs, which are no longer considered carnosaurs. True carnosaurs had limbs comparable in size to those of more basal theropods. Sauropod vertebrae have been found with carnosaur tooth marks in them, which attests to the predatory habits of these dinosaurs.

The coelurosaurs ("hollow-tailed reptiles") include generally small to medium-size theropods, though the recent inclusion of tyrannosaurs would seem to discount this generalization. Coelurosauria is defined as birds and all tetanurans more closely related to birds than to the carnosaurs. The first known members, including birds, appear in the Late Jurassic. The great Cretaceous diversification of the other coelurosaurs ended with the Cretaceous extinctions.

In coelurosaurs the pelvis is modified so that the ischium is reduced to two-thirds or less the size of the pubis. The eyes are larger, and no more than 15 tail vertebrae bear transverse projections. Each of the various coelurosaurian groups has very distinct features that sets it apart from the others. The most basal known form, the Late Jurassic *Compsognathus*, was the size of a chicken and contemporaneous with the first known bird, *Archaeopteryx*. However, the two animals were not as closely related as some other coelurosaurs were to birds.

Tyrannosaurs and the related albertosaurs were the largest of the Late Cretaceous theropods of the northern continents. They are distinguished by an exceptionally large, high skull and teeth with a much more rounded cross section than the typical daggerlike teeth of other theropods. Their forelimbs are very short, and the third finger is reduced to a splint or lost entirely. Tyrannosaurs are thought to have migrated to North America from Asia, because early relatives first appear on the latter continent. Although there has been some debate about whether tyrannosaurs were active predators or more passive scavengers, the distinction is not usually strong in living predatory animals, and frequently larger carnivores will chase smaller ones away from fresh kills. However, some skeletons of plant-eating dinosaurs evidently have healed wounds caused by tyrannosaur bites, so active predation appears to be sustained.

Ornithomimids were medium-size to large theropods. Almost all of them were toothless, and apparently their jaws were covered by a horny beak. They also had very long legs and arms. A well-known example is *Struthiomimus*. Most were ostrich-sized and were adapted for fast running, with particularly long foot bones, or metatarsals. The largest was *Deinocheirus* from Asia, known only from one specimen consisting of complete arms and hands almost 3 metres (10 feet) long—nearly four times longer than those of *Struthiomimus*. These animals' speed, toothlessness, and long hands with relatively symmetrical fingers leave their lifestyle and feeding habits unclear, but they may have been fairly omnivorous like ostriches, although they are not directly related.

Oviraptorids, therizinosaurids, and caenagnathids appear to form a clade slightly more related to birds than to the coelurosaurs. Oviraptorids, known from the Late Cretaceous of Mongolia, had very strange skulls, often with high crests and a reduced dentition in an oddly curved jaw. The name oviraptor means "egg stealer," and it was given because remains of this carnivorous dinosaur were found along with fossil eggs presumed to belong to a small ceratopsian, *Protoceratops*, which lay nearby. Recent discoveries in Mongolia of oviraptorids sitting in birdlike positions on nests of eggs formerly thought to belong to *Protoceratops* reveal that the parentage was misplaced and that oviraptorids, like their bird relatives, apparently tended their young. Therizinosaurids, or segnosaurs, were medium-size Asian theropods known only from a few examples. The mouth had bladelike teeth at the back but apparently no teeth at the front. The pelvis differed markedly from the normal saurischian design. They are very inadequately understood but seem to have been unlike all other theropods. Caenagnathids are not well known either but appear to have had rounded jaws that, lacking or bearing reduced teeth, are sometimes mistaken for the jaws of birds.

The maniraptorans comprise birds, dromaeosaurs, and troodontids. Dromaeosaurs were medium-size predators with long, grasping arms and hands, moderately long legs, and a specialized stiffened tail that could be used for active balance control. Their feet bore large talons on one toe that were evidently used for raking and slicing prey. A famous discovery known as the "fighting dinosaurs of Mongolia" features a small dromaeosaur, *Velociraptor*, locked in petrified combat with a small protoceratopsian. The hands of the dromaeosaur are grasping the beaked dinosaur's frill, and the foot talons are apparently lodged in its throat. The best-known examples are *Deinonychus* of North America and *Velociraptor* of Asia.

Ornithischia

The Ornithischia were all plant eaters, as far as is known. In addition to a common pelvic structure, they share a number of other unique features, including a bone that joined the two lower jaws and distinctive leaf-shaped teeth crenulated along the upper edges. They had at least one palpebral, or "eyelid," bone, reduced skull openings near the eyes and in the lower jaw (antorbital and mandibular), five or more sacral vertebrae, and a pubis whose main shaft points backward and down, parallel to the ischium. The earliest and most basal form is the incompletely known *Pisanosaurus*, from the Late Triassic of Argentina. Some teeth and footprints and some fragmentary skeletal material of ornithischians are known from Late Triassic sediments, but it is only in the Early Jurassic that they become well known. Basal Jurassic forms include *Lesothosaurus* and other fabrosaurids, small animals that are the best-known basal ornithischians. They have the ornithischian features mentioned above but few specializations beyond these. Otherwise, the two main ornithischian lineages are the Cerapoda and Thyreophora.

Cerapoda

Cerapoda is divided into three groups: Ornithopoda, Pachycephalosauria, and Ceratopsia. The latter two are sometimes grouped together as Marginocephalia because they share a few features, including a bony shelf on the back of the skull.

Ornithopoda

Ornithopods include heterodontosaurs, known from southern Africa; the slightly larger hypsilophodontids, about 3 metres (9.8 feet) in length; the much larger iguanodontids, about 9 metres (29.5 feet) long, mostly from North America and Europe; and the large duck-billed hadrosaurs of North America and Eurasia. In all these forms, the front teeth are set slightly lower than the cheek teeth; the jaw joint is set lower than where the teeth meet in the jaws (the occlusal plane); and the nasal bone is excluded by a separate bone (the premaxilla) from contacting the upper jaw (maxilla).

The postcranial anatomy of the ornithopods reflects the bipedal ancestry of the group, but the giant hadrosaurs and some iguanodontids may have been as comfortable on four legs as on two, especially while feeding on low vegetation. All members had hind legs that were much longer and sturdier than their forelegs. The thighbone (femur) was nearly always shorter than the shinbones (tibia and fibula), especially in all but the largest forms, and it usually bore a prominent process, called the fourth trochanter, just above mid-length for the attachment of the retractor, or walking, muscles. The pelvis was expanded, usually with an elongated and broad blade of the ilium for the attachment of the protractor, or recovery, leg muscles. The pubis, as in all ornithischians, had migrated backward to lie parallel to the ischium, as described above. But in all but the most basal forms, a new prepubic process began to grow forward from the pubis, eventually reaching far in front of the forward edge of the ilium and becoming expanded into a paddlelike shape in hadrosaurs. It is generally thought that this process supported abdominal muscles and connective tissues of internal organs, but little is demonstrably known. The tail was long and sometimes quite deep and flat-sided. The vertebral spines of the tail and trunk region were reinforced by a rhomboidal latticework of bony (ossified) tendons running in criss-cross fashion between adjacent spines. They suggest a certain degree of stiffening of the tail and backbone, which were balanced over the massive hips.

Ornithopod feet were modified from the primitive five-toed pattern in a way that resembled similar modifications in theropod feet. The three middle toes served as the functional foot. The inside toe was shortened and often held off the ground, and the outside toe was greatly reduced or absent altogether. The resemblance to theropod feet is so strong that the footprints of the two groups are easily confused, especially if poorly preserved. The toes of all but the most basal ornithopods terminated in broad, almost hooflike bones, especially in the duckbills, as opposed to the sharp claws of theropods, and this is one way to distinguish their footprints. The hand reflected the primitive five-digit design, and, as was generally true in archosaurs, the fourth and fifth digits were shorter than the other three, with the third being longest. In iguanodontids and hadrosaurs, the fingers ended in broad, blunt bones rather than in claws, much like the toes. It is thought that these middle fingers and toes were covered by blunt, hooflike structures. In the duckbills the fingers apparently were encased in a mittenlike structure that could have broadened the hand for better support of the animal's weight on soft ground.

The Ornithopoda differ from one another mainly in the structure of their skulls, their jaws and teeth, their hands and feet, and their pelvises. Ornithopods constitute an excellent case study in evolution because, as the various lineages arise and die out from the latest Triassic to the latest Cretaceous, trends in size, complications and elaborations of teeth and chewing mechanisms, adaptations for quadrupedal posture in some forms, and other changes emerge clearly from their phylogenetic patterns.

In the fabrosaurids the teeth were simple leaf-shaped, laterally compressed elements arranged in a single front-to-back row in each jaw. They were not set in from the outer cheek surface as in most ornithopods. Small incisor-like teeth were borne on the premaxillary bones above, but (as always) no teeth were present on the predentary below. One pair of incisors had been lost. The lower jaw had no coronoid process for large muscle attachment, and the upper temporal opening (the jaw muscle site), like the mandibular opening, was relatively smaller than in theropods and other archosaurs. Upper and lower teeth alternated in position when the jaw was closed; they did not occlude directly.

In heterodontosaurs the cheek teeth were crowded together into long rows and set inward slightly from the outer cheek surface. The inset, which persisted through all later ornithopods, has been interpreted to suggest the presence of cheeks that may have held plant food in the mouth for further processing by the cheek teeth. They occluded directly to form distinct chisel-like cutting edges with a self-sharpening mechanism maintained by hard enamel on the outer side of the upper teeth and the inner side of the lower. There were prominent upper and lower tusklike teeth at the front of the mouth (the upper set in the premaxillary bones, the lower on the dentary bones). At least two pairs of incisors seem to have been retained. Certain features of the skull suggest much larger jaw muscles in heterodontosaurs than in the fabrosaurids.

The hypsilophodonts had cheek teeth arranged in tightly packed rows set well inward from the outer cheek surfaces. The teeth occluded directly, and the opposing rows formed a long shearing edge similar to that of the heterodontosaurs. There was, however, no "tusk" either above or below. The premaxillaries had small simple incisor-like teeth above the beak-covered, toothless predentary. Strong projections of bone extended up from the lower jaw toward the moderate-size upper temporal fenestrae.

The skulls of iguanodonts accommodated still larger jaw muscles, but the cheek teeth were less regular and compacted than in the primitive ornithopods and consequently did not occlude as uniformly. Both the premaxillaries and the predentary were toothless but probably were sheathed in horny beaks.

Specialization of the teeth and jaws reached a pinnacle in the hadrosaurs, or duck-billed ornithopods. In this group a very prominent, robust projection jutted from the back of the stout lower jaw. Large chambers housing muscles were present above this process and beneath certain openings in the skull (the lateral and upper temporal fenestrae). These chambers are clear evidence of powerful jaw muscles. The dentition consisted of numerous tightly compacted teeth crowded into large grinding batteries. The battery in each jaw was composed of as many as 200 functional and replacement teeth with distinct, well-defined wear, or grinding, surfaces that resulted from very exact occlusion. As teeth were lost from the front of the jaws in iguanodontids and hadrosaurs, the snouts expanded into a bulbous shape, especially in the "duck-billed" hadrosaur, and may have been covered by a horny beak that improved feeding. These bills apparently had edges sharp enough to shred and strip leaves or needles from low shrubs and branches. Pine needles have been identified in duck-billed dinosaur remains and presumably represent stomach contents.

Other interesting specializations may have assisted iguanodontids and hadrosaurs in feeding. In both groups there was a marked increase in mobility (kinesis) among the joints of the bones of the facial region. As the jaws clamped down, some cheek bones were allowed to rotate outward slightly, perhaps to cushion the stress of chewing tough foods. The hands were also unusually modified in the two groups, though in different ways. In iguanodontids the wrist bones were coalesced into a single blocky structure that was less mobile than in more primitive wrist configurations. The joints of the thumb were similarly coalesced into a single conelike spike that had limited mobility on the wrist. The middle three digits flexed in the normal way and bore broad flat, spatulate claws. The fifth digit actually had two additional joints and became somewhat opposable to the rest of the hand. It is thought that the hands may have been adapted to grasp and strip vegetation, and the spikelike thumb has been suggested to have been an effective weapon against predators. These features were more or less continued in hadrosaurs, except in this group the blocky wrist was reduced and the thumb was lost completely.

Some varieties of hadrosaurs are also noted for the peculiar crests and projections on the top of the head. These structures were expansions of the skull composed almost entirely of the nasal bones. In genera such as *Corythosaurus*, *Lambeosaurus*, *Parasaurolophus*, (and a few others), the crests were hollow, containing a series of middle and outer chambers that formed a convoluted passage from the nostrils to the trachea. Except for passing air along to the lungs, the function of these crests is not widely agreed upon. Sound production (honking), an improved sense of smell, and a visually conspicuous ornament for species recognition are some suggestions. Because these animals are no longer considered to have been amphibious, ideas such as snorkeling and extra air storage space have generally been discarded. Besides, the crests had no opening at their ends and consequently would not have been able to work as snorkels. Even the largest crests held only an estimated 2 percent of the volume of the lungs, hardly enough to justify the construction of such an elaborate structure.

Pachycephalosauria

In important respects the pachycephalosaurs conformed to the basic ornithopod body plan, and there is some evidence that pachycephalosaurs actually evolved from (and are therefore members of) ornithopods, perhaps similar to hypsilophodontids. All of them appear to have been bipedal. They bore the typical ornithopod ossified tendons along the back, and they had simple leaf-shaped teeth, although the teeth were enameled on both sides. The ornithischian type of pelvis was present, but a portion of the ischium was not.

The pachycephalosaurs are known as domeheads because of their most distinctive feature—a marked thickening of the frontoparietal (forehead) bones of the skull. The thickness of bone was much greater than might be expected in animals of their size. The suggestion has been made that this forehead swelling served as protection against the impact of the type of head-butting activities seen today in animals such as bighorn sheep, but microscopic studies of the bone structure of these thick domes suggest that they are poorly designed to divert stresses away from the braincase. Also, the great variety of pachycephalosaur domes—from thin, flat skull tops to pointed ridges with large spikes and knobs facing down and back—suggests no single function in defense or combat.

Stegoceras and *Pachycephalosaurus* of the North American Cretaceous were, respectively, the smallest and largest members of the group, the former attaining a length of about 2.5 metres (8 feet) and the latter twice that.

Pachycephalosaurs are known almost entirely from the Late Cretaceous (although *Yaverlandia* is from the Early Cretaceous) and have been found in North America and Asia. They are generally rare and still are relatively poorly known among dinosaur groups.

Ceratopsia

The first ceratopsian ("horn-faced") dinosaur remains were found in the 1870s by the American paleontologist Edward D. Cope, who named the animal *Agathaumus*, but the material was so fragmentary that its unusual design was not at once recognized. The first inkling that there had been horned dinosaurs did not emerge until the late 1880s with the discovery of a large horn core, first mistaken for that of a bison. Shortly afterward, dozens of large skulls with horns were found—the first of many specimens of *Triceratops*.

Ceratopsians first appeared in the modest form of psittacosaurids, or parrot-reptiles, in the Early Cretaceous and survived to the "great extinction" at the end of the Cretaceous Period *Triceratops*, together with *Tyrannosaurus*, was one of the very last of all known Mesozoic Era dinosaurs in North America, where the fossil record of the latest Cretaceous is best known. Ceratopsians had a peculiar geographic distribution: the earliest and most primitive kinds, such as *Psittacosaurus*, are known only from Asia—Mongolia and China, specifically *Protoceratops* and its relatives are known from both Asia and North America. All the advanced ceratopsids (chasmosaurines and centrosaurines), with the exception of a few fragmentary and doubtful specimens, have been found only in North America.

Ceratopsians ranged in size from relatively small animals the size of a dog to the nearly 9-metre- (30-foot-) long, four- to five-ton *Triceratops*. Although commonly compared to the modern rhinoceros, *Triceratops* grew to a weight and bulk several times that of the largest living rhinoceros, and its behaviour probably was correspondingly different. The most distinctive feature of nearly all members of the group was the horns on the head, hence the name *ceratops.* Correlated with the various arrays of head horns in the different taxa was the unusually large size of ceratopsian heads. Great bony growths extended from the back of the skull, reaching well over the neck and shoulders. This neck shield, or frill, resulted in the longest head that ever adorned any land animal; the length of the *Torosaurus* skull was almost 3 metres (10 feet), longer than a whole adult *Protoceratops.*

Several hypotheses have been proposed to explain this frill structure: a protective shield to cover the neck region, an attachment site of greatly enlarged jaw muscles, an attachment site of powerful neck muscles for wielding the head horns, or a sort of ornament to present a huge, frightening head-on profile to potential attackers. The most unusual thought is that the structure was none of these, but rather acted as a giant heat-control apparatus, with its entire upper surface covered in a vast network of blood vessels pulsing with overheated blood or absorbing solar heat.

Most of these hypotheses are difficult to test. One important fact to keep in mind was that the frill was little more than a frame of bone, sometimes ornamented with knobs and spikes around large openings behind and above the skull. An exception to this pattern was *Triceratops*, which had a solid and relatively short frill, but *Triceratops* is so well known that its frill is often mistakenly considered typical of ceratopsians. The open frill of other ceratopsians would have provided only poor protection for the neck region and only a modest area of attachment for jaw or neck muscles. If skin and soft tissues spanned the area framed by the bony frill, it would have created a formidable presence when the head was lowered in threatening display. Such a large structure would naturally have absorbed and reflected sunlight that warmed the tissue and its internal blood vessels, but it is questionable whether this was an important or necessary function of the frill, since other dinosaurs do not have similar structures.

The Ceratopsia are divided into groups that mirror their evolutionary trends through time: the primitive psittacosaurids, such as *Psittacosaurus*; the protoceratopsids, including *Protoceratops* of Asia and *Leptoceratops* of North America; and the ceratopsids, encompassing all the advanced and better-known kinds such as the chasmosaurines *Triceratops* and *Torosaurus* as well as the centrosaurines such as *Centrosaurus* (or *Monoclonius*)—all from North America.

Like the pachycephalosaurs, the most basal ceratopsians, such as *Psittacosaurus*, look much like typical ornithopods, largely because of their relatively long hind limbs and short front limbs (probably resulting in bipedal stance and locomotion) and the persistence of upper front teeth and a fairly unspecialized pelvis. Resembling ornithopods in body form, *Psittacosaurus* had a shorter neck and tail and was much smaller (only 2 metres [6.5 feet] long) than the most advanced ornithopods such as the iguanodonts and hadrosaurs *Psittacosaurus*, however, possessed a beak, the beginnings of a characteristic neck frill at the back of the skull, and teeth that prefigured those of the more advanced ceratopsians. It is also recognized diagnostically as a ceratopsian by the presence of a unique bone called the rostral, a toothless upper beak bone that opposed the lower predentary found in all ornithischians.

The best-known of the protoceratopsids is the genus *Protoceratops*. Dozens of skeletal specimens, ranging from near hatchlings to full-size adults, have been found and studied. This rare treasure, the first to include very young individuals unmistakably associated with mature individuals, was the result of the series of American Museum of Natural History expeditions in the 1920s to the Gobi Desert of Mongolia. Their collection provided the first valid growth series of any dinosaur. Their discovery of several nests of eggs loosely associated with *Protoceratops* skeletons was the first finding of eggs that were unquestionably dinosaurian. Originally attributed to *Protoceratops*, the eggs only recently were correctly attributed to the theropod *Oviraptor* (as noted in the section Tetanurae).

The skeletal anatomy of the protoceratopsids foreshadowed that of the more advanced ceratopsids. The ceratopsian skull was disproportionately large for the rest of the animal, constituting about one-fifth of the total body length in *Protoceratops* and at least one-third in *Torosaurus*. The head frill of *Protoceratops* was a modest backward extension of two cranial arches, but it became the enormous fan-shaped ornament of later forms. *Protoceratops* also displayed a short but stout horn on the snout due to development of the nasal bones. This too was a precursor of the prominent nasal horns of ceratopsids such as *Centrosaurus*, *Chasmosaurus*, *Styracosaurus*, *Torosaurus*, and *Triceratops*. The last two genera evolved two additional larger horns above the eyes. These horns undoubtedly were covered by horny sheaths or soft tissue, as is evidenced by impressions on them of superficial vascular channels for nourishing blood vessels. These advanced ceratopsids are sometimes divided into centrosaurines, which had a prominent nose horn but small or absent eye horns, and chasmosaurines, which had larger eye horns but reduced nose horns.

Ceratopsian jaws were highly specialized. The lower jaw was massive and solid to support a large battery of teeth similar to those of the duckbills. The lower jawbones were joined at the front and capped by a stout beak formed of the toothless predentary bone. This structure itself must have been covered by a sharp, horny, turtlelike beak. Continuous dental surfaces extended over the rear two-thirds of the jaw. The tooth batteries, however, differed from those of the hadrosaurs in forming long, vertical slicing surfaces as upper and lower batteries met, operating much like self-sharpening shears.

As in the hadrosaurs, each dental battery consisted of about two dozen or more tooth positions compressed together into a single large block. At each tooth position there was one functional, or occluding, tooth (the duckbills had two or three) along with several more unerupted replacement teeth beneath. (All toothed vertebrates, living and extinct, except mammals, have a lifelong supply of replacement teeth.) The suggestion is that they fed on something exceedingly tough and fibrous, such as the fronds of palms or cycads, both of which were plentiful during late Mesozoic times.

With the exception of the bipedal *Psittacosaurus*, and perhaps the facultatively bipedal protoceratopsids, all ceratopsians were obligate quadrupeds with a heavy, ponderous build. The leg bones were stout and the legs themselves muscular; the feet were semiplantigrade for graviportal stance and progression; and all the toes ended in "hooves" rather than claws. As in most other four-legged animals, the rear legs were significantly longer than the front legs (which again suggests their bipedal ancestry). The hind legs were positioned directly beneath the hip sockets and held almost straight and vertical. The front legs, on the other hand, projected out to each side from the shoulder sockets in a "push-up" position. Consequently, the head was carried low and close to the ground. This mixed posture was perhaps related to the large horned head and its role in combat, the bent forelegs providing a wide stance and stable base for directing the horns at an opponent and resisting attack.

The first four neck vertebrae of ceratopsians were fused (co-ossified), presumably to support the massive skull. The first joint of the neck was unusual in that the bone at the base of the skull formed a nearly perfect sphere that fit into a cuplike socket of the fused neck vertebrae. Such an arrangement would seem to have provided solid connections along with maximum freedom of the head to pivot in any direction without having to turn the body. Presumably ceratopsians used their horns in an aggressive manner, but whether they used them as defense against possible predators, in rutting combat with other male ceratopsians, or in both is not so clear. Evidence of puncture wounds in some specimens suggests rutting encounters, but the fact that both sexes apparently had horns seems to indicate defense or species recognition as their primary uses.

Thyreophora

The Thyreophora consist mainly of the well-known Stegosauria, the plated dinosaurs, and Ankylosauria, the armoured dinosaurs, as well as their more basal relatives, including *Scutellosaurus* and *Scelidosaurus*. *Scutellosaurus* was a small bipedal dinosaur, only about a metre (3.3 feet) in length, known from the Early Jurassic Period of Arizona, U.S. It was first classified as a fabrosaurid because of its primitive skeletal structures. However, it differed from fabrosaurids in some important respects, including the possession of small bony plates, or scutes, of various shapes along the back and sides of its body. These scutes are also found in the slightly larger *Scelidosaurus*, which was up to 3 metres (9.8 feet) in length and quadrupedal. This dinosaur is known from the Early Jurassic of England and Arizona.

In the Middle and Late Jurassic, the first stegosaurs and ankylosaurs appeared. Like the previously described forms, they are distinguished by bony scutes. Scutes are maintained and elaborated all over the body in ankylosaurs but are reduced to a series of plates and spikes along the backbone in stegosaurs, though their basic structure remains the same in both groups. Thyreophorans also have low, flat skulls, simple S-shaped tooth rows with small leaf-shaped tooth crowns, and spout-shaped snouts.

Stegosauria

With their unique bony back plates, the stegosaurs are very distinctive. Relatively few specimens have been found, but they were widespread, with remains being found in North America, Africa, Europe, and Asia. Stegosaurian remains have appeared in Early Jurassic to Early Cretaceous strata. The most familiar genus is *Stegosaurus*, found in the Morrison Formation (Late Jurassic) of western North America. *Stegosaurus* was 3.7 metres (12 feet) in height and 9 metres (29.5 feet) in length, probably weighed two tons, and had a broad, deep body. Not all varieties of the Stegosauria were this large. For example, *Kentrosaurus* , from eastern Africa, was less than 2 metres (6.5 feet) high and 3.5 metres (11.5 feet) long.

All stegosaurs were graviportal and undoubtedly quadrupedal, although the massive legs were of greatly disparate lengths—the hind legs being more than twice the length of the forelegs. Whatever walking and running skills were possessed by the stegosaurs, their limb proportions must have made these movements extremely slow. The humerus of the upper arm was longer than the bones of the forearm, the femur much longer than the shinbones, and certain bones of the feet very short, which means that the stride must have been short. In addition, the feet were graviportal in design and showed no adaptations for running.

The stegosaurian skull was notably small, long, low, and narrow, with little space for sizable jaw muscles. The weakly developed dentition consisted of small, laterally compressed, leaf-shaped teeth arranged in short, straight rows. This combination of features seems odd in comparison with the large, bulky body. The weak dentition suggests that the food eaten must have required little preparation by the teeth and yet provided adequate nourishment. Perhaps the digestive tract contained fermenting bacteria capable of breaking down the cellulose-rich Jurassic plant tissues. Digestion may also have been assisted by a crop or gizzard full of pulverizing stomach stones (gastroliths), though none has yet been discovered in stegosaurian specimens. A collection of disklike bones is found in the throat region of *Stegosaurus*, but these are likely to have been embedded in the skin, not used in the gut. Even so, it is still difficult to understand how these animals, with such small and poorly equipped mouths, could have fed themselves adequately to sustain their great bulk. The same problem has been encountered in speculations about the feeding habits of sauropods.

The most distinctive stegosaurian feature was the double row of large diamond-shaped bony plates on the back. A controversy as to their purpose and how they were arranged has raged ever since the first *Stegosaurus* specimen was collected (1877, Colorado, U.S.). The evidence and a general consensus argue in favour of the traditional idea that the plates projected upward and were set in two staggered (alternating) rows on either side of the backbone. In other stegosaurs, such as *Kentrosaurus*, the plates are more symmetrical and may have been arranged side by side. The suggestion that the plates did not project above the back at all, but lay flat to form flank armour, has been rejected on the basis of studies of the microstructure of the bone of the plates, in which attachment fibres are embedded in a manner consistent with an upright position. In *Stegosaurus* itself, the end of the tail bore at least two pairs of long bony spikes, which suggests some sort of defensive role for the tail but not necessarily for the back plates. However, other stegosaurs, such as *Kentrosaurus*, had relatively small plates along the front half of the spine and spikes along the back half of the spine and the tail.

The discovery in 1976 that the bony plates of *Stegosaurus* were highly vascularized led to the suggestion that these "fins" functioned as cooling vanes to dissipate excess body heat in much the same way that the ears of elephants do. The staggered arrangement in parallel rows might have maximized the area of cooling surface by minimizing any downwind "breeze shadow" that would have resulted from a paired configuration. Asymmetry is a bizarre anatomic condition, and, right or wrong, this certainly is an imaginative explanation of its presence in this animal. No other stegosaur, however, had such a peculiar feature. Rather, all other taxa had a variety of paired body spikes that seem best explained as passive defense or display adaptations rather than cooling mechanisms.

Ankylosauria

The ankylosaurs are known from the Late Jurassic and Cretaceous periods. They are called "armoured dinosaurs" for their extensive mosaic of small and large interlocking bony plates that completely encased the back and flanks. Most ankylosaurs, such as *Euoplocephalus*, *Nodosaurus*, and *Palaeoscincus*, were relatively low and broad in body form and walked close to the ground on short, stocky legs in a quadrupedal stance. As in stegosaurs, the hind legs were longer than the front legs, but they were not as disproportionate as those of *Stegosaurus*. Like the stegosaurs, however, their limbs were stout and columnar, the thighbone and upper arm were longer than the shin and forearm, and the metapodials were stubby. These features point to a slow, graviportal mode of locomotion. The feet were semiplantigrade and possibly supported from beneath by pads of cartilage. The bones at the ends of the digits (terminal phalanges) were broad and hooflike rather than clawlike.

The ankylosaur skull was low, broad, and boxlike, with dermal scutes (osteoderms) that were often fused to the underlying skull bones. In *Euoplocephalus* even the eyelid seems to have developed a protective bony covering. The jaws were weak, with a very small predentary and no significant projections of bone for jaw muscle attachment. The small jaw muscle chamber was largely covered by dermal bones rather than having openings. The teeth were small, loosely spaced, leaf-shaped structures reminiscent of the earliest primitive ornithischian teeth. All taxa had very few teeth in either jaw, in marked contrast to the highly specialized, numerous teeth of other ornithischians. These features of the jaws and teeth lead to the impression that the animals must have fed on some sort of soft, pulpy plant food.

Apparently neither very diverse nor abundant, the ankylosaurs are known only from North America, Europe, and Asia. They are divided into the more basal Nodosauridae and the more advanced Ankylosauridae, which may have evolved from nodosaurs. The most conspicuous difference between the two groups is the presence of a massive bony club at the end of the tail in the advanced ankylosaurs. No such tail structure is present in the nodosaurs. The patterns of the armour also generally differ between the two groups, and ankylosaurids tend to have even broader, more bone-encrusted skulls than did the nodosaurs.

The End of the Dinosaurs

A misconception commonly portrayed in popular books and media is that all the dinosaurs died out at the same time—and apparently quite suddenly—at the end of the Cretaceous Period. This is not entirely correct, and not only because birds are a living branch of dinosaurian lineage. The best records, which are almost exclusively from North America, show that dinosaurs were already in decline during the latest portion of the Cretaceous. The causes of this decline, as well as the fortunes of other groups at the time, are complex and difficult to attribute to a single source. In order to understand extinction, it is necessary to understand the basic fossil record of dinosaurs.

Final Changes in Dinosaur Communities

During the 160 million years or so of the Mesozoic Era from which dinosaurs are known, there were constant changes in dinosaur communities. Different species evolved rapidly and were quickly replaced by others throughout the Mesozoic. It is rare that any particular type of dinosaur survived from one geologic formation into the next. The fossil evidence shows a moderately rich fauna of plateosaurs and other prosauropods, primitive ornithopods, and theropods during the Late Triassic Period. Most of these kinds of dinosaurs are also represented in strata of the Early Jurassic Period (about 200 million to 176 million years ago), but following a poorly known Middle Jurassic, the fauna of the Late Jurassic (about 161 million to 145.5 million years ago) was very different. By this time sauropods, more advanced ornithopods, stegosaurs, and a variety of theropods predominated. The Early Cretaceous (145.5 million to 99.6 million years ago) then contained a few sauropods (albeit they were all new forms), a few stegosaurian holdovers, new kinds of theropods and ornithopods, and some of the first well-known ankylosaurs. By the Late Cretaceous, sauropods, which had disappeared from the northern continents through most of the Early and mid-Cretaceous, had reinvaded the northern continents from the south, and advanced ornithopods (duckbills) had become the dominant browsers. A variety of new theropods of all sizes were widespread; stegosaurs no longer existed; and the ankylosaurs were represented by a collection of new forms that were prominent in North America and Asia. New groups of dinosaurs, the pachycephalosaurs and ceratopsians, had appeared in Asia and had successfully colonized North America. The overall picture is thus quite clear: throughout Mesozoic time there was a continuous dying out and renewal of dinosaurian life.

It is important to note that extinction is a normal, universal occurrence. Mass extinctions often come to mind when the term extinction is mentioned, but the normal background extinctions that occur throughout geologic time probably account for most losses of biodiversity. Just as a new species constantly split from existing ones, existing species are constantly becoming extinct. The speciation rate of a group must, on balance, exceed the extinction rate in the long run, or that group will become extinct. The history of animal and plant life is replete with successions as early forms are replaced by new and often more advanced forms. In most instances the layered (stratigraphic) nature of the fossil record gives too little information to show whether the old forms were actually displaced by the new successors (from the effects of competition, predation, or other ecological processes) or if the new kinds simply expanded into the declining population's ecological niches.

Because the fossil record is episodic rather than continuous, it is very useful for asking many kinds of questions, but it is not possible to say precisely how long most dinosaur species or genera actually existed. Moreover, because the knowledge of the various dinosaur groups is somewhat incomplete, the duration of any particular dinosaur can be gauged only approximately—usually by stratigraphic boundaries and presumed "first" and "last" occurrences. The latter often coincide with geologic age boundaries. In fact, the absence of particular life-forms has historically defined most geologic boundaries ever since the geologic record was first compiled and analyzed in the late 18th century. The "moments" of apparently high extinction levels among dinosaurs were near the ends of two stages of the Late Triassic, perhaps at the end of the Jurassic, and of course at the end of the Cretaceous. Undoubtedly, there were lesser extinction peaks at other times in between, but there are poor terrestrial records for most of the world in the Middle Triassic, Middle Jurassic, and mid-Cretaceous.

The K–T Boundary Event

It was not only the dinosaurs that disappeared at the Cretaceous–Tertiary (K–T), or Cretaceous–Paleogene (K–Pg), boundary. Many other organisms became extinct or were greatly reduced in abundance and diversity, and the extinctions were quite different between, and even among, marine and terrestrial organisms. Land plants did not respond in the same way as land animals, and not all marine organisms showed the same patterns of extinction. Some groups died out well before the K–T boundary, including flying reptiles (pterosaurs) and sea reptiles (plesiosaurs, mosasaurs, and ichthyosaurs). Strangely, turtles, crocodilians, lizards, and snakes were either not affected or affected only slightly. Effects on amphibians and mammals were mild. These patterns seem odd, considering how environmentally sensitive and habitat-restricted many of these groups are today. Many marine groups—such as the molluscan ammonites, the belemnites, and certain bivalves—were decimated. Other greatly affected groups were the moss animals (phylum Bryozoa), the crinoids, and a number of planktonic life-forms such as foraminifera, radiolarians, coccolithophores, and diatoms.

Whatever factors caused it, there was undeniably a major, worldwide biotic change near the end of the Cretaceous. But the extermination of the dinosaurs is the best-known change by far, and it has been a puzzle to paleontologists, geologists, and biologists for two centuries. Many hypotheses have been offered over the years to explain dinosaur extinction, but only a few have received serious consideration. Proposed causes have included everything from disease to heat waves and resulting sterility, freezing cold spells, the rise of egg-eating mammals, and X rays from a nearby exploding supernova. Since the early 1980s, attention has focused on the so-called asteroid theory put forward by the American geologist Walter Alvarez, his father, physicist Luis Alvarez, and their coworkers. This theory is consistent with the timing and magnitude of some extinctions, especially in the oceans, but it does not fully explain the patterns on land and does not eliminate the possibility that other factors were at work on land as well as in the seas.

One important question is whether the extinctions were simultaneous and instantaneous or whether they were nonsynchronous and spread over a long time. The precision with which geologic time can be measured leaves much to be desired no matter what means are used (radiometric, paleomagnetic, or the more traditional measuring of fossil content of stratigraphic layers). Only rarely does an "instantaneous" event leave a worldwide—or even regional—signature in the geologic record in the way that a volcanic eruption does locally. Attempts to pinpoint the K–T boundary event, even by using the best radiometric dating techniques, result in a margin of error on the order of 50,000 years. Consequently, the actual time involved in this, or any of the preceding or subsequent extinctions, has remained undetermined.

The Asteroid Theory

The discovery of an abnormally high concentration of the rare metal iridium at, or very close to, the K–T boundary provides what has been recognized as one of those rare instantaneous geologic time markers that seem to be worldwide. This iridium anomaly, or spike, was first found by Walter Alvarez in the Cretaceous–Tertiary stratigraphic sequence at Gubbio, Italy, in the 1970s. The spike has subsequently been detected at hundreds of localities in Denmark and elsewhere, both in rock outcrops on land and in core samples drilled from ocean floors. Iridium normally is a rare substance in rocks of the Earth's crust (about 0.3 part per billion). At Gubbio the iridium concentration is more than 20 times greater (6.3 parts per billion), and it exceeds this concentration at other sites.

Because the levels of iridium are higher in meteorites than on the Earth, the Gubbio anomaly is thought to have an extraterrestrial explanation. If this is true, such extraterrestrial signatures will have a growing influence on the precision with which geologic time boundaries can be specified. The level of iridium in meteorites has been accepted as representing the average level throughout the solar system and, by extension, the universe. Accordingly, the iridium concentration at the K–T boundary is widely attributed to a collision between the Earth and a huge meteor or asteroid. The size of the object is estimated at about 10 km (6.2 miles) in diameter and one quadrillion metric tons in weight. The velocity at the time of impact is reckoned to have been several hundreds of thousands of kilometres (miles) per hour. The crater resulting from such a collision would be some 100 km (62 miles) or more in diameter. Such an impact site (called an astrobleme), known as the Chicxulub crater, may have been identified in the Yucatán Peninsula.

The asteroid theory is widely accepted as the most probable explanation of the K–T iridium anomaly, but it does not appear to account for all the paleontological data. An impact explosion of this kind would have ejected an enormous volume of terrestrial and asteroid material into the atmosphere, producing a cloud of dust and solid particles that would have encircled the Earth and blocked out sunlight for many months, possibly years. The loss of sunlight could have eliminated photosynthesis and resulted in the death of plants and the subsequent extinction of herbivores, their predators, and scavengers.

The K–T mass extinctions, however, do not seem to be fully explained by this hypothesis. The stratigraphic record is most complete for extinctions of marine life—foraminifera, ammonites, coccolithophores, and the like. These apparently died out suddenly and simultaneously, and their extinction accords best with the asteroid theory. The fossil evidence of land dwellers, however, suggests a gradual rather than a sudden decline in dinosaurian diversity (and possibly abundance). Alterations in terrestrial life seem to be best accounted for by environmental factors, such as the consequences of seafloor spreading and continental drift, resulting in continental fragmentation, climatic deterioration, increased seasonality, and perhaps changes in the distributions and compositions of terrestrial communities. But one phenomenon does not preclude another. It is entirely possible that a culmination of ordinary biological changes and some catastrophic events, including increased volcanic activity, took place about the end of the Cretaceous.

Dinosaur Descendants

Contrary to the commonly held belief that the dinosaurs left no descendants, the rare (seven) specimens of *Archaeopteryx* (the earliest bird known) provide compelling evidence that birds (class Aves) evolved from small theropod dinosaurs. Following the principles of genealogy that are applied to humans as much as to other organisms, organisms are classified at a higher level within the groups from which they evolved. *Archaeopteryx* is therefore classified as both a dinosaur and a bird, just as humans are both primates and mammals.

The specimens of *Archaeopteryx* contain particular anatomic features that also are exclusively present in certain theropods (*Oviraptor*, *Velociraptor*, *Deinonychus*, and *Troodon*, among others). These animals share long arms and hands, a somewhat shorter, stiffened tail, a similar pelvis, and an unusual wrist joint in which the hand is allowed to flex sideways instead of up and down. This wrist motion is virtually identical to the motion used by birds (and bats) in flight, though in these small dinosaurs its initial primary function was probably in catching prey.

Beginning in the 1990s, several specimens of small theropod dinosaurs from the Early Cretaceous of Liaoning province, China, were unearthed. These fossils are remarkably well preserved, and because they include impressions of featherlike, filamentous structures that covered the body, they have shed much light on the relationship between birds and Mesozoic dinosaurs. Such structures are now known in a compsognathid (*Sinosauropteryx*), a therizinosaurid (*Beipiaosaurus*), a dromaeosaur

(*Sinornithosaurus*), and an alvarezsaurid (*Shuvuuia*). The filamentous structures on the skin of *Sinosauropteryx* are similar to the barbs of feathers, which suggests that feathers evolved from a much simpler structure that probably functioned as an insulator. True feathers of several types, including contour and body feathers, have been found in the 125-million-year-old feathered oviraptorid *Caudipteryx* and the apparently related *Protarchaeopteryx*. Because these animals were not birds and did not fly, it is now evident that true feathers neither evolved first in birds nor developed for the purpose of flight. Instead, feathers may have evolved for insulation, display, camouflage, species recognition, or some combination of these functions and only later became adapted for flight. In the case of *Caudipteryx*, for example, it has been established that these animals not only sat on nests but probably protected the eggs with their feathers.

Until comparatively recent times, the two groups of birds from Cretaceous time that received the most attention because of their strange form were the divers, such as *Hesperornis*, and the strong-winged *Ichthyornis*, a more ternlike form. Because they were the first well-known Cretaceous birds, having been described by American paleontologist O. C. Marsh in 1880, they were thought to represent typical Cretaceous birds. Recent discoveries, however, have changed this view. For example, members of one Early Cretaceous bird group, the Confuciusornithidae, showed very little advancement compared with *Archaeopteryx* and the Enantiornithes (a major group of birds widely distributed around the world through most of the Cretaceous Period). Because representatives of living bird groups have long been known among the fossil species from the Paleocene and Eocene epochs (about 66 million to 34 million years ago), it has seemed evident that bird groups other than those including *Hesperornis* and *Ichthyornis* must have existed during the Cretaceous. Knowledge of these, based on fragments of fossil bone, has slowly come to light, and there is now a fairly definite record from Cretaceous rock strata of other ancestral birds related to the living groups of loons, grebes, flamingos, cranes, parrots, and shorebirds—and thus indication of early avian diversity. Therefore, it is clear that birds did not go through a "bottleneck" of extinction at the end of the Cretaceous that separated the archaic groups from the extant groups. Rather, the living groups were mostly present by the latest Cretaceous, and by this time the archaic groups seem to have died out.

CHAPTER 2
The Triassic Period

In geologic time the first period of the Mesozoic Era is known as the Triassic Period. It began 251 million years ago, at the close of the Permian Period, and ended 199.6 million years ago, when it was succeeded by the Jurassic Period.

The Triassic Period marked the beginning of major changes that were to take place throughout the Mesozoic Era, particularly in the distribution of continents, the evolution of life, and the geographic distribution of living things. At the beginning of the Triassic, virtually all the major landmasses of the world were collected into the supercontinent of Pangea. Terrestrial climates were predominately warm and dry (though seasonal monsoons occurred over large areas), and the Earth's crust was relatively quiescent. At the end of the Triassic, however, plate tectonic activity picked up, and a period of continental rifting began. On the margins of the continents, shallow seas, which had dwindled in area at the end of the Permian, became more extensive. As sea levels gradually rose, the waters of continental shelves were colonized for the first time by large marine reptiles and reef-building corals of modern aspect.

The Triassic followed on the heels of the largest mass extinction in the history of the Earth. This event occurred at the end of the Permian, when 85 to 95 percent of marine invertebrate species and 70 percent of terrestrial vertebrate genera died out. During the recovery of life in the Triassic Period, the relative importance of land animals grew. Reptiles increased in diversity and number, and the first dinosaurs appeared, heralding the great radiation that would characterize this group during the Jurassic and Cretaceous periods. Finally, the end of the Triassic saw the appearance of the first mammals—tiny, fur-bearing, shrewlike animals derived from reptiles.

Another episode of mass extinction occurred at the end of the Triassic. Though this event was less devastating than its counterpart at the end of the Permian, it did result in drastic reductions of some living populations—particularly of the ammonoids, primitive mollusks that have served as important index fossils for assigning relative ages to various strata in the Triassic System of rocks.

The name Trias (later modified to Triassic) was first proposed in 1834 by the German paleontologist Friedrich August von Alberti for a sequence of rock strata in central Germany that lay above Permian rocks and below Jurassic rocks. (The name Trias referred to the division of these strata into three units: the Bunter [or Buntsandstein], Muschelkalk, and Keuper.) Alberti's rock sequence, which became known as the "Germanic facies," had many drawbacks as a standard for assigning relative ages to Triassic rocks from other regions of the world, and so for much of the 19th and 20th centuries Triassic stages were based mainly on type sections from the "Alpine facies" in Austria, Switzerland, and northern Italy. Since the mid-20th century more complete sequences have been discovered in North America, and these now serve as the standard for Triassic time in general. Meanwhile, studies of seafloor spreading and plate tectonics have yielded important new information on the paleogeography and paleoclimatology of the Triassic, allowing for a better understanding of the evolution and extinction of life-forms and of the paleoecology and paleobiogeography of the period. In addition, paleontologists continue to be occupied with defining the lower and upper boundaries of the Triassic System on a worldwide basis and with understanding the reasons for the mass extinctions that took place at those boundaries.

THE TRIASSIC ENVIRONMENT

The environment at the beginning of the Triassic Period had relatively little variation. All of the Earth's continents were joined into a continuous swath of land that nearly stretched from one pole to the other, whereas the remainder of the Earth's surface during this time was occupied by a large ocean. This arrangement simplified ocean circulation and thus the distribution of heat and moisture. In addition, since the temperature gradient between the poles and the Equator was relatively small, the Triassic world contained fewer distinct habitats than during other periods.

Paleogeography

At the beginning of the Triassic Period, the land was grouped together into one large C-shaped supercontinent. Covering about one-quarter of the Earth's surface, Pangea stretched from 85° N to 90° S in a narrow belt of about 60° of longitude. It consisted of a group of northern continents collectively referred to as Laurasia and a group of southern continents collectively referred to as Gondwana. The rest of the globe was covered by Panthalassa, an enormous world ocean that stretched from pole to pole and extended to about twice the width of the present-day Pacific Ocean at the Equator. Scattered across Panthalassa within 30° of the Triassic Equator were islands, seamounts, and volcanic archipelagoes, some associated with deposits of reef carbonates now found in western North America and other locations.

Projecting westward between Gondwana and Laurasia along an east-west axis approximately coincident with the present-day Mediterranean Sea was a deep embayment of Panthalassa known as the Tethys Sea (previously discussed in chapter 1). This ancient seaway was later to extend farther westward to Gibraltar as rifting between Laurasia and Gondwana began in the Late Triassic (about 229 million to 200 million years ago). Eventually, by Middle to Late Jurassic times, it would link up with the eastern side of Panthalassa, effectively separating the two halves of the Pangea supercontinent. Paleogeographers reconstruct these continental configurations using evidence from many sources, the most important of which are paleomagnetic data and correspondences between continental margins in shape, rock types, orogenic (mountain-building) events, and distribution of fossilized plants and land vertebrates that lived prior to the breakup of Pangea. In addition, the apparent polar-wandering curves (plots of the apparent movement of the Earth's magnetic poles with respect to the continents through time) for modern-day Africa and North America converge between the Carboniferous and Triassic periods and then begin to diverge in the Late Triassic, which indicates the exact time when the two continents began to separate and the Tethys Sea began to open up.

Thick sequences of clastic sediments accumulated in marginal troughs bordering the present-day circum-Pacific region as well as the northern and southern margins of the Tethys, while shelf seas occupied parts of the Tethyan, circum-Pacific, and circum-Arctic regions but were otherwise restricted in distribution. Much of the circum-Pacific region and the northeastern part of Tethys were bordered by active (that is, convergent) plate margins, but the northwestern and southern margins of Tethys were passive (that is, divergent) during the Triassic. At the end of the Triassic, increased tectonic activity contributed to rising sea levels and an increase in the extent of shallow continental shelf seas.

Along the western margin of modern North America, a major subduction zone was present where the eastward-moving oceanic plate of eastern Panthalassa slid under the continental plate of Pangea. The Panthalassa plate carried fragments of island arcs and microcontinents that, because of their lesser density, could not be subducted along with the oceanic plate. As these fragments reached the subduction zone, they were sutured onto the Cordilleran belt of North America, forming what geologists refer to as allochthonous terranes (fragments of crust displaced from their site of origin). This process of "accretionary tectonics" (or obduction) created more than 50 terranes of various ages in the Cordilleran region, including the Sonomia and Golconda terranes of the northwestern United States, both of which were accreted in the Early Triassic (about 251 million to 246 million years ago). The former microcontinent of Sonomia occupies what is now southeastern Oregon and northern California and Nevada.

Paleoclimate

Worldwide climatic conditions during the Triassic seem to have been much more homogeneous than at present. No polar ice existed. Temperature differences between the Equator and the poles would have been less extreme than they are today, which would have resulted in less diversity in biological habitats.

Beginning in the Late Permian and continuing into the Early Triassic, the emergence of the supercontinent Pangea and the associated reduction in the total area covered by continental shelf seas led to widespread aridity over most land areas. Judging from modern conditions, a single large landmass such as Pangea would be expected to experience an extreme, strongly seasonal continental climate with hot summers and cold winters. Yet the paleoclimatic evidence is conflicting. There are several indicators of an arid climate, including the following: red sandstones and shales that contain few fossils, lithified dune deposits with cross-bedding, salt pseudomorphs in marls, mudcracks, and evaporites. On the other hand, there is evidence for strong seasonal precipitation, including braided fluvial (riverine) sediments, clay-rich deltaic deposits, and red beds of alluvial and fluvial origin. This dilemma is best resolved by postulating a monsoonal climate, particularly during the Middle and Late Triassic, over wide areas of Pangea. Under these conditions, cross-equatorial monsoonal winds would have brought strong seasonal precipitation to some areas, especially where these winds crossed large expanses of open water.

Another indication of temperate and tropical climates is coal deposits. Their presence invariably indicates humid conditions with relatively high rainfall responsible for both lush vegetational growth and poor drainage. The resultant large swamps would act as depositional basins wherein the decomposing plant material would be transformed gradually into peat. Such humid conditions must have existed in high latitudes during the later stages of the Triassic Period, on the basis of the occurrence of coals in Triassic formations in Arctic Canada, Russia, Ukraine, China, Japan, South America, South Africa, Australia, and Antarctica.

It has been postulated that, because of the large size of Panthalassa, oceanic circulation patterns during the Triassic would have been relatively simple, consisting of enormous single gyres in each hemisphere. East-west temperature extremes would have been great, with the western margin of Panthalassa being much warmer than the eastern. A permanent westerly equatorial current would have provided warm waters to Tethys, enabling reefs to develop there wherever substrates and depths were favourable.

Additional important evidence regarding paleoclimate is provided by the nature of Triassic fossils and their latitudinal distribution. The biotas of the period are fairly modern in aspect, and so their life habits and environmental requirements can be reconstructed with relative confidence from comparisons to living relatives. For example, the presence of colonial stony corals as framework builders in Tethyan reefs of Late Triassic age suggests an environment of warm shelf seas at low latitudes. These seas must have been sufficiently shallow and clear to allow penetration of adequate light for photosynthesis by zooxanthellae, a type of protozoa inferred to be, perhaps for the first time in geologic history, symbiotically associated with reef-building corals and aiding in their calcification.

The geographic distribution of modern-day animals indicates, with few exceptions, that faunal diversity decreases steadily in both hemispheres as one approaches the poles. For example, ectothermic (cold-blooded) amphibians and reptiles show a much higher diversity in the warmer low latitudes, reflecting the strong influence of ambient air temperatures on these animals, which are unable to regulate their internal temperature. The evidence from Triassic fossils, however, is equivocal: the distribution of Triassic amphibians and reptiles shows only a slight change with latitude, although the distribution of ammonoids from the upper part of the Lower Triassic shows a much stronger geographic gradient. It may be that Triassic marine invertebrates were more sensitive to differences in ambient temperature than land vertebrates or that ambient temperature differences were greater in the ocean than on land. There is also the possibility that both of these conditions existed.

TRIASSIC LIFE

The boundary between the Paleozoic and Mesozoic eras was marked by the Earth's third and largest mass extinction episode, which occurred immediately prior to the Triassic. As a result, Early Triassic biotas were impoverished, though diversity and abundance progressively increased during Middle and Late Triassic times. The fossils of many Early Triassic life-forms tend to be Paleozoic in aspect, whereas those of the Middle and Late Triassic are decidedly Mesozoic in appearance and are clearly the precursors of things to come. New land vertebrates appeared throughout the Triassic. By the end of the period, both the first true mammals and the earliest dinosaurs had appeared.

Mass Extinctions of the Triassic

Periodic large-scale mass extinctions have occurred throughout the history of life. Indeed, it is on this basis that the geologic eras were first established. Of the five major mass extinction events, the one best known is the last, which took place at the end of the Cretaceous Period and killed the dinosaurs. However, the largest of all extinction events occurred between the Permian and Triassic periods at the end of the Paleozoic Era, and it is this third mass extinction that profoundly affected life during the Triassic. The fourth episode of mass extinction occurred at the end of the Triassic, drastically reducing some marine and terrestrial groups, such as ammonoids, mammal-like reptiles, and primitive amphibians, but not affecting others.

The Permian-Triassic Extinctions

Though the Permian-Triassic mass extinction was the most extensive in the history of life on Earth, it should be noted that many groups were showing evidence of a gradual decline long before the end of the Paleozoic. Nevertheless, 85 to 95 percent of marine invertebrate species became extinct at the end of the Permian. On land, four-legged vertebrates and plants suffered significant reductions in diversity across the Permian-Triassic boundary. Only 30 percent of terrestrial vertebrate genera survived into the Triassic.

Many possible causes have been advanced to account for these extinctions. Some researchers believe that there is a periodicity to mass extinctions, which suggests a common, perhaps astronomical, cause. Others maintain that each extinction event is unique in itself. Cataclysmic events, such as intense volcanic activity and the impact of a celestial body, or more gradual trends, such as changes in sea levels, oceanic temperature, salinity, or nutrients, fluctuations in oxygen and carbon dioxide levels, climatic cooling, and cosmic radiation, have been proposed to explain the Permian-Triassic crisis. Unlike the end-Cretaceous event, there is no consistent evidence in rocks at the Permian-Triassic boundary to support an asteroid impact hypothesis, such as an anomalous presence of iridium and associated shocked quartz (quartz grains that have experienced high temperatures and pressures from impact shock). A more plausible theory is suggested by finely laminated pyritic shales, rich in organic carbon, that are commonly found at the Permian-Triassic transition in many areas. These shales may reflect oceanic anoxia (lack of dissolved oxygen) in both low and high latitudes over a wide range of shelf depths, perhaps caused by weakening of oceanic circulation. Such anoxia could devastate marine life, particularly the bottom-dwellers (benthos). Any theory, however, must take into account that not all groups were affected to the same extent by the extinctions.

The trilobites, a group of arthropods long past their zenith, made their last appearance in the Permian, as did the closely related eurypterids. Rugose and tabulate corals became extinct at the end of the Paleozoic. Several superfamilies of Paleozoic brachiopods, such as the productaceans, chonetaceans, and richthofeniaceans, also disappeared at the end of the Permian. Fusulinid foraminiferans, useful as late Paleozoic index fossils, did not survive the crisis, nor did the cryptostomate and fenestrate bryozoans, which inhabited many Carboniferous and Permian reefs. Gone also were the blastoids, a group of echinoderms that persisted in what is now Indonesia until the end of the Permian, although their decline had begun much earlier in other regions. However, some groups, such as the conodonts (a type of tiny marine invertebrate), were little affected by this crisis in the history of life, although they were destined to disappear at the end of the Triassic.

The End-Triassic Extinctions

The end-Triassic mass extinction was less devastating than its counterpart at the end of the Permian. Nevertheless, in the marine realm some groups such as the conodonts became extinct, while many Triassic ceratitid ammonoids disappeared. Only the phylloceratid ammonoids were able to survive, and they gave rise to the explosive radiation of cephalopods later in the Jurassic. Many families of brachiopods, gastropods, bivalves, and marine reptiles also became extinct. On land a great part of the vertebrate fauna disappeared at the end of the Triassic, although the dinosaurs, pterosaurs, crocodiles, turtles, mammals, and fishes were little affected by the transition. Plant fossils and palynomorphs (spores and pollen of plants) show no significant changes in diversity across the Triassic-Jurassic boundary. Sea-level changes and associated anoxia, coupled with climatic change, were the most likely causes for the end-Triassic extinction.

Invertebrates

The difference between Permian and Triassic faunas is most noticeable among the marine invertebrates. At the Permian-Triassic boundary the number of families was reduced by half, with an estimated 85 to 95 percent of all species disappearing.

Ammonoids were common in the Permian but suffered drastic reduction at the end of that period. Only a few genera belonging to the prolecanitid group survived the crisis, but their descendants, the ceratitids, provided the rootstock for an explosive adaptive radiation in the Middle and Late Triassic. Ammonoid shells have a complex suture line where internal partitions join the outer shell wall. Ceratitids have varying external ornamentation, but all share the distinctive ceratitic internal suture line of rounded saddles and denticulate lobes, as shown by such Early Triassic genera as *Otoceras* and *Ophiceras*. The group first reached its acme and then declined dramatically in the Late Triassic. In the Carnian Stage (the first stage of the Late Triassic) there were more than 150 ceratitid genera. In the next stage, the Norian, there were fewer than 100, and finally in the Rhaetian Stage there were fewer than 10. In the Late Triassic evolved bizarre heteromorphs with loosely coiled body chambers, such as *Choristoceras*, or with helically coiled whorls, such as

Cochloceras. These aberrant forms were short-lived, however. A small group of smooth-shelled forms with more complex suture lines, the phylloceratids, also arose in the Early Triassic. They are regarded as the earliest true ammonites and gave rise to all post-Triassic ammonites, even though Triassic ammonoids as a whole almost became extinct at the end of the period.

Other marine invertebrate fossils found in Triassic rocks, albeit much reduced in diversity compared with those of the Permian, include gastropods, bivalves, brachiopods, bryozoans, corals, foraminiferans, and echinoderms. These groups are either poorly represented or absent in Lower Triassic rocks but increase in importance later in the period. Most are bottom-dwellers (benthos), but the bivalve genera *Claraia*, *Posidonia*, *Daonella*, *Halobia*, and *Monotis*, often used as Triassic index fossils, were planktonic and may have achieved widespread distribution by being attached to floating seaweed.

Fossilized echinoids (sea urchins). Shutterstock.com

Colonial stony corals became important reef-builders in the Middle and Late Triassic. For example, the Rhaetian Dachstein reefs from Austria were colonized by a diverse fauna of colonial corals and calcareous sponges, with subsidiary calcareous algae, echinoids, foraminiferans, and other colonial invertebrates. Many successful Paleozoic articulate brachiopod superfamilies (those having valves characterized by teeth and sockets) became extinct at the end of the Permian, which left only the spiriferaceans, rhynchonellaceans, terebratulaceans, terebratellaceans, thecideaceans, and some other less important groups to continue into the Mesozoic. The brachiopods, however, never again achieved the dominance they held among the benthos of the Paleozoic, and they may have suffered competitively from the adaptive radiation of the bivalves in the Mesozoic.

Fossil echinoderms are represented in the Triassic by crinoid columnals and the echinoid *Miocidaris*, a holdover from the Permian. The crinoids had begun to decline long before the end of the Permian, by which time they were almost entirely decimated, with both the flexible and camerate varieties dying out. The inadunates survived the crisis. They did not become extinct until the end of the Triassic and gave rise to the articulates, which still exist today.

Vertebrates

Fishes and Marine Reptiles

Vertebrate animals appear to have been less affected by the Permian-Triassic crisis than were invertebrates. The fishes show some decline in diversity and abundance at the end of the Paleozoic, with acanthodians (spiny sharks) becoming extinct and elasmobranchs (primitive sharks and rays) much reduced in diversity. Actinopterygians (ray-finned fishes), however, continued to flourish during the Triassic, gradually moving from freshwater to marine environments, which were already inhabited by subholostean ray-finned fishes (genera intermediate between palaeoniscoids and holosteans). The shellfish-eating hybodont sharks, already diversified by the end of the Permian, continued into the Triassic.

Fossils of marine reptiles such as the shell-crushing placodonts (which superficially resembled turtles) and the fish-eating nothosaurs occur in the Muschelkalk, a rock formation of Triassic marine sediments in central Germany. The nothosaurs, members of the sauropterygian order, did not survive the Triassic, but they were ancestors of the large predatory plesiosaurs of the Jurassic. The largest inhabitants of Triassic seas were the early ichthyosaurs, superficially like dolphins in profile and streamlined for rapid swimming. These efficient hunters, which were equipped with powerful fins, paddlelike limbs, a long-toothed jaw, and large eyes, may have preyed upon some of the early squidlike cephalopods known as belemnites. There also is evidence that these unusual reptiles gave birth to live young.

Terrestrial Reptiles and the First Mammals

On land the vertebrates are represented in the Triassic by labyrinthodont amphibians and reptiles, the latter consisting of cotylosaurs, therapsids, eosuchians, thecodontians, and protorosaurs. All these tetrapod groups suffered a sharp reduction in diversity at the close of the Permian. In fact, 75 percent of the early amphibian families and 80 percent of the early reptilian families disappeared at or near the Permian-Triassic boundary. Whereas Early Triassic forms were still Paleozoic in aspect, new forms appeared throughout the period, and by Late Triassic times the tetrapod fauna was distinctly

Mesozoic in aspect. Modern groups whose ancestral forms appeared for the first time in the Middle and Late Triassic include lizards, turtles, rhynchocephalians (lizardlike animals), and crocodilians.

The mammal-like reptiles, or therapsids, suffered pulses of extinctions in the Late Permian. The group survived the boundary crisis but became virtually extinct by the end of the Triassic, possibly because of competition from more efficient predators, such as the thecodonts. The first true mammals, which were very small, appeared in the Late Triassic (the shrewlike *Morganucodon*, for example). Although their fossilized remains have been collected from a bone bed in Great Britain dating from the Rhaetian Stage at the end of the Triassic, the evolutionary transition from therapsid reptiles to mammals at the close of the Triassic is nowhere clearly demonstrated by well-preserved fossils.

From Reptiles to Dinosaurs

First encountered in the Early Triassic, the thecodonts became common during the Middle Triassic (about 246 million to 229 million years ago) but disappeared before the beginning of the Jurassic some 176 million years ago. Typical of this group of archosaurs (or "ruling reptiles") in the Triassic were small bipedal forms belonging to the pseudosuchians. Forms such as *Lagosuchus* were swift-running predators that had erect limbs directly under the body, which made them more mobile and agile. This group presumably gave rise to primitive dinosaurs belonging to the saurischian and ornithischian orders during the Late Triassic to Early Jurassic. The early dinosaurs were bipedal, swift-moving, and relatively small compared with later Mesozoic forms, but some, such as *Plateosaurus*, reached lengths of 8 metres (26 feet). *Coelophysis* was a Late Triassic carnivorous dinosaur about 2 metres (6 to 8 feet) long. Its fossils have been found in the Chinle Formation in the Petrified Forest National Park of northeastern Arizona in the United States. The dinosaur group was to achieve much greater importance later in the Mesozoic, resulting in the era being informally called the "Age of Reptiles."

Flying Reptiles

Some of the earliest lizards may have been the first vertebrates to take to the air. Gliding lizards, such as the small Late Triassic *Icarosaurus* , are thought to have developed an airfoil from skin stretched between extended ribs, which would have allowed short glides similar to those made by present-day flying squirrels. Similarly, *Longisquama* had long scales that could have been employed as primitive wings, while the Late Triassic *Sharovipteryx* was an active flyer and may have been the first true pterosaur (flying reptile). All these forms became extinct at the end of the Triassic, their role as fliers being taken over by the later pterosaurs of the Jurassic and Cretaceous.

Plants

Land plants were affected by the Permian-Triassic crisis, but less so than were the animals, since the demise of late Paleozoic floras had begun much earlier. The dominant understory plants in the Triassic were the ferns, while most middle-story plants were gymnosperms (plants having exposed seeds)—the cycadeoids (an extinct order) and the still-extant cycads and ginkgoes. The upper story of Triassic forests consisted of conifers; their best-known fossil remains are preserved in the Upper Triassic Chinle Formation.

While extensive forests did exist during the Triassic, widespread aridity on the northern continents in the Early and Middle Triassic limited their areal extent, which resulted in generally poor development of floras during this period. However, in the Late Triassic the occurrence of water-loving plants, such as lycopods (vascular plants now represented only by the club mosses), horsetails, and ferns, suggests that the arid climate changed to a more moist monsoonal one and that this climatic belt extended as high as latitude 60° N. Subtropical to warm-temperate Eurasian flora lay in a belt between about 15° and 60° N, while north of this belt were the temperate Siberian (Angaran) flora, extending to within 10° of the Triassic North Pole. In the southern continents the Permian *Glossopteris* and *Gangamopteris* seed fern flora, adapted to cool, moist conditions, were replaced by a Triassic flora dominated by *Dicroidium* , a seed fern that preferred warm, dry conditions—which indicates major climatic changes at the Permian-Triassic boundary. *Dicroidium*, a genus of the pteridosperm order, was part of an extensive Gondwanan paleoflora that was discovered in the Late Triassic Molteno Formation of southern Africa and elsewhere. This paleoflora extended from 30° to well below 60° S. Few fossil remains exist from the Triassic for the equatorial zone between 15° N and 30° S.

In the oceans the coccolithophores, an important group of still-living marine pelagic algae, made their first appearance during the Late Triassic, while dinoflagellates underwent rapid diversification during the Late Triassic and Early Jurassic. Dasycladacean marine green algae and cyanobacteria were abundant throughout the Triassic.

Significant Dinosaurs of the Triassic Period

Most of the dinosaurs of this period were smaller than those that appeared later in the era. *Coelophysis* and *Herrerasaurus* were small agile dinosaurs that possessed several morphological features adapted to hunting prey.

Some Triassic dinosaurs, such as *Plateosaurus*, did grow to relatively large sizes, however.

Coelophysis

This is the name of a genus of small carnivorous dinosaurs found as fossils from the Late Triassic Period of North America.

Coelophysis was a primitive theropod dinosaur. Usually growing to a length of about 2 metres (6.6 feet), it was very light, weighing only about 18–23 kg (40–50 pounds), and had a long, slender neck, tail, and hind leg. The head was long and narrow, and the jaws were equipped with many sharp teeth.

Coelophysis, like other predatory dinosaurs, was an agile, lightly built predator that possibly fed on other small reptiles and early relatives of mammals. It is representative of the basal stock from which later, more derived theropod dinosaurs evolved. *Coelophysis* is known from a massive death assemblage of hundreds of skeletons found at Ghost Ranch, near Abuquiu, New Mexico, and first excavated in 1947.

Herrerasaurus

Herrerasaurus, a genus of primitive carnivorous dinosaur or close relative of the dinosaurs, was found as a fossil in Argentine deposits from the Late Triassic Period. It had long, powerful hind legs for running and short forelimbs equipped with three recurved claws for grasping and raking. The lower jaw possessed large inward-curving teeth and was flexible for holding prey. *Herrerasaurus* reached a length of about 3 metres (10 feet) and weighed about 180 kg (400 pounds).

Herrerasaurus flourished at a time just before dinosaurs became the dominant land animals. Its remains help clarify the sequence of anatomic changes that occurred during early dinosaur evolution. It closely resembled the common ancestor of all dinosaurs, and it retained the carnivorous habits and features of predatory animals that were ancestral to dinosaurs and their relatives. Although some features, such as their three-toed feet, resemble those of true theropod dinosaurs, they lack some features that distinguish theropods from saurischians, such as overlapping wrist bones and an opposable thumb.

Fragmentary fossil remains of *Herrerasaurus* were first discovered in the early 1960s, but it was not until 1988, when several skeletons were discovered in the Ischigualasto Formation of northwestern Argentina, that researchers could complete the first picture of the animal.

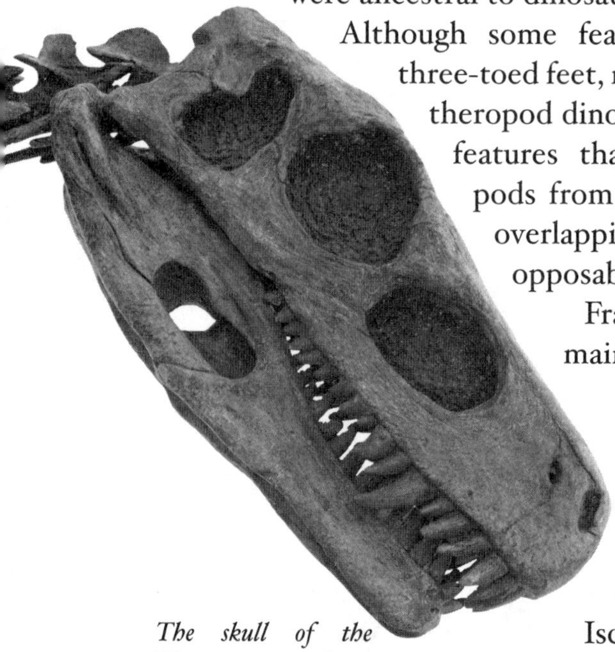

The skull of the Herrerasaurus *shows its lower jaw and inner-curving teeth.* © www.istockphoto.com/breckeni

Plateosaurus

This dinosaur genus is known from extensive fossil material found in Europe dating to the Late Triassic Period. The fossils were representative of the prosauropods, an early group that might have been ancestral to the giant sauropod dinosaurs of later time periods.

Plateosaurus was among the earliest dinosaurs to attain a relatively large size, growing to about 8 metres (26 feet) long. It was more massive than earlier dinosaurs and had bones that were stocky and thick. Although *Plateosaurus*

could rise up on its two very strong hind legs, its forelimbs also were relatively well developed and strong, and it may have walked on two or four legs for various purposes. The small skull was perched atop a long, flexible neck and contained flat teeth serrated on the front and back edges.

Plateosaurs were the first known large herbivores among the dinosaurs. Dinosaurs related to *Plateosaurus* have been found in South Africa, North America, and China. The prosauropod group of dinosaurs is not found after the Early Jurassic Period (about 200 million to 176 million years ago), which is when the first of the large "true" sauropod dinosaurs appeared. This fact, along with the increasing trend to large size among prosauropods, supports the idea that sauropods evolved directly from prosauropods, although some authorities regard the two as separate groups.

Other Significant Life-Forms of the Triassic Period

In addition to the dinosaurs that evolved during the period, the Triassic was the time of several notable mammal-like reptiles. The genera *Bauria*, *Cynognathus*, *Thrinaxodon*, and *Tritylodon* give important clues to paleontologists studying the emergence of mammals. The Triassic also saw the arrival of the pterosaurs, ichthyosaurs, as well as the possible precursors to teleost fishes and the ancestors of the present-day sturgeon (*Acipenser*).

Bauria

This genus of mammal-like reptiles that inhabited parts of present-day South Africa during the Early Triassic Period. The skull of *Bauria* had several mammal-like features. A secondary palate separates air and food passages. The teeth show specialization and are differentiated into a set of incisor-like, caninelike, and molarlike cheek teeth. A single bone, the dentary, dwarfs the other lower jawbones, a trend toward the mammalian condition of only one bone, the dentary. *Bauria* and its relatives did not survive the Early Triassic.

Chondrosteiformes

The Chondrosteiformes were an extinct order of ray-finned saltwater fishes (class Actinopterygii) comprising a single family Chondrosteidae. These fishes were prominent in seas during the Early Triassic to Late Jurassic (from 251 million to 145.5 million years ago). Some species were suctorial feeders that probably gave rise to present-day sturgeon.

Cynognathus

Members of this genus of extinct advanced therapsids (mammals and their relatives) were found as fossils in Lower Triassic deposits in South Africa and South America. *Cynognathus* is representative of the Theriodontia, a group of cynodont therapsids that gave rise to the earliest mammals.

Cynognathus was approximately as large as a modern wolf and, like the wolf, was an active predator. The body of *Cynognathus* was not massively constructed. The tail was short, and the limbs were tucked well under and close to the body, providing the potential for rapid and efficient locomotion. The skull was long and had openings for the attachment of strong muscles used in opening and closing the jaws. The lower jaw was dominated by the dentary bone. The other lower-jaw elements, characteristic of reptiles, were relatively reduced, as in mammals and their near relatives. The teeth were regionally specialized on the jaw into different forms, as in mammals. Incisors adapted to nipping were followed by strongly developed canines, important features in predatory animals. Separated from the canines by a gap, or diastema, was a series of cheek teeth that sliced the animal's food into smaller, more easily swallowed particles. A well-developed secondary palate separated food passages from breathing passages. The vertebral column was well differentiated.

DAONELLA

This genus of extinct pelecypods (clams) serves as a guide, or index, fossil in Triassic rocks. The shell is characterized by a wide dorsal region and by fine, radiating, riblike lineations. The shell is circular in outline and may show fine growth lines.

EUPARKERIA

This genus of extinct reptiles is very closely related to the ancestral archosaurs (a group containing present-day crocodiles and birds and ancestral dinosaurs and pterosaurs). Specimens are found as fossils in Middle Triassic rocks of South Africa (245 million to 240 million years ago). *Euparkeria* was about 1 metre (3 feet) long and lightly built. It probably progressed on all four limbs or on only two back limbs. Like other archosaurs, *Euparkeria* had an opening in the skull between its eyes and nasal breach (the antorbital opening) and two additional apertures in the skull behind one eye (the upper and lower temporal openings). Its teeth were set in sockets, rather than being attached to the side of the jawbone or perched atop it. These teeth were long, sharp, and recurved, which attested to the carnivorous habit that seems to have been common among the first archosaurs. *Euparkeria* also possessed teeth on its palate, which was also common among earlier reptiles and amphibians.

Ichthyosaurs

Most members of this group of extinct aquatic reptiles were very similar to porpoises in appearance and habits. Ichthyosaurs were distant relatives of lizards and snakes (lepidosaurs) and were the most highly specialized aquatic reptiles, but ichthyosaurs were not dinosaurs.

Ichthyosaurs had a very wide geographic distribution, and their fossil remains span almost the entire Mesozoic Era. However, they were most abundant and diverse during the Triassic and Jurassic periods (251 million to 145 5 million years ago). Excellent fossil specimens occur in the fine-grained Early Jurassic shales of southern Germany. In one specimen, the entire outline of the body is preserved, including the outline of a well-developed, fleshy dorsal fin. Several specimens are known in which the skeletal remains of small, immature ichthyosaurs are fossilized within the bodies of larger individuals, even within the birth canal.

Ichthyosaurus, a representative genus from which the larger group takes its name, was about 3 metres (10 feet) long and was probably able to move through the water at high speeds. Very fishlike in appearance, it is especially well known from Early Jurassic deposits in England. The body was streamlined. No distinct neck was present, and the head blended smoothly into the body. The limbs were

The cast of a Lower Jurassic ichtyosaur depicts the skeletal structure, while the overlaid shadow approximates the original body shape. Shutterstock.com

modified into paddlelike appendages used to steer the animal. It propelled itself by using a well-developed fishlike tail and by undulating the body. The vertebral column, which was formed from disklike structures, bent downward into the lower lobe of the caudal, or tail, fin. The upper lobe was unsupported by bone. Early reconstructions of ichthyosaurs showed them with the spinal column straightened, and it was not until well-preserved evidence was found that the bent condition of the backbone became apparent. The skull and jaws of *Ichthyosaurus* were long and contained numerous sharp teeth. The eyes were very large, and the nostrils were positioned far back on the top of the skull (another specialized adaptation to an aquatic existence). They probably fed largely upon fish as well as other marine animals. It is unlikely that they ventured onto land, and they certainly reproduced in the water. If stranded ashore, they would have been as helpless as beached whales.

Ichthyosaurs are first known from the Triassic Period of Asia, where they began as long-bodied, undulating swimmers without many of the specializations seen in later species. By the Late Triassic some lineages had achieved great size. Fossils from the western United States and Canada indicate that some ichthyosaurs could exceed 13 metres (43 feet) in length. Deep-bodied and with long fins, these appear to have been ambush predators that fed on fishes. The typical ichthyosaur form was fully realized by the Early Jurassic, when the tunalike body plan suggestive of high-speed pursuit and great mobility asserted itself. By this time, however, the other lineages of ichthyosaurs had become extinct. Ichthyosaurs persisted into Late Cretaceous times and may have been well adapted for deep diving as well as near-shore predation, but all species became extinct well before the end of the Cretaceous Period.

Leptolepis

Scientists might be able to trace the origins of the teleosts, the dominant group of fishes in the world today, back to *Leptolepis*, genus of marine fishes very closely related to the first teleosts. *Leptolepis* was abundant in the world's Mesozoic seas and was herringlike in size and appearance. Fragmentary remains from earlier and later rocks may indicate an earlier origin and longer persistence for the genus than the Jurassic period dates indicate. In many anatomical details, *Leptolepis* is intermediate between the more primitive holosteans and the more advanced teleost fish.

Marasuchus

Marasuchus, a genus of archosaurian reptiles, inhabited part of present-day South America during the Ladinian Stage (some 237 million to 229 million years ago) of the Middle Triassic Epoch. *Marasuchus* fossils were discovered in the Los Chañares Formation of the Ischigualasto–Villa Union Basin in northwestern Argentina. *Marasuchus* was not a dinosaur. Members of this genus and others (such as *Silesaurus* and *Eucoelophysis*) are classified as basal dinosauromorphs, or direct precursors to the dinosaurs. Together the basal dinosauromorphs and the dinosaurs make up the Dinosauromorpha, a group containing all reptiles more closely related to dinosaurs than to pterosaurs.

Marasuchus was lightly built and small, growing to 30–40 cm (about 12–16 inches). It was bipedal, walking with an upright (parasagittal) gait, like that of modern mammals and birds. All parts of the reptile's skeletal anatomy are known from fossils except for the skull and lower jaw. One of the diagnostic features of dinosaurs, a hole in the hip socket (acetabulum) of the pelvis for the femur (thigh bone), is absent in *Marasuchus*; however, it possessed characteristics, such as an elongate pubis and the presence of an anterior trochanter on the femur, similar to those found in dinosaurs. The presence of these characteristics in *Marasuchus* shows that some of the features limited to dinosaurs and their close relatives had begun to evolve in the Middle Triassic prior to the formal origin of dinosaurs in the Late Triassic.

Until 2003, *Marasuchus* was thought to be one of the closest relatives of the dinosaurs. At present, it has been supplanted by other dinosauromorphs such as *Silesaurus.* Nonetheless, *Marasuchus* remains an important animal for understanding the origin and evolution of dinosaur characteristics.

Myophoria

Myophoria, a genus of extinct clams found as fossils in Triassic rocks, is readily identified by its distinctive shell form and ornamentation. As a result, it is a useful guide, or index, fossil for the Triassic Period. The shell in *Myophoria* is angular, with prominent ribs that radiate from its apex. Fine growth lines encircle the shell at right angles to the ribs.

Nothosaurus

Members of this genus of marine reptiles have been found as fossils from the Triassic Period in southwestern and eastern Asia, North Africa, and especially Europe.

Nothosaurus was characterized by a slender body, long neck and tail, and long limbs. Although the animal was aquatic, the limbs were less specialized for swimming than they were in more advanced sauropterygians such as pistosaurs, pliosaurids, and plesiosaurids. The palate in the nothosaurs was closed, the air passages being separated from the food passages—an adaptation that aided feeding while in the water. The skull was long and flat with large openings. Numerous pointed teeth were present along the margins of the jaws. *Nothosaurus* moved through the water by undulating its body and by swimming with its limbs. As did the other sauropterygians, *Nothosaurus* evolved from terrestrial reptiles distantly related to lizards and snakes.

Phytosaurs

Phytosaurs were a group of heavily armoured semiaquatic reptiles. These animals were found as fossils from the Late Triassic Period. Phytosaurs were not dinosaurs. Both groups, rather, were archosaurs.

Phytosaurs were able to move about easily on land, and, although they were not ancestral to the crocodiles, they were distantly related and resembled crocodiles in appearance and probably in habits as well. The long, pointed jaws were armed with numerous sharp teeth, and it is probable that the phytosaurs preyed largely upon fishes. Like crocodiles, they had several rows of bony armour embedded in the skin along the back. The nostrils in the phytosaurs were set on a crest high on the skull in front of the eyes. This adaptation allowed them to float just underneath the water's surface, with only the nostrils protruding above it.

Phytosaur fossils occur in North America, Europe, and India, but their remains have not been found in the southern continents. Familiar genera include *Phytosaurus*, *Belodon*, and *Rutiodon*, which was more than 3 metres (10 feet) long and whose skull alone measured about 1 metre.

Pleuromeia

Pleuromeia, a genus of extinct lycopsid plants from the Triassic Period, is characterized by an unbranched trunk up to 2 metres (6.6 feet) tall. Unlike other arborescent lycopsids of the Carboniferous Period (about 360 million to 300 million years ago), such as *Lepidodendron* and *Sigillaria*, *Pleuromeia* had a four-lobed bulblike base rather than a branching underground rhizome. A crown of long, thin leaves persisted near the growing tip of the trunk. Leaves and leaf bases were lost from lower portions of the plant. Like its relatives, *Pleuromeia* reproduced by spores. Some species produced a single large cone at the trunk apex, and others may have produced many smaller cones. Nonetheless, the details of how *Pleuromeia* reproduced remain unclear. The genus was widely distributed, and specimens are known from Russia, Europe, China, and Australia.

Pterosaurs

Pterosaurs were a group of flying reptiles that flourished during all periods (Triassic, Jurassic, and Cretaceous) of the Mesozoic Era. Although pterosaurs are not dinosaurs, both are archosaurs, or "ruling reptiles," a group to which birds and crocodiles also belong.

Ancestors of pterosaurs tended toward a bipedal gait, which thus freed the forelimbs for other uses. These limbs evolved into wings in birds and pterosaurs, but, instead of feathers, pterosaurs developed a wing surface formed by a membrane of skin similar to that of bats. In bats, however, all of the fingers except the thumb support the membrane. In pterosaurs, the membrane was attached solely to the elongated fourth finger (there was no fifth finger). The first three fingers were slender, clawed, clutching structures. When the pterosaur was not in flight, the finger and membrane were extended rearward along the flanks. In addition to the main flight membrane, an accessory membrane stretching between the shoulder and wrist reduced turbulence on the wing. The pterosaur wing appears to have been well adapted to flight. Embedded within it was a system of fine, long, keratinous fibers that ran parallel to one another like the feather shafts of birds. This arrangement enhanced strength and maneuverability in flight.

The body was compact, and the hind legs were long and slender, like those of birds, and were easily able to support the animal on land. Despite the considerable size of the forelimbs, the bones were hollow and thin-walled, which kept weight low. The skull, with its long, slender beak, was delicate but strong, with most of the component bones being fused. The eyes were large, and the eyeball was reinforced by a series of bony plates (sclerotic ring).

The brain was large and apparently comparable in structure to that of birds, and, as in that group, sight rather than smell appears to have been the dominant sense. Most pterosaur remains are found in sediments close to what were bodies of water (fossils are well preserved in such places), so little is known about the diversity of forest or plains pterosaurs.

Traditionally, two major groups of pterosaurs have been recognized. Rhamphorhynchoidea is a term that has included all the basal forms up to the Late Jurassic Period (about 161 million to 145 5 million years ago). These are typified by relatively long tails, long fifth toes, sharply pointed teeth, and only slightly elongated wing metacarpals (palm bones). Rhamphorhynchoids were the first pterosaurs, and they are found in deposits from the Late Triassic Period Genera of this group include *Eudimorphodon* and *Peteinosaurus*, both found in Italian Triassic deposits; these had wingspans of less than 1 metre (3.3 feet) *Dimorphodon*, from the Early Jurassic of England, was about 1.5 metres (5 feet) from wingtip to wingtip *Rhamphorhynchus* was a late form from the Late Jurassic Period and had a wingspan of about 1 metre (3.3 feet). It has long been realized, however, that

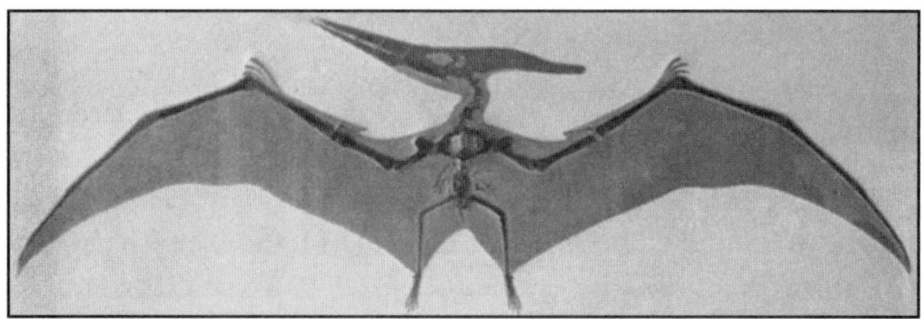

Pteranodon skeleton and restoration of wings. Courtesy of the American Museum of Natural History, New York

Rhamphorhynchoidea is an artificial grouping of primitive forms, as some members are actually more closely related to the other major group of pterosaurs, the Pterodactyloidea. Pterodactyloids appeared in the Late Jurassic and survived into the Cretaceous, when the earlier forms of pterosaurs had become extinct. The earliest Late Jurassic pterodactyloid is *Pterodactylus*, of which numerous individuals are known from Solnhofen Limestone of Bavaria, Germany. *Pteranodon*, which grew to 7 metres (23 foot), was also a Pterodactyloid. *Lacusovagus* (family Chaoyangopteridae, a group of toothless pterodactyloids) is known from a single fossilized skull discovered in Cretaceous rocks in Brazil. It possessed a 5-metre (16.4-feet) wingspan and is the only member of Chaoyangopteridae found outside China. No pterosaur remains are more recent than the Cretaceous; their ecological roles were eventually taken over by birds.

TETRACTINELLA

Remarkable for its distinctive shell, *Tetractinella* is a genus of extinct brachiopods (lamp shells) found as fossils in Triassic marine rocks. Its shell has prominent ribs and intervening troughs radiating from its apex and margins extending in a weblike fashion between the ribs; the shell is compressed in profile. One species of *Tetractinella* is an excellent example of a phenomenon known as homeomorphy, in which an organism simulates an unrelated organism in form and function. *Tetractinella trigonella,* a Middle Triassic species from Italy, is remarkably similar to the unrelated *Cheirothyris fleuriausa,* from the Late Jurassic (about 150 million years ago) marine rocks of Germany. The two forms are separated by a great geographic distance and by a large span of time.

Thrinaxodon

Thrinaxodon is an extinct genus of cynodont, a close mammal relative. Members of this genus have been found as fossils in continental deposits formed during the Early Triassic Period in southern Africa. *Thrinaxodon* was a lightly built animal about 0.5 metre (2 feet) long.

Tritylodon

Tritylodon, a genus of extinct cynodont therapsids (mammal relatives), have been found as fossils in Late Triassic and Early Jurassic rocks in southern Africa and North America. These fossils have been dated to between 208 million and 200 million years ago. Tritylodonts are characterized by a distinctive dentition: the anterior incisors are separated from the complicated cheek teeth by a pronounced gap. The cheek teeth possess two to four rows of cusps arranged longitudinally. In features of skull construction and general overall skeletal construction the tritylodonts closely approached true mammals, though they were too specialized to have given rise to the mammals and may have been contemporary with some of the earliest of them. In jaw construction and articulation tritylodonts were not mammalian. The lower jaw retained components from earlier amniotes rather than the single bone, the dentary, that is characteristic of the mammals. It is probable that the habits of *Tritylodon* were similar to those of the later rodents and multituberculates.

Tropites

One example of a notable mollusk appearing during the period is *Tropites*, a genus of extinct cephalopods (animals similar to the modern squid and octopus but with an external shell) found as fossils in marine rocks of the Late Triassic Period. Because of its narrow time range, *Tropites* is a good index fossil (useful for stratigraphic correlations). *Tropites* is characterized by a distinctive, easily recognizable, globular shell within a central keel.

Voltzia

One link in the evolution of cone-bearing plants is exemplified by the genus *Voltzia*, a group dating to the Early Triassic epoch. It belongs to the family Voltziaceae, order Coniferales (sometimes Voltziales). The genus showed interesting modifications of the seed-cone complex of earlier forms. The pollen-bearing cone was an axis with spirally arranged pollen cases. The seed-bearing cone had three ovules on five flattened and fused scales, a trend of fusion and simplification that continued in later coniferous genera.

Triassic Geology

The Triassic Period is characterized by few geologic events of major significance, in contrast to the subsequent periods of the Mesozoic Era (the Jurassic and Cretaceous periods), when the supercontinent Pangea fragmented and the new Atlantic and Indian oceans opened up. This does not mean, however, that the period was geologically silent.

Continental Rifting in the Triassic

The beginning of continental rifting in the Late Triassic caused stretching of the crust in eastern North America along the Appalachian Mountain belt from the Carolinas to Nova Scotia, resulting in normal faulting in this region. There, grabens (fault-bounded basins) received thick clastic (rock fragment) sequences from the erosion of the nearby Appalachians, which were later intruded by igneous dikes and sills. In similar fault-controlled basins between Africa and Laurasia, evaporite deposits were formed in arid or semiarid environments as seawater from the Tethys Sea periodically spilled into these newly formed troughs and then evaporated, leaving behind its salts. Evaporites of Late Triassic and Early Jurassic age in Morocco and off eastern Canada were apparently deposited in such tectonically formed basins.

Mountain-Building Activity in the Triassic

Mountain building was restricted during the Triassic, with relatively minor orogenic activity taking place along the Pacific coastal margin of North America and in China and Japan. The unmetamorphosed nature of the Triassic rocks of the Newark Group, a rock sequence in eastern North America known for its dinosaur tracks and fossils of freshwater organisms, indicates that its sediments were deposited after the main phase of the Appalachian orogeny in the late Paleozoic.

The Stages of the Triassic Period

The three rock series of the Triassic Period are made up of seven stages. The Lower and Middle Triassic Series contain two stages each, whereas the Upper Triassic Series is divided into three stages. More specifically, the Induan and Olenekian stages make up the Lower Triassic Series, and the Anisian and Ladinian stages make up the Middle Triassic Series. In contrast, the Upper Triassic Series is divided into the Carnian, Norian, and Rhaetian stages.

Induan Stage

The lowermost of two divisions of the Lower Triassic Series are those of the Induan Stage, representing those rocks deposited worldwide during Induan time (from 251 million to 249.5 million years ago). The stage name is derived from the Indus River in the Salt Range of Pakistan. The stratotype for the Induan, as originally defined, is the strata above the Chhideru beds and below the Upper Ceratite Limestone of the Salt Range. The Induan stage is subdivided into two substages, which in ascending order are the Griesbachian and Dienerian. Induan marine strata are correlated worldwide by six biozones containing ammonoid cephalopod index fossils. Five of these biozones have designated type localities in North America. These zones cannot be used for nonmarine rocks, however the Induan Stage underlies the Olenekian Stage of the Lower Triassic Series and overlies the Changhsingian Stage of the Permian Series.

Olenekian Stage

The uppermost of two divisions of the Lower Triassic Series is the Olenekian Stage, representing those rocks deposited worldwide during Olenekian time (249.5 million to 245.9 million years ago). The stage name is derived from the Olenyok, or Olenek, River of Siberia. The stratotype for the Olenekian, which was defined in 1956, is the strata in the lower course of the Olenyok River that rest upon deposits of the Induan Stage and that are overlain by those of the Anisian Stage. The Olenekian Stage is subdivided into two substages, which in ascending order are the Smithian and Spathian. Olenekian marine strata are correlated worldwide by five ammonoid cephalopod biozones, four of which have designated type localities in North America. These zones cannot be used for nonmarine rocks, however. The Olenekian Stage underlies the Anisian Stage of the Middle Triassic Series and overlies the Induan Stage of the Lower Triassic Series.

Anisian Stage

The lowermost of two divisions of the Middle Triassic Series is the Anisian Stage, representing those rocks deposited worldwide during Anisian time (245.9 million to 237 million years ago). The stage name is derived from an area of limestone formations along the Anisus River at Grossreifling in the Austrian Alps. The Anisian Stage is subdivided, in ascending order, into the Aegean, Bithynian, Pelsonian, and Illyrian substages. Anisian marine strata are correlated worldwide by seven biozones containing ammonoid cephalopod index fossils. All these biozones have designated type localities in North America. These zones cannot be used for nonmarine strata, however. The Anisian Stage underlies the Ladinian Stage of the Middle Triassic Series and overlies the Olenekian Stage of the Lower Triassic Series.

Ladinian Stage

The Ladinian Stage is the uppermost of two divisions of the Middle Triassic Series. It represents those rocks deposited worldwide during Ladinian time (237 million to 228.7 million years ago). The stage name is derived from the Ladini people of the Dolomites in northern Italy. The stratotypes for the Ladinian are the Buchenstein and Wengen beds of the Dolomites. The Ladinian is subdivided into two substages, which in ascending order are the

Fassanian and Longobardian. Ladinian marine strata are correlated worldwide by five distinct ammonoid cephalopod biozones, all of which have designated type localities in North America. These zones cannot be used for nonmarine strata, however. The Ladinian Stage underlies the Carnian Stage of the Upper Triassic Series and overlies the Anisian Stage of the Middle Triassic Series.

Carnian Stage

The lowermost of three divisions of the Upper Triassic Series is the Carnian Stage, representing those rocks deposited worldwide during Carnian time (228.7 million to 216.5 million years ago). The stage name is probably derived from the Austrian state of Kärnten (Carinthia), where the stratotype is located. The Carnian Stage is subdivided into two substages, which in ascending order are the Julian and Tuvalian. Carnian marine strata are correlated worldwide by six ammonoid cephalopod biozones, all of which have designated type localities in North America. These zones cannot be used for nonmarine strata, however. The Carnian Stage underlies the Norian Stage of the Upper Triassic Series and overlies the Ladinian Stage of the Middle Triassic Series.

Norian Stage

The Norian Stage is second of three divisions in the Upper Triassic Series. It represents those rocks deposited worldwide during Norian time (216.5 million to 203.6 million years ago). The stage was named after an ancient Roman province south of the Danube River in present-day Austria. The stratotype for the Norian is a formation known as the beds with *Cyrtopleurites bicrenatus* (an ammonoid index fossil) at Sommeraukogel, Hallstatt, Austria. The Norian Stage is subdivided into three substages, which in ascending order are the Lacian, Alaunian, and Sevatian. Norian marine strata are correlated worldwide by six ammonoid cephalopod biozones, all of which have designated type localities in North America. These zones cannot be used for nonmarine strata, however. The Norian Stage underlies the Rhaetian Stage of the Upper Triassic Series and overlies the Carnian Stage of the Upper Triassic Series.

Rhaetian Stage

The uppermost of three divisions in the Upper Triassic Series is the Rhaetian Stage, representing those rocks deposited worldwide during Rhaetian time (203.6 million to 199.6 million years ago). The stage name is derived from the Rhaetian Alps of Italy, Switzerland, and Austria; the stratotype is the Kössen beds at Kendelbachgraben, Sankt

The Lower Norian rock formations of the Petrified Forest National Park, Arizona, U.S. Shutterstock.com

Wolfgang, Austria. Rhaetian rocks are transitional in age and sometimes placed in the Lower Jurassic. In Great Britain the Rhaetian (or Rhaetic) consists of lagoonal deposits, such as limestones, shales, and marls, as well as bone beds that contain fragments of amphibians and reptiles. Elsewhere Rhaetian marine strata are correlated worldwide by two distinct ammonoid cephalopod biozones, both of which have designated type localities in North America. Rhaetian rocks may also consist of shelf limestones with characteristic brachiopods, conodonts, and other shelly forms. The Rhaetian Stage underlies the Hettangian Stage of the Lower Jurassic Series and overlies the Norian Stage of the Upper Triassic Series.

CHAPTER 3

The Jurassic Period

The Jurassic Period is the second of three periods of the Mesozoic Era, extending from 199.6 million to 145.5 million years ago. It immediately followed the Triassic Period and was succeeded by the Cretaceous Period. The Morrison Formation of the United States and the Solnhofen Limestone of Germany, both famous for their exceptionally well-preserved fossils, are geologic features that were formed during Jurassic times.

The Jurassic was a time of significant global change in continental configurations, oceanographic patterns, and biological systems. During this period the supercontinent Pangea split apart, allowing for the eventual development of what are now the central Atlantic Ocean and the Gulf of Mexico. Heightened plate tectonic movement led to significant volcanic activity, mountain-building events, and attachment of islands onto continents. Shallow seaways covered many continents, and marine and marginal marine sediments were deposited, preserving a diverse set of fossils. Rock strata laid down during the Jurassic Period have yielded gold, coal, petroleum, and other natural resources.

During the Early Jurassic (about 200 million to 176 million years ago), animals and plants living both on land and in the seas recovered from one of the largest mass extinctions in Earth history. Many groups of vertebrate and invertebrate organisms important in the modern world made their first appearance during the Jurassic. Life was especially diverse in the oceans—thriving reef ecosystems, shallow-water invertebrate communities, and large swimming predators, including reptiles and squidlike animals. On land, dinosaurs and flying pterosaurs dominated the ecosystems, and birds made their first appearance. Early mammals also were present, though they were still fairly insignificant. Insect populations were diverse, and plants were dominated by the gymnosperms, or "naked-seed" plants.

The Jurassic Period was named early in the 19th century, by the French geologist and mineralogist Alexandre Brongniart, for the Jura Mountains between France and Switzerland. Much of the initial work by geologists in trying to correlate rocks and develop a relative geologic time scale was conducted on Jurassic strata in western Europe.

THE JURASSIC ENVIRONMENT

The Jurassic environment was primarily characterized by the movements of various tectonic plates. At the start of the interval, the continents were grouped into two vast regions: Laurasia and Gondwana. Later each of these regions showed signs of breaking up into smaller pieces. Collisions between continents and other smaller landmasses contributed to the development of the Rocky and Andes mountain ranges. The temperature differences between the poles and the Equator remained small throughout Jurassic times, possibly due to the release of large amounts of greenhouse gases from volcanism and tectonic activity. The period was also a time of fluctuating sea levels.

Paleogeography

Although the breakup of the supercontinent Pangea had already started in the Triassic Period, the continents were still very close together at the beginning of Jurassic time.

The landmasses were grouped into a northern region—Laurasia—consisting of North America and Eurasia, and a southern region—Gondwana—consisting of South America, Africa, India, Antarctica, and Australia. These two regions were separated by Tethys, a tropical east-west seaway. During the Jurassic, spreading centres and oceanic rifts formed between North America and Eurasia, between North America and Gondwana, and between the various segments of Gondwana itself. In the steadily opening, though still restricted, ocean basins, there was a continuous accumulation of thick flood basalts and a subsequent deposition of sediments. Some of these deposits, such as salt deposits in the Gulf of Mexico and oil-bearing shales of the North Sea, are economically important today. In addition to ocean basin spreading, continental rifting initiated during the Jurassic, eventually separating Africa and South America from Antarctica, India, and Madagascar. The numerous microplates and blocks making up the complex Caribbean region today can be traced to this time interval.

To accommodate the production of new seafloor along the proto-Atlantic Ocean, significant subduction zones (where seafloor is destroyed) were active along virtually all the continental margins around Pangea as well as in southern Tibet, southeastern Europe, and other areas. All along the west coast of North, Central, and South America, plate tectonic activity in the subduction zones brought on the initial formation of north-south mountain ranges such as the Rocky Mountains and the Andes. Along western North America, several terranes (islands or microcontinents riding on a moving plate) were brought east on oceanic crust and collided with the continent, including parts of a microcontinent that collided into the Alaskan and Siberian regions in the northern Pacific. These collisions added to the growth of the North American continent and its mountain chains. One mountain-build-

Cross-bedded Jurassic sandstone in Zion National Park, Utah, U.S. Peter L. Kresan

ing event, known as the Nevadan orogeny, resulted in the emplacement of massive igneous and metamorphic rocks from Alaska to Baja California. Granites formed in the Sierra Nevadas during this time can be seen today in Yosemite National Park, California.

In the Early Jurassic the western interior of North America was covered by a vast sand sea, or erg—one of the largest deposits of dune sands in the geologic record. These deposits (including the Navajo Sandstone) are prominent in a number of places today, including Zion National Park, Utah. In Middle and early Late Jurassic times (161.2 million to 145.5 million years ago), the western regions of North America were covered by shallow seaways that advanced and retreated repeatedly, leaving successive accumulations of marine sandstones, limestones, and shales. By Late Jurassic time the seaway had retreated, and strata bearing dinosaur fossils were deposited in river floodplains and stream channel environments, such as those recorded in the Morrison Formation, Montana.

Records of sea level changes can be found on every continent. However, because of the significant tectonic activity occurring around the world, it is not clear which of these local changes can be correlated to global sea level change. Because there is no evidence of major glaciations in the Jurassic, any global sea level change must have been due to thermal expansion of seawater or plate tectonic activity (such as major activity at seafloor ridges). Some geologists have proposed that average sea levels increased from Early to Late Jurassic time.

Paleoclimate

Jurassic climates can be reconstructed from the analyses of fossil and sediment distribution and from geochemical analyses. Fossils of warm-adapted plants are found up to 60° N and 60° S paleolatitude, suggesting an expanded tropical zone. In higher paleolatitudes, ferns and other frost-sensitive plants indicate that there was a less severe temperature difference between the Equator and the poles than exists today. Despite this decreased temperature gradient, there was a marked difference in marine invertebrates from northern higher latitudes—the boreal realm—and the tropical Tethyan realm. Decreased latitudinal temperature gradients probably led to decreased zonal winds.

Large salt deposits dating from the Jurassic represent areas of high aridity, while extensive coal deposits suggest areas of high precipitation. It has been suggested that an arid belt existed on the western side of Pangea, while more-humid conditions existed in the east. These conditions may have been caused by large landmasses affecting wind and precipitation in a manner similar to that of modern continents.

Analyses of oxygen isotopes in marine fossils suggest that Jurassic global temperatures were generally quite warm. Geochemical evidence suggests that surface waters in the low latitudes were about 20 °C (68 °F), while deep waters were about 17 °C (63 °F). Coolest temperatures existed during the Middle Jurassic (175.6 million to 161.2 million years ago) and warmest temperatures in the Late Jurassic. A drop in temperatures occurred at the Jurassic-Cretaceous boundary.

It has been suggested that increased volcanic and seafloor-spreading activity during the Jurassic released large amounts of carbon dioxide—a greenhouse gas—and led to higher global temperatures. Warm temperatures and decreased latitudinal gradients also may be related to the Tethys Sea, which distributed warm, tropical waters around the world. Ocean circulation was probably fairly sluggish because of the warm temperatures, lack of ocean density gradients, and decreased winds. As stated above, there is no evidence of glaciation or polar ice caps in the Jurassic. This may have been caused by the lack of a continental landmass in a polar position or by generally warm conditions. However, because of the complex relationships between temperature, geographic configurations, and glaciations, it is difficult to state a definite cause and effect.

JURASSIC LIFE

The Triassic-Jurassic boundary is marked by one of the five largest mass extinctions on Earth. About half of the marine invertebrate genera went extinct at this time. Whether land plants or terrestrial vertebrates suffered a similar extinction during this interval is unclear. In addition, at least two other Jurassic intervals show heightened faunal turnover affecting mainly marine invertebrates—one in Early Jurassic time and another at the end of the period.

Jurassic rock strata preserve the first appearances of many important modern biological groups. In the oceans, life on the seafloor became more complex and modern, with an abundance of mollusks and coral reef builders by Middle Jurassic time. While modern fishes became common in Jurassic seas, they shared the waters with ammonites and other squidlike organisms as well as large reptiles that are all extinct today. On land a new set of plants and animals was dominant by the Early Jurassic. As previously mentioned, gymnosperms ("naked-seed" plants such as conifers) replaced the seed ferns that dominated older ecosystems. Similarly, dinosaurs and mammals, as well as amphibians and reptiles resembling those of modern times, replaced the ancestral reptiles and mammal groups common in Late Triassic times. The earliest bird fossils were found in Jurassic rocks. However, although groups now living were present in Jurassic terrestrial ecosystems, Jurassic communities would still have been very different because dinosaurs were the dominant animals.

Marine Life

The earliest Jurassic marine ecosystems show signs of recovery from the major mass extinction that occurred at the Triassic-Jurassic boundary. This extinction eliminated about half of marine invertebrate genera and left some groups with very few surviving species. Diversity increased rapidly for the first four million years (the Hettangian Age) following this extinction and then slowed through the next five million years. Another extinction event occurred among benthic (bottom-dwelling) invertebrates at the Pliensbachian-Toarcian boundary in the Early

Jurassic, interrupting the overall recovery and diversification. The last spiriferid brachiopod (abundant during the Paleozoic Era) went extinct at this time, and in some regions 84 percent of bivalve species went extinct. Although best documented in Europe, biodiversity during this period seems to have decreased around the globe. The extinctions may be related to an onset of low-oxygen conditions in epicontinental seas, as evidenced by the presence today of layers of organic-rich shales, which must have been formed in seas with so little oxygen that no burrowing organisms could survive and efficient breakdown of organic matter could not occur. Full recovery from this extinction did not occur until the Middle Jurassic. It has been proposed that a final interval of heightened extinction took place at the end of the Jurassic, although its magnitude and global extent are disputed. This final turnover may have been limited to Eurasian regions affected by local sea level decreases, or it may be related to a decrease in the quality of fossil preservation through the Late Jurassic.

Except for the extinction events outlined above, in general, marine invertebrates increased their diversity and even modernized through the Jurassic. Some previously abundant Paleozoic groups were extinct by the Jurassic, and other groups were present but no longer dominant. Moreover, many important modern groups first appeared in the fossil record during the Jurassic, and many important groups experienced high levels of diversification (a process known as evolutionary radiation).

A diverse group of vertebrates swam in Jurassic seas. Cartilaginous and bony fishes were abundant. Large fishes and marine reptiles were common. The largest bony fish ever to live, measuring 20 metres (66 feet) long, *Leedsichthys*, existed at this time, and Jurassic pliosaurs are some of the largest carnivorous reptiles ever discovered.

Protists and Invertebrates

Among the plankton—floating, single-celled, microscopic organisms—two significant new groups originated and radiated rapidly: coccolithophores and foraminifera. In addition, diatoms are considered by some scholars to have originated in the Late Jurassic and radiated during the Cretaceous. The skeletons of all three groups are major contributors to deep-sea sediments. Before the explosion of skeletonized planktonic organisms, carbonates were mainly deposited in shallow-water, nearshore environments. Today the tests (shells) of coccolithophores and foraminifera account for significant volumes of carbonate sediments in the deep sea, while diatom tests create silica-rich sediments. Thus, the advent of these groups has significantly changed the geochemistry of the oceans, the nature of the deep-sea floor, and marine food webs.

Mollusks became dominant in marine ecosystems, both among swimmers in the water column (nekton) and organisms living on the seafloor (benthos). Nektic cephalopods, such as shelled ammonites and squidlike belemnites with internal skeletons, were very common. Although only one group of ammonites survived the Triassic-Jurassic mass extinction, they radiated rapidly into many different forms. Because their shells have elaborate suture lines, they are easily identifiable. This quality, along with their abundance and rapid evolution, make them useful as index fossils for correlating and sequencing rocks. Thus, ammonites are a major tool for developing relative time scales and dividing the Jurassic into finer time intervals. Other common mollusks include bivalves (pelecypods) and snails (gastropods). These forms diversified into a number of different niches. Among the bivalves, scallops (pectinids) and oysters show marked radiation. Some bivalves also are used as index fossils.

Common echinoderms include crinoids (sea lilies), echinoids (sea urchins), and sea stars (starfish). Jurassic crinoids are descendants from the one group that survived the Permian-Triassic mass extinction. Their circular or star-shaped stem ossicles (plates) can be quite abundant in Jurassic sediments. Under special circumstances, articulated Jurassic crinoids are preserved. Some of these fossils suggest that certain species may have lived on floating logs and not on the seafloor. One group of regular sea urchins, radially symmetrical and living on the surface of the seafloor, radiated into a number of irregular echinoid groups (heart urchins) that could burrow into sediment.

Some lophophorates (brachiopods, or lamp shells) and bryozoa (moss animals) underwent recovery and diversification in the Jurassic but never became as dominant as they were in the Paleozoic Era. Spiriferid brachiopods went extinct during the Early Jurassic extinction event, but rhynchonellid and terebratulid brachiopods can be found throughout the period.

Among bryozoans that survived into the Jurassic, cyclostomes are found encrusting hard substrates Cheilostomes (the most common modern bryozoan) appeared in the Late Jurassic. With the extinction of trilobites, a new set of arthropods developed. The first true crabs and lobsters appeared, bearing large front claws adapted for predation. Shrimp burrows are not uncommon in Jurassic sediments, and fossil shrimp are occasionally preserved. Ostracods—small crustaceans—radiated during the Jurassic and are used today as index fossils.

Unlike today's world, where virtually all reefs are formed by scleractinian corals, Jurassic reefs and mounds were constructed by a variety of invertebrate organisms. Buildups were constructed by siliceous sponges and serpulid tube worms as well as corals. Stromatolite mounds were formed by communities of algae, bacteria, and other microorganisms. These reefs also had a diverse set of fauna associated with them.

The ecology of the seas was changed by the diversification of marine fauna and by the adaptations of these new organisms. With the evolution and radiation of more-effective predators (crabs, snails, echinoderms, and marine vertebrates), predation pressures began to increase rapidly. For this reason, the Jurassic marks the start of the "Mesozoic Marine Revolution"—an arms race between predators and prey that led to increased diversification of marine fauna. For example, increased levels of burrowing are found in Jurassic sediments, along with an increase in the maximum depth of burrowing. These increases may have developed as a predator-avoidance adaptation, with organisms evolving that were capable of burrowing into sediment, but the activity had far-reaching effects. Burrowing changed the nature of the seafloor, the utilization of resources and space, and sedimentation style.

Vertebrates

Along with invertebrate fauna, a diverse group of vertebrates inhabited Jurassic seas. Some of them are related to modern groups, while others are now completely extinct. Chondrichthians (cartilaginous fishes including sharks) and bony fishes were common. Teleosts—the dominant type of fish today—began to acquire a more modern look as they developed bony (ossified) vertebrae and showed considerable change in their bone structure, fins, and tail. The largest bony fish of all time, *Leedsichthys*, measuring 20 metres (66 feet) long, lived during the Jurassic.

Large marine reptiles were common denizens of Jurassic seas. Ichthyosaurs had sleek profiles similar to those of modern fast-swimming fish and had large eye orbits, perhaps the largest of any vertebrate ever. Jurassic pliosaurs (short-necked plesiosaurs) could be about 15 metres (50 feet) long and are some of the largest carnivorous reptiles ever found—even rivaling *Tyrannosaurus*, which lived during the subsequent Cretaceous Period. Fossils of large crocodiles and elasmosaurs (long-necked plesiosaurs) are also found in Jurassic marine rocks.

Terrestrial Life

Invertebrates

Insects constitute the most abundant terrestrial invertebrates found in the Jurassic fossil record. Groups include the odonates (damselflies and dragonflies), coleopterans (beetles), dipterans (flies), and hymenopterans (bees, ants, and wasps). The discovery of Jurassic bees—which today are dependent upon flowering plants (angiosperms)—suggests either the early presence of angiosperms or that bees were originally adapted to other strategies. Snails, bivalves, and ostracods are preserved in freshwater deposits.

Vertebrates

Because of poor preservation of terrestrial deposits and their fossils, it is unclear whether the mass extinction at the end of the Triassic had the same impact on terrestrial ecosystems as it did in the oceans. However, there was a distinct change in vertebrate fauna by the Early Jurassic. In Triassic terrestrial ecosystems, synapsids and therapsids—ancestors of modern mammals and their relatives, often called "mammal-like reptiles"—were dominant. They occupied several ecological niches and grew to large sizes. By the start of the Jurassic, these groups became rare, a minor component of fossil assemblages. Individuals were very small—no larger than squirrel-sized—and their teeth and skeletal anatomy show that the early mammals were probably omnivorous (eating plants and animals) or insectivorous. Instead, the archosaurs (dinosaurs, crocodiles, and pterosaurs) were the dominant terrestrial vertebrates. It is not clear why this change from synapsid-dominated to archosaur-dominated faunas occurred. It could be related to the Triassic-Jurassic extinctions or to adaptations that allowed the archosaurs to outcompete the mammals and mammalian ancestors (at least until the end of the Mesozoic Era). In the Late Jurassic, while some marine invertebrates were going extinct, terrestrial vertebrates may also have experienced a drop in diversity, but the evidence here, too, is inconclusive.

Pterosaurs were common throughout the Jurassic. With light skeletons and wing structure supported by a single digit on each "hand," they were adapted to flying and gliding.

The dinosaurs are divided into two groups based on a number of skeletal characteristics: the saurischians (lizard-hipped) and the ornithischians (bird-hipped). The pubic bone of the saurischians pointed forward, while the ornithischians had an extension that pointed backward.

The saurischians, including sauropods and all carnivorous dinosaurs, were the earliest dinosaurs. Sauropods (including *Apatosaurus*) appeared in the Early Jurassic and reached the peak of their diversity, abundance, and body size in the Late Jurassic. Sauropods were generally long-necked and probably adapted to browsing on the leaves of tall gymnosperms. Their decline in the latest Jurassic appears to have corresponded to a decline in this type of vegetation.

Carnivorous saurischians, the theropods, include *Allosaurus*. The earliest allosaur is from the Middle Jurassic. Many of the theropods were globally distributed in the Jurassic. The origin of birds is still debated, but it is generally accepted that birds descended from small theropods during the Jurassic. The earliest undisputed bird fossil discovered is *Archaeopteryx*. Despite its feathers, this bird was saurischian in appearance: it had teeth, a tail like that of a lizard, and claws at the wing tips, and it lacked a strong breastbone keel for flight muscle attachment.

The ornithischians were all herbivorous and included *Stegosaurus* and *Seismosaurus*. By the Jurassic the earliest bipedal ornithopods had diversified into armoured dinosaurs and quadrupedal forms. The presence of heavy plates, spikes, and horns on various dinosaurs suggests that predatory pressures from the theropods may have been intense. However, some of the ornamentation also may have been used against other dinosaurs of the same species.

Stegosaurus, model by Stephen Czerkas, 1986. © Stephen Czerkas; photograph, courtesy of the Natural History Museum of Los Angeles County

Other reptiles, including turtles, were present throughout the Jurassic, while modern forms of lizards made their appearance in the Late Jurassic. Amphibians present during the Triassic Period declined drastically by the Jurassic, and more modern forms developed, such as the first frog with the type of skeletal characteristics seen today.

Plants

Although no new major plant groups originated during this time, Jurassic plant communities differed considerably from their predecessors. The seed-fern floras, such as Glossopteris of Gondwana, disappeared at or near the Triassic-Jurassic boundary. Their demise may be related to the mass extinction seen in marine ecosystems. True ferns were present during the Jurassic, but gymnosperms ("naked-seed" plants) dominated the terrestrial eco-

Cycas media, a treelike cycad that produces large terminal seed cones. G.R. Roberts

system. Gymnosperms originated in the Paleozoic Era and include three groups: cycads and cycadeoids, conifers, and ginkgos. All have exposed seeds and rely on wind dispersal for reproduction. The cycads (including the modern sago palm) and the extinct cycadeoids are palmlike gymnosperms. They proliferated to such an extent that the Jurassic has been called the "Age of Cycads." The conifers (cone-bearing plants such as modern pine trees) also made up a large part of Jurassic forests. Almost all modern conifers had originated by the end of the Jurassic. The ginkgo, a fruit-bearing gymnosperm that is represented today by only one living species, was fairly widespread during the Jurassic.

The first undisputed fossil evidence for angiosperms (flowering plants) is not found until the Cretaceous Period. However, some pollen material similar to that of angiosperms has been reported in rocks of Jurassic age. Also present are fossils of insects whose present-day descendants depend upon angiosperms, suggesting that angiosperms may indeed have been present by Jurassic times.

Significant Dinosaurs of the Jurassic Period

During this interval, several of the more popular groups of dinosaurs emerged. Such predatory dinosaurs as *Allosaurus*, *Ceratosaurus*, and the tyranosaurs lived during Jurassic times, as well as the herbivorous *Apatosaurus*, formerly known as *Brontosaurus*, and *Stegosaurus*. The Jurassic also witnessed the arrival of *Archaeopteryx*, a genus of animals widely believed to be the first birds.

Allosaurus

Allosaurus, formerly known as *Antrodemus*, is a genus of large carnivorous dinosaurs that lived from 150 million to

144 million years ago during the Late Jurassic Period; they are best known from fossils found in the western United States, particularly from the Cleveland-Lloyd Quarry in Utah and the Garden Park Quarry in Colorado.

Allosaurus weighed two tons and grew to 10 5 metres (35 feet) in length, although fossils indicate that some individuals could have reached 12 metres (39 feet). Half the body length consisted of a well-developed tail, and *Allosaurus,* like all theropod dinosaurs, was a biped. It had very strong hind limbs and a massive pelvis with strongly forward- (anteriorly) and rearward- (posteriorly) directed projections. The forelimbs were considerably smaller than the hind limbs but not as small as those of tyrannosaurs. The forelimbs had three fingers ending in sharp claws and were probably used for grasping.

The allosaur skull is distinguished by a large roughened ridge just in front of the eye. The skull was large and had sizable laterally compressed teeth, which were sharp and recurved. *Allosaurus* likely preyed upon ornithischian dinosaurs, small sauropod dinosaurs, and anything else that it could trap and kill. It is possible that *Allosaurus* was also a scavenger, feeding upon carcasses of dead or dying animals. The name *Allosaurus* subsumes *Antrodemus*, which was named earlier but was based only on an undiagnostic tail vertebra. Descendants of *Allosaurus* lived from 144 million to 135 million years ago, during the Early Cretaceous Period, and are known from fossils found in North America, Africa, and Australia.

Apatosaurus

Apatosaurus, formerly known as *Brontosaurus*, is a genus of giant herbivorous sauropod dinosaur, one of the largest land animals of all time, that lived between 147 million and 137 million years ago during the Late Jurassic and Early

Cretaceous periods. Its fossil remains are found in North America and Europe.

Apatosaurus weighed as much as 30 tons and measured up to 21 metres (70 feet) long, including its long neck and tail. It had four massive and pillarlike legs, and its tail was extremely long and whiplike. Although some scientists have suggested that the tail could have been cracked supersonically like a bullwhip, this is unlikely, as damage to the vertebrae would have been a more probable result.

The size, shape, and features of the *Apatosaurus* head were disputed for more than a century after its remains were first uncovered. Certainty was clouded in part by incomplete fossil finds and by a suspected mix-up of fossils during shipment from an excavation site. The head was originally and mistakenly represented in models like that of a camarasaurid, with a square, snubnosed skull and spoonlike teeth. In 1978, however, scientists rediscovered a long-lost skull in the basement of the Carnegie Museum in Pittsburgh, Pennsylvania. This was the skull that actually belonged to an *Apatosaurus* skeleton. It was slender and elongated and contained long peglike teeth, like those of a diplodocid. Henceforth, *Apatosaurus* skull models in museums around the world were changed accordingly.

Much discussion has centred on whether *Apatosaurus* and related forms were able to support their great bulk on the land or were forced to adopt aquatic habits. Many lines of evidence, including skeletal structure and footprints, show that *Apatosaurus* and all sauropods were terrestrial, like elephants. No skeletal features are indicative of an aquatic existence, and analyses suggest that the dinosaur's bones could easily have supported its great weight Footprints show that the toes were covered in horny pads like those of elephants. Furthermore, the ribcage was heart-shaped in cross-section like those of elephants, not barrel-shaped like that of the amphibious hippopotamus. Even the massive *Brachiosaurus*, which weighed about 80 tons, was probably more often on land than in the water.

Archaeopteryx

This genus contains the oldest-known fossil animals generally accepted as birds. The eight known fossil specimens date to the Late Jurassic Period, and all were found in the Solnhofen Limestone Formation in Bavaria, Germany. Here a very fine-grained Jurassic limestone formed in a shallow tropical marine environment (probably a coral lagoon), where lime-rich muds slowly accumulated and permitted fossil material to be exceptionally well preserved. Several of the fossils show clear impressions of feathers. The sizes of the specimens range from that of a blue jay to that of a large chicken.

Archaeopteryx shared many anatomic characters with coelurosaurs, a group of theropods (carnivorous dinosaurs). In fact, only the identification of feathers on the first known specimens indicated that the animal was a bird. Unlike living birds, however, *Archaeopteryx* had well-developed teeth and a long well-developed tail similar to those of smaller dinosaurs, except that it had a row of feathers on each side. The three fingers bore claws and moved independently, unlike the fused fingers of living birds.

Archaeopteryx had well-developed wings, and the structure and arrangement of its wing feathers—similar to that of most living birds—indicate that it could fly. Skeletal structures related to flight are incompletely developed, however, which suggests that *Archaeopteryx* may not have been able to sustain flight for great distances. *Archaeopteryx* is known to have evolved from small carnivorous dinosaurs, as made evident by the retention of many features, including the teeth and long tail mentioned above. It also retained a wishbone, a breastbone, hollow, thin-walled bones, air sacs in the backbones, and feathers, which are also found in the nonavian coelurosaurian relatives of birds. These structures, therefore, cannot be said to have evolved for the purpose of flight, because they were already present in dinosaurs before either birds or flight evolved.

Brachiosaurs

Brachiosaurs are a group containing any member or relative of the dinosaur genus *Brachiosaurus*, which lived 150 million to 130 million years ago from the Late Jurassic to the Early Cretaceous Period. Brachiosaurs were the heaviest and tallest sauropod dinosaurs for which complete skeletons exist. Larger fossil bones belonging to other (and possibly related) sauropods have been found, but these specimens are incomplete. Fossilized remains of brachiosaurs are found in Africa, North America, and Europe.

Brachiosaurs were built like huge giraffes. They had immensely long necks and relatively short tails. Their morphology is unusual among dinosaurs in that the forelimbs were longer than the hind limbs. These adaptations apparently enabled them to lift their heads to about 12 metres (39 feet) above the ground in order to browse the branches of tall trees. Brachiosaurs attained a maximum length approaching 25 metres (82 feet) and a weight of nearly 80 metric tons (88 tons). Their nasal bones were

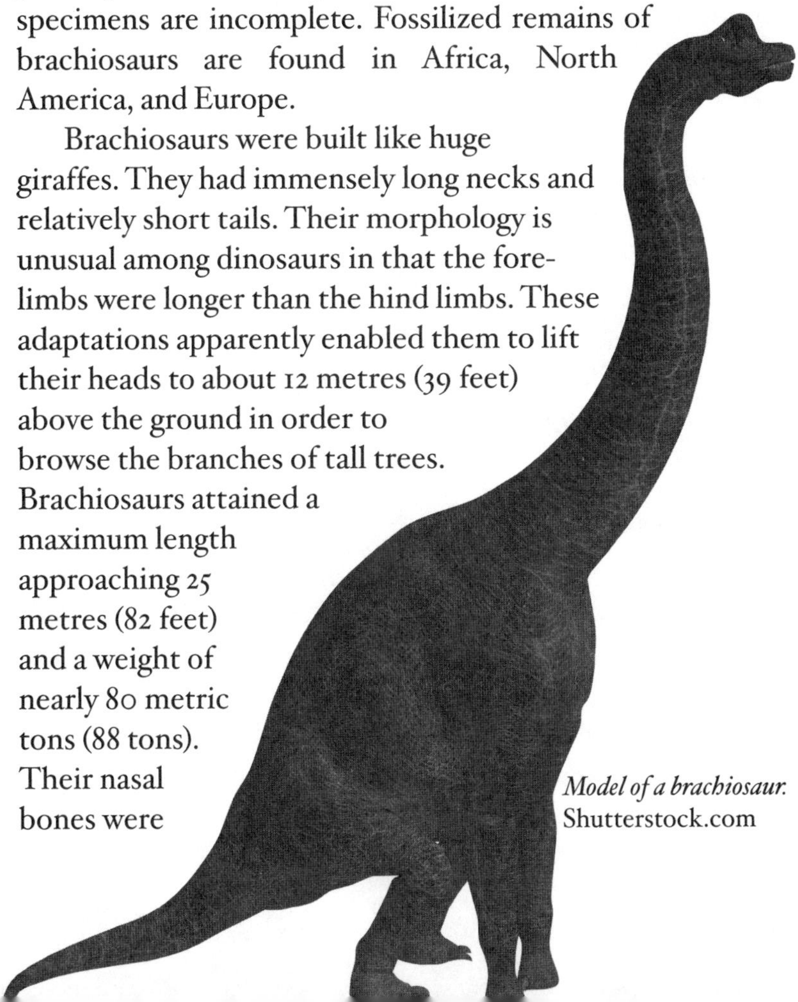

Model of a brachiosaur. Shutterstock.com

expanded into a broad arch that presumably allowed them to maintain some distance between the vegetation and the nasal openings so that they could breathe easily while feeding. The mouth contained a few dozen pencil-like teeth with beveled edges. Like most other dinosaurs, brachiosaurs did not chew their food but used their jaws to collect food, which the tongue presumably forced into the throat. Considering their massive size, their small heads, and the relatively poor quality of their forage, scientists have inferred that brachiosaurs must have spent nearly all their waking hours feeding.

As mentioned above, the huge size of brachiosaurs led some researchers to suggest that they spent most of their time submerged in water, which would have served to buoy up their great weight. The location of the nasal openings—on top of the head and above the eyes—lent additional support to this idea. However, water pressure at the depths needed to cover these dinosaurs would have crushed their lungs and thus made breathing difficult or impossible. Other features of their skeleton show that brachiosaurs were well adapted to a life spent on land browsing the high treetops. Their skeletons were strong but not massive, so their weight could be supported without any help from water. Their great neckbones, for example, are so deeply excavated that they function as a lightweight framework of struts and plates.

Camarasaurus

This genus of dinosaurs lived during the Late Jurassic Period. Its fossils, which have been uncovered in western North America, are among the most commonly found of all sauropod remains.

Camarasaurs grew to a length of about 18 metres (59 feet) and were somewhat smaller than other sauropods of the time such as diplodocids and brachiosaurs. Camarasaurs were further distinguished by their shorter necks and tails, shorter, snubnosed skulls, and large spoon-shaped teeth. The nostrils were positioned in front of the eyes—not above the eyes as in brachiosaurs, or at the tip of the snout as in the diplodocids.

When *Apatosaurus* (formerly *Brontosaurus*) was first found in the late 1800s, its skull was missing, and the skull of a camarasaur was often used in museum mounts. In 1978, however, the actual apatosaur skull was found, and it showed a distinct resemblance to diplodocids. *Apatosaurus* was therefore reclassified as a diplodocid rather than a camarasaur. Camarasaurs have comparatively shorter necks than brachiosaurs, and they have shorter necks and tails than diplodocids.

CAMPTOSAURUS

Specimens of *Camptosaurus*, a genus of large herbivorous dinosaurs, have been found as fossils in western Europe and western North America. *Camptosaurus* lived from the Late Jurassic to the Early Cretaceous Period.

Camptosaurus grew to a length of up to 6 metres (20 feet). Juvenile skeletons have also been found. It had very strong hind limbs and smaller forelimbs that were strong enough to support the animal if it chose to progress on all fours, as it might have done while feeding.

Camptosaurus was an ornithopod related to tenontosaurids and iguanodontids. It had the distinctive "blocky" wrist of iguanodontids that facilitated four-legged progression. Nevertheless, the hand was also prehensile and could have grasped vegetation as it was feeding. The thumb was a small spur rather than the conelike spike developed in *Iguanodon*. In other respects, *Camptosaurus* was a fairly generalized iguanodontid. The skull was low, long, and massive, with long rows of broad leaf-shaped cheek teeth. A beaklike structure (probably covered by horny pads) was effective in getting plant material into the mouth, where it was cut by the cheek teeth. *Camptosaurus* lacked the deep dorsal spines of many other iguanodontids, and its claws were more normally curved and less hooflike than those of other iguanodontids and hadrosaurs.

Carnosaurs

These animals consist of any of the dinosaurs belonging to the taxonomic group Carnosauria, a subgroup of the bipedal, flesh-eating theropods that evolved into predators of large herbivorous dinosaurs.

Most were large predators with high skulls and dagger-shaped teeth that were recurved and compressed laterally with serrated keels on their front and back edges for slicing through flesh. Carnosaurs include *Allosaurus* and relatives that are more closely related to allosaurs than to birds. Carnosaurs are thus contrasted with coelurosaurs, which include birds and all other theropod dinosaurs more closely related to birds than to allosaurs. (The tyrannosaurs are considered to be members of Coelurosauria, not Carnosauria, despite their large size.) The carnosaurs lived during the late Jurassic Period and survived into the Cretaceous Period.

Ceratosaurus

Fossils of *Ceratosaurus*, a genus of large carnivorous dinosaurs, date from the Late Jurassic Period in North America and Africa.

Ceratosaurus lived at about the same time as *Allosaurus* and was similar in many general respects to that dinosaur, but the two were not closely related. *Ceratosaurus* belongs to a more primitive theropod stock that includes the coelophysids and abelisaurids. Although it weighed up to two tons, this dinosaur was slightly smaller than *Allosaurus* and bore a distinctive "horn" (actually an expanded nasal crest) on its snout and a row of bony plates down the middle of its back. *Ceratosaurus* also differed from allosaurs in that it retained remnants of a fourth clawed finger, unlike the three typical of most theropods.

Compsognathus

Compsognathus, a group of very small predaceous dinosaurs, lived in Europe during the Late Jurassic Period.

One of the smallest dinosaurs known, *Compsognathus* grew only about as large as a chicken, but with a length of about 60–90 cm (2–3 feet), including the long tail, and a weight of about 55 kg (12 pounds). A swift runner, it was lightly built and had a long neck and tail, strong hind limbs, and very small forelimbs. Of special interest is a tiny skeleton preserved within the rib cage of one *Compsognathus* fossil. This skeleton was once mistakenly thought to be that of an embryo, but further study has shown it to be a lizard's and thus documents the predatory habits of *Compsognathus.*

Recently, a closely related theropod dinosaur was discovered in China dating from the Early Cretaceous Period This fossil, dubbed *Sinosauropteryx* , has filamentous structures on the skin similar to the barbs of feathers, which suggests that feathers evolved from a much simpler structure that probably functioned as an insulator. Since this discovery, several such dinosaurs related to other known theropods have also been found in China.

Confuciusornis

This genus of extinct crow-sized birds lived during the Late Jurassic and Early Cretaceous. *Confuciusornis* fossils were discovered in the Chaomidianzi Formation of

Liaoning province, China, in ancient lake deposits mixed with layers of volcanic ash. These fossils were first described by Hou Lianhai and colleagues in 1995. *Confuciusornis* was about 25 cm (roughly 10 inches) from beak to pelvis. It possessed a small triangular snout and lacked teeth.

Confuciusornis held a number of physical characteristics in common with modern birds but possessed some striking differences. Beautifully preserved specimens show impressions of its feathers, from which it can be inferred that the wings were of comparable size to those of similar flying birds today. Unlike modern birds, however, the forearm of *Confuciusornis* was shorter than both its hand and upper arm bone (humerus). It also retained the feature of having three free fingers on the hand, like *Archaeopteryx* and other theropod dinosaurs. In contrast, the fingers of more-derived birds are fused into an immobile element. *Confuciusornis* had a short tail, a common feature in modern birds, and its caudal vertebrae were reduced in size and number. The terminal vertebrae were fused to form a structure known as the pygo-

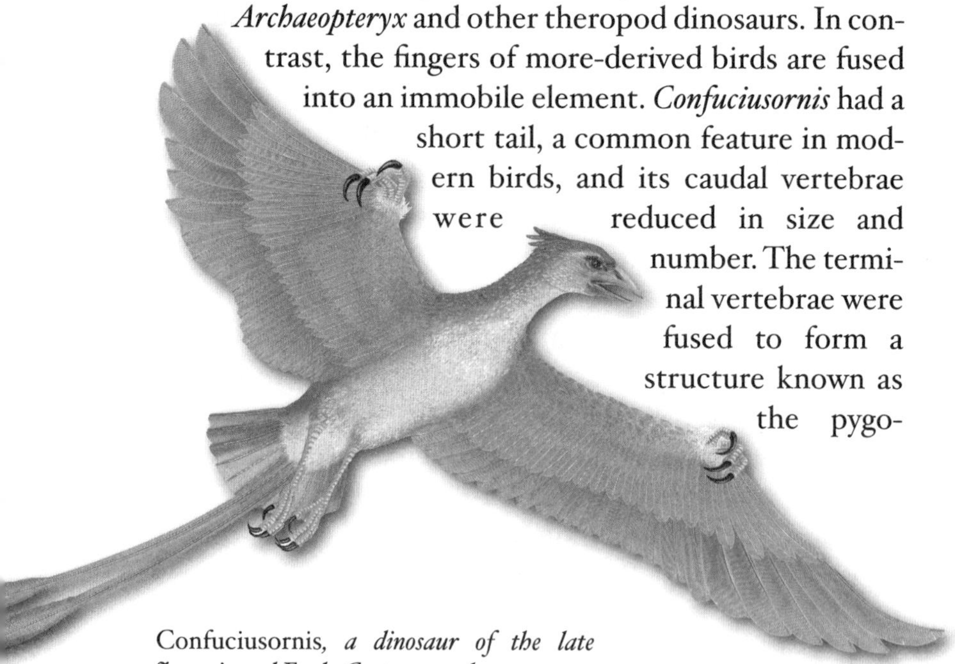

Confuciusornis, *a dinosaur of the late Jurassic and Early Cretaceous, shares a number of physical characteristics with modern birds.* Encyclopædia Britannica, Inc.

style. In some specimens, as in the related *Changchengornis*, a pair of long, thin feathers proceeded from each side of the tail and expanded distally into a teardrop-shaped surface. It has been suggested that these feathers were sexually dimorphic structures and possibly indicative of males. To date, this hypothesis has not been tested statistically or corroborated by other dimorphic features.

Whereas most living birds (including the ostrich) reach full size within a year, the internal bone structure of *Confuciusornis* shows that it grew more slowly. Like other small dinosaurs, *Confuciusornis* probably took several years to mature. This evidence suggests that birds apparently did not evolve their rapid growth rates until sometime in the Late Cretaceous.

Local farmers living in or near the Chaomidianzi Formation collected the first known remains of *Confuciusornis*. Although a good number of specimens have been deposited in Chinese museums, many more have been sold illegally to commercial fossil dealers.

Dimorphodon

The remains of *Dimorphodon*, a genus of primitive flying reptiles, have been found as fossils in European deposits from the Early Jurassic Period. *Dimorphodon* is among the earliest known pterosaurs, an extinct group of reptiles related to the dinosaurs. It was about 1 metre (3.3 feet) long and had a wingspan of about 1.7 metres (5.5 m).

The head was very lightly built but large and deep; the skull had several wide openings; and the eyes were large. In the front of *Dimorphodon*'s jaws were several large pointed teeth, but in the back there were many smaller ones. The limbs were well developed, and, like its ancestors (which were closely related to the first dinosaurs), it probably walked on two legs. The wings consisted of thin membranes of skin stretching from the enormously elongated fourth finger of each hand rearward to the hip or hind limbs. On the ground, the animal probably folded its wings in the manner of present-day birds and bats. The first three fingers of each hand were well developed, with large claws that were probably used for grasping.

Dimorphodon, like other early pterosaurs, had a long tail that probably helped stabilize it during flight. It also had a large breastbone and a large crest on the humerus to which the powerful flight muscles were attached. Like all but the largest pterosaurs, *Dimorphodon* was well suited for flapping flight.

Diplodocus

Fossil remains of *Diplodocus*, a genus of dinosaurs known for their gigantic size, have been found in North America in rocks dating from the Late Jurassic Period. *Diplodocus* is perhaps the most commonly displayed dinosaur. It, along with sauropods such as *Apatosaurus* (formerly *Brontosaurus*), belong to a related subgroup of dinosaurs called diplodocids, members of which were some of the longest land animals that ever lived.

The skull of *Diplodocus* was unusually small and rather light. Elongate like that of a horse, it sat atop a very long neck. The brain was extremely small. The body was comparatively light and was well supported by limb girdles and pillarlike legs. While most of these dinosaurs weighed slightly more than 30 tons, some members of the genus may have weighed as much as 80 tons.

The tail was very long and probably extremely flexible. It most likely provided an anchoring site for the powerful hind leg muscles. The tail may also have functioned as a defensive weapon that could lash out at predators with great force. At some distance down the tail, certain arched structures beneath the tail vertebrae change in shape from spoonlike to canoelike. This flattening of the arches occurs at approximately the same height as where the base of the tail is located above the ground, which suggests that the tail could have been used as a prop for the hindlimbs. This arrangement may have enabled the animal to rear up on its back legs to feed on high vegetation.

Docodon

This extinct genus of mammals was originally known only from fossilized teeth. The dentition patterns of the cusps and other molar structures are complex and distinct, resembling those of modern mammals. However, *Docodon* and its close relatives, the docodonts, are only distantly related to living mammal groups. Whether or not these animals are considered mammals is a controversial matter—*Docodon* fits only the broadest definition of mammal, having the typical mammalian jaw joint between the dentary and squamosal bones.

Docodonts are found in European and North American deposits of the Middle and Late Jurassic Period. The best-known docodont is *Haldanodon* from the Late Jurassic of Portugal. *Haldanodon* is recognized from a virtually complete skeleton that suggests that it was fossorial, or burrowing.

Iguanodon

Fossil remains belonging to the genus *Iguanodon*, a group of large herbivorous dinosaurs, dating from the Late Jurassic and Early Cretaceous periods (roughly 161 million to 100 million years ago) have been found in a wide area of Europe, North Africa, North America, Australia, and Asia; a few have been found from Late Cretaceous deposits of Europe and southern Africa.

Iguanodon was the largest, best known, and most widespread of all the iguanodontids (family Iguanodontidae), which are closely related to the hadrosaurs, or duck-billed dinosaurs. *Iguanodon* was 9 metres (30 feet) long, stood nearly 2 metres (6.5 feet) tall at the hip, and weighed four to five tons. The animal probably spent its time grazing while moving about on four legs, although it was able to walk on two. Iguanodontid forelimbs had an unusual five-fingered hand. The wrist bones were fused into a block; the joints of the thumb were fused into a conelike spike; the three middle fingers ended in blunt, hooflike claws; and the fifth finger diverged laterally from the others. Furthermore, the smallest finger had two small additional phalanges, a throwback to more primitive dinosaurian configuration. The teeth were ridged and formed sloping surfaces whose grinding action could pulverize its diet of low-growing ferns and horsetails that grew near streams and rivers. Most bones of the skull and jaws were not tightly fused but instead had movable joints that allowed flexibility when chewing tough plant material.

In 1825 *Iguanodon* became the second species to be described scientifically as a dinosaur, the first having been *Megalosaurus*. *Iguanodon* was named for its teeth, whose similarity to those of modern iguanas also provided the dinosaur's discoverer, the English physician Gideon Mantell, with the first clue that dinosaurs had been reptiles. In his first reconstruction of the incomplete remains of *Iguanodon*, Mantell restored the skeleton in a quadrupedal pose with the spikelike thumb perched on its nose. This reconstruction persisted in London's famous Crystal Palace dinosaur sculptures by Waterhouse Hawkins (1854) until many complete skeletons were found in Bernissart, Belgium, during the 1880s. Reconstructions of the Belgian skeletons mistakenly placed the animal in an upright, kangaroo-like stance with its tail on the ground—a misconception not corrected until the late 20th century, when a posture based upon a nearly horizontal backbone was adopted.

The fossil remains of many individuals have been found, some in groups, which suggests that iguanodontids traveled in herds. Fossilized tracks of iguanodontids are also relatively common and are widespread in Late Jurassic and Early Cretaceous deposits.

Ornitholestes

Ornitholestes is a genus of small, lightly built carnivorous dinosaurs found as fossils from the Late Jurassic Period in North America. *Ornitholestes* is known from a nearly complete skeleton found in Wyoming, U.S. It was about 2 metres (6.6 feet) long, with a long skull, neck, and tail. The neck was apparently very flexible. The forelimbs were well developed and ended in three long clawed fingers, which indicates that *Ornitholestes* could catch quick and elusive prey. Its name means "bird robber," but it probably ate small, speedy lizards and even early mammals. The hind limbs were well developed, with strong running muscles. Some authorities have equated *Ornitholestes* and *Coelurus*, but they appear to be separate genera.

Pterodactyls

"Pterodactyl" is an informal term for a subgroup of flying reptiles (Pterosauria) known from the Late Jurassic through Late Cretaceous periods.

Pterodactyls, or, more correctly, pterodactyloids, are distinguished from basal pterosaurs by their reduced teeth, tail, and fifth toe. Pterodactyloid metacarpals (palm bones) were more elongated than those of earlier pterosaurs, which instead had elongated phalanges (finger bones). There are also proportional differences in the skull, neck, pelvis, and wing bones. Pterodactyloid genera include *Pterodactylus*, a Late Jurassic form from Germany with a wingspan ranging from 50 cm (20 inches) to well over 1 metre (3.3 feet). It is likely that all fossils of *Pterodactylus* represent different stages of growth within a single species *Pteranodon*, a Late Cretaceous form found in North America, had a long cranial crest and a wingspan exceeding 7 metres (23 feet). Other crested genera are found in Late Cretaceous deposits of Brazil and include *Tupuxuara*, *Anhanguera*, and *Santanadactylus*. *Dsungaripterus* and several other crested forms have been discovered in China. A group of Late Cretaceous pterodactyloids called azhdarchids includes *Montanazhdarcho* and *Quetzalcoatlus* from North America, Europe, and Africa. The wingspan of these reptiles ranged from 2 to 11 metres (6.5–36 feet), which makes them the largest-known flying animals.

Rhamphorhynchus

Specimens of *Rhamphorhynchus*, a genus of flying reptiles (pterosaurs), were uncovered as fossils from the Late Jurassic Period in Europe. The finds suggest that the animal had a diamond-shaped rudder at the tip of its tail. *Rhamphorhynchus* was about 50 cm (20 inches) long, with a long skull and large eyes; the nostrils were set back on the beak. The teeth slanted forward and interlocked and were probably used to eat fish. The body was short, and each thin wing membrane stretched from a long fourth finger. The wing membrane probably attached near the hind limbs.

Scutellosaurus

This genus of small ornithischian dinosaurs from the Early Jurassic Period is characterized by the presence of small scutes along the back and sides of the body. *Scutellosaurus* had small forelimbs and robust hind limbs indicative of a bipedal stance. However, some authorities maintain that its forearms were strong enough to support quadrupedal movement. *Scutellosaurus* reached lengths of 1.5 to 2 metres (about 5 to 6.5 feet). Its skull grew to about 9 cm (about 3.5 inches) in length, and it contained several broad incisors and a row of fluted leaf-shaped cheek teeth that appear to be adapted for feeding on plants.

The first remains of *Scutellosaurus*, which made up a nearly complete skeleton, were found in the Kayenta Formation of Arizona by Douglas Lawler in 1971. Lawler, then a graduate student at the University of California, Berkeley, took the remains to American paleontologist E.H. Colbert at the Museum of Northern Arizona in Flagstaff. In 1981 Colbert described the remains (collected by a Harvard University field party in 1977), along with a second specimen, as *Scutellosaurus lawleri*. The remains of six additional specimens were recovered from other Kayenta localities in Arizona in 1983 by American paleontologist James M. Clark.

Colbert identified the new find and inferred that it was closely related to *Lesothosaurus diagnosticus*, a basal ornithischian, and so he placed it in the family Fabrosauridae. However, *Scutellosaurus* possessed scutes, whereas the fabrosaurs did not. The presence of scutes and other features of the skeleton, such as the curve and shape of the lower jaw, demonstrated that *Scutellosaurus* is more closely related to the stegosaurs and the ankylosaurs in suborder Thyreophora.

Most authorities now recognize *Scutellosaurus* as the most primitive known member of the Thyreophora. In fact, it is so basal that it does not belong to either subgroup. Ankylosaurs improved upon the body armour seen in *Scutellosaurus* by making it more robust and massive, which resulted in a sculpted, tanklike appearance. Stegosaurs, on the other hand, lost all the armour except a single row of parasagittal scutes alternating along the spinal column. These scutes were successively modified into various combinations of broad plates and narrow spikes. Although many authorities have long noted the defensive and thermoregulatory functions of these structures may have principally served as indicators that allowed different species of stegosaurs to recognize each other. In *Scutellosaurus*, however, the scutes were far too small to serve these functions. Embedded in the skin like those of crocodiles, the scutes were probably barely visible.

Stegosaurus

Stegosaurus, one genus of various plated dinosaurs (Stegosauria), lived during the Late Jurassic Period. Fossil remains of this animal are recognizable by the presence of a spiked tail and series of large triangular bony plates along the back. *Stegosaurus* usually grew to a length of about 6.5 metres (21 feet), but some reached 9 metres (30 feet). The skull and brain were very small for such a large animal. The forelimbs were much shorter than the hind limbs, which gave the back a characteristically arched appearance. The feet were short and broad.

Various hypotheses have attempted to explain the arrangement and use of the plates. Paleontologists had long thought that *Stegosaurus* had two parallel rows of plates, either staggered or paired, and that these afforded protection to the animal's backbone and spinal cord. However, new discoveries and reexamination of existing *Stegosaurus* specimens since the 1970s suggest that the plates alternated along the backbone, as no two plates from the same animal have exactly the same shape or size. Because the plates contained many blood vessels, the alternating placement appears consistent with a hypothesis of thermoregulation. This hypothesis proposes that the plates acted as radiators, releasing body heat to a cooler ambient environment. Conversely, the plates could also have collected heat by being faced toward the sun like living solar panels

Two pairs of pointed bony spikes were present on the end of the tail. These are presumed to have served as defensive weapons, but they may have been ornamental. The spinal cord in the region of the sacrum was enlarged and was actually larger than the brain, a fact that gave rise to the misconception that *Stegosaurus* possessed two brains. It is more likely, however, that much of the sacral cavity was used for storing glycogen, as is the case in many present-day animals.

Stegosaurus and its relatives are closely related to the ankylosaurs, with which they share not only dermal armour but several other features, including a simple curved row of small teeth. Both groups evolved from a lineage of smaller armoured dinosaurs such as *Scutellosaurus* and *Scelidosaurus* of the Early Jurassic Period. Stegosaurs lost the armour from the flanks of the body that these early relatives had. Plating among different stegosaurs varied: some forms apparently had parallel rather than alternating plates, and some, such as *Kentrurosaurus*, had plates along the front half of the back and spikes along the back half and tail. These variations cast doubt on the hypothesis of a strong thermoregulatory function for the plates of *Stegosaurus*, because such structures were not optimized in all stegosaurs for collecting or releasing heat. Furthermore, it is puzzling why other stegosaurs and other dinosaurs lacked elaborate thermoregulatory structures. Display and species recognition remain likely functions for the plates, although such hypotheses are difficult to investigate.

Steneosaurus

Steneosaurus is a genus of extinct crocodiles that inhabited shallow seas and whose fossils are found in sediments of the Jurassic Period in South America, Europe, and North Africa. The skull of *Steneosaurus* was very light and narrow, with large openings and a long and narrow snout. The nostrils were at the tip of the snout and connected to the throat by a long bony tube. Many sharp teeth were present, which were probably used to eat fish.

Tyrannosaurs

This group of predatory dinosaurs lived from the Late Jurassic Period to the latest Cretaceous Period, at which time they reached their greatest dominance. Most tyrannosaurs were large predators, with very large, high skulls approaching or well exceeding a full metre (more than three feet) in length. The best-known and largest member of the group is *Tyrannosaurus rex* , or *T. rex*. The "king of the tyrant lizards," as its Latin name is usually translated, walked on powerfully developed hind limbs. If the animal had stood upright, it would have been more than 6.5 metres (21 feet) tall, but the usual posture was horizontal, with the body carried parallel to the ground and the tail held off the ground as a counterbalance. In this position a large adult, weighing 4,000 to 7,000 kg (about 9,000 to 15,000 pounds), could measure 14 metres (46 feet) long.

The longest known tyrannosaur skull is 1.3 metres (more than 4 feet) long. The skull bones of large tyrannosaurs are often several centimetres thick and are strongly braced to each other, which suggests a resistance to the forces of biting, both inflicted upon and received from other tyrannosaurs. Engineering models, in fact, show that the bite force of *T. rex* would easily have been capable of ripping through a car roof, as portrayed in the 1993 motion picture *Jurassic Park*, directed by Steven Spielberg. The huge mouth contained some 60 teeth, which could protrude as far as 15 cm (6 inches). The crowns of the teeth were shed and regrown frequently (every 250 days or so, on the basis of microscopic lines visible within the teeth). Serrations of the teeth bear deep pocketlike recesses in which bacteria may have flourished to provide an infectious bite.

Robotic adult and baby Tyrannosaurus rex *models used in a live show titled "Walking with Dinosaurs," performed in 2009.* Oli Scarff/Getty Images

Tyrannosaur teeth are distinctive. The front teeth are small and U-shaped. The side teeth are large, and in adults they become even larger, fewer in number, and D-shaped in cross section rather than daggerlike as in most theropods, or flesh-eating dinosaurs. In juveniles the teeth are laterally compressed and serrated front and back, like those of other theropods. In mature individuals, however, the teeth fall neatly into three general classes: upper front teeth, upper side teeth, and lower jaw teeth. Gut contents and coprolites (fossilized feces) of tyrannosaurs, as well as remains of other dinosaurs preserved with tyrannosaurid bite marks, show that tyrannosaurs were voracious predators that could easily bite through skulls, pelvises, and limbs of other dinosaurs.

In contrast to the powerful jaws and legs, the forelimbs of tyrannosaurs were very small (less than the length of the shoulder blade), and in some forms the hands were reduced to only two digits. Although a mechanical reconstruction suggests that the musculature of the arms of *T. rex* and some other large tyrannosaurs could have lifted about 180 kg (400 pounds), the hands would not have been able to reach the mouth or grasp prey. The hind limb bones appear massive but are lightly constructed: the thickness of the bone wall is only about 20 percent of the bones' diameter—a figure approaching that of many birds.

The age of individual dinosaurs and other vertebrates can be determined by counting the annual growth rings that are laid down in the long bones, in a manner somewhat analogous to counting tree rings. By using a series of bones from early growth stages to adulthood, the life history of an animal species can be reconstructed. Such studies have shown that *T. rex* effectively reached full size in less than 20 years—approximately the same period as for human beings. Of course, at a length of 6.5 metres (21 feet) and a mass of six tons, *T. rex* reached a much larger size than humans in 20 years. But its growth rate was not as high as that of some herbivorous dinosaurs such as the hadrosaurs (duck-billed dinosaurs), which reached full size in seven or eight years, or the sauropods (the largest plant-eating dinosaurs), which attained most of their gigantic size in 14 years or so. On the other hand, the growth rate of *T. rex* was higher than that of the African elephant, which has a similar mass yet a longer time to maturity. Some of the known specimens of *T. rex* did not quite reach full size. Others do not seem to have survived long after achieving it. This may testify to the hard life of Mesozoic dinosaurs.

Although it was once thought that male and female tyrannosaurs could be distinguished by the shape of the tail vertebrae near the pelvis, this feature turns out not to be diagnostic. However, one subsequently discovered feature does establish sex. During the reproductive cycles of female birds, a layer of bone (medullary bone) is often deposited on the inner wall of the long bones. This process has been recognized in some fossils of tyrannosaurs (and of a few other dinosaurs), indicating that these specimens are female.

Fossils of *T. rex* are found only in the Hell Creek Formation of Garfield county, Montana, and adjacent areas of the United States, in deposits dating from the Maastrichtian Age, the last time unit of the Cretaceous Period—although slightly earlier relatives such as *Tarbosaurus* are known from Asia. Found in the same deposits as *T. rex* are fossils of the ceratopsians (giant horned dinosaurs) on which they likely preyed. There is some question about whether tyrannosaurs killed their food or simply scavenged it. However, neither predatory nor scavenging behaviour need be excluded, since *T. rex*, like many large carnivores today, probably fed opportunistically, scavenging when it could and hunting when it had to. One argument for predation emphasizes *T. rex*'s vision. The eye sockets tend to be keyhole-shaped and directed forward, which has been taken as evidence for accurate depth perception, because the fields of view of the eyes would overlap. Other evidence supporting predation is the well-protected skull and formidable jaws. Wounds in the bones of its prey indicate that *T. rex* ate by using a "puncture and tear" stroke, planting its feet and using the powerful muscles of the neck and legs to anchor itself and pull flesh off bones.

Before 1980 all knowledge of *T. rex* was based on only four skeletons, none very complete. The Latin name was given to the first specimen by American paleontologist Henry Fairfield Osborn in 1905 and was based on partial specimens collected from the Hell Creek Formation by renowned fossil hunter Barnum Brown. Remains found by Brown are on display at the Carnegie Museum of Natural History in Pittsburgh, Pa., the American Museum of Natural History in New York City, and the Natural History Museum in London. Since 1980 more than two dozen other specimens of *T. rex* have been discovered in western North America, some very complete. However, some are in private collections and are therefore lost to science and education. Two of the best specimens, consisting of almost complete adult skeletons, were unearthed in 1990. One, the 85-percent-complete "Wankel" *T. rex*, is on display at the Museum of the Rockies in Bozeman, Mont., and the other, the 90-percent-complete "Sue," is displayed at the Field Museum in Chicago. Other *T. rex* specimens are mounted at other natural history museums in North America, such as the Denver Natural History Museum, the University of California Museum of Paleontology in Berkeley, the Natural History Museum of Los Angeles County, and the Royal Tyrrell Museum in Drumheller, Alta., near Dinosaur Provincial Park.

Sue, a 76-million year-old Tyrannosaurus rex *skeleton, is displayed in Washington, D.C.'s Union Station in 2000.* Mark Wilson/Getty Images

In 2000 five *T. rex* specimens were discovered in the Hell Creek Formation. Several are now on display at the Museum of the Rockies. One of them, the "B-rex," preserves soft tissues and also medullary bone that indicates the specimen was female. The soft tissues preserve transparent, flexible, hollow blood vessels that contain small round microstructures highly reminiscent in structure of red blood cells. The preservation of these structures is one of the most amazing features of the entire known fossil record.

Tyrannosaurs are generally divided into the large but more lightly built and slightly earlier albertosaurines and the still larger, more robust, and later tyrannosaurines. Most tyrannosaurs are known from the latest Cretaceous, but some basal forms are now known from the Early Cretaceous and even the Late Jurassic, though these earlier forms share few features with their later, well-known relatives *Guanlong*, an animal about 3 metres (10 feet) long from the Late Jurassic of Xinjiang province, western China, is the earliest well-known member of the group. It has some primitive and unique features—the most notable being a complex skull crest consisting of a hollow bone running atop the midline of its skull. *Dilong*, an early tyrannosaur 1.5 metres (5 feet) long from the spectacular Liaoning deposits of northeastern China, is preserved with a covering of simple, filamentous "protofeathers" like those seen on many other Early Cretaceous theropod dinosaurs. *Eotyrannus*, from Early Cretaceous deposits on Britain's Isle of Wight, is also lightly built and relatively small (some 4.5 metres, or 15 feet, long). These three tyrannosaurs are so primitive that they retain three fingers on their hands.

Several small tyrannosaur fossils from the latest Cretaceous of western North America were once assigned to separate taxa, but most scholars now consider them to be merely young tyrannosaurs. For example, specimens once given the names *Nanotyrannus* and *Stygivenator* are now considered to be juvenile tyrannosaurs, and the former *Dinotyrannus* is now seen as a subadult *T. rex*. *T. rex* is the only tyrannosaur known from the late Maastrichtian Age (i.e., the latest Cretaceous Period) in North America. As is mentioned above, *Tarbosaurus* is a slightly earlier and very similar form from the latest Cretaceous of Mongolia.

Tyrannosaurs were long thought to be one of the carnosaurs ("flesh-eating lizards"), related to other large theropods such as the allosaurs. These resemblances have proved to be superficial, related to large size alone. Today tyrannosaurs are considered to be gigantic members of the coelurosaurs ("hollow-tailed lizards"), a group largely composed of smaller, more-gracile forms. Frequently they have been related to the largely toothless, ostrichlike ornithomimids, mainly because tyrannosaurs and ornithomimids share a peculiar foot with "pinched" foot bones. Tyrannosaurs may turn out to be closely related to the dromaeosaurs, the "raptors" of Jurassic Park, though evidence for this hypothesis is as elusive as any other.

Yinlong

This ceratopsian dinosaur genus is known from a single nearly complete skeleton taken from the Junggar Basin of western China. *Yinlong* was discovered in rock deposits dating from 159 million to 154 million years ago, during the Oxfordian and Kimmeridgian stages of the Late Jurassic Epoch. The genus is recognized as the most primitive ceratopsian dinosaur known, and it is also the earliest indisputable ceratopsian described from the Jurassic Period. The genus name is derived from Chinese words meaning "hiding dragon," because the fossil was found near a filming location of the movie Crouching Tiger, *Hidden Dragon, directed by Ang Lee* (2000). The genus contains only one species, *Yinlong downsi*, named for the American vertebrate paleontologist William R. Downs III.

In addition to being the earliest ceratopsian, *Yinlong* is distinctive because its skeleton shares many features with *Heterodontosaurus*, a genus of ornithopod dinosaurs, and the pachycephalosaurians (such as *Pachycephalosaurus*). These features are important for determining the evolutionary relationships between all ornithischian dinosaurs.

Yinlong was herbivorous and measured 1.2 metres (about 4 feet) long. Like the pachycephalosaurians, *Yinlong* walked bipedally, whereas most ceratopsians relied on quadrupedal locomotion. It also shared a number of pachycephalosaurian skull characteristics not seen in other, more advanced ceratopsians. The combination of ceratopsian and pachycephalosaurian skeletal features in *Yinlong* strengthens the argument that the pachycephalosaurians were the closest relatives of the ceratopsian dinosaurs. It also suggests that later pachycephalosaurians retained more of the primitive characteristics initially shared between the two groups, while the skeletons of ceratopsians became much more derived with time.

Other Significant Life-Forms of the Jurassic Period

Although the Jurassic was a time of great dinosaur speciation, other forms of life (mammals, fishes, mollusks, etc.) also continued to evolve. Several interesting examples of mammalian dentition also emerged during the Jurassic. *Diarthrognathus* retained both mammal-like and reptile-like features in its jaw. Other mammals, such as the multituberculates, *Spalacotherium* and *Triconodon*, developed specialized molar shapes and configurations. The Jurassic also marked the beginning of the halcyon times of pliosaurs, enormous reptilian carnivores that stalked Jurassic seas.

Aucella

This genus of clams is characteristically found as fossils in marine rocks of the Jurassic Period (between about 176 million and 145.5 million years old). The shell has a distinctive teardrop shape and is ornamented with a concentric pattern of ribs. The apex of one valve (shell half) is often curved over the other. A distinctive and commonly found Jurassic species is *Aucella piochii.*

Cardioceras

An extinct genus of ammonite cephalopods, *Cardioceras* is related to the modern pearly nautilus. *Cardioceras* appears as fossils in rocks of the Late Jurassic Period. The several species known are excellent index, or guide, fossils for Jurassic rocks, enabling them to be correlated over widely separated areas. The shell of *Cardioceras* is circular in outline and ribbed, with a prominent crest along the outer margin.

Diarthrognathus

Diarthrognathus is a genus of extinct, advanced mammal-like reptiles found as fossils in Early Jurassic terrestrial deposits about 200 million years old in southern Africa. *Diarthrognathus* was contemporaneous with a host of other mammal relatives but is nearer than many of them to the line leading to the true mammals because of its unspecialized features of skeletal anatomy and dentition. In true mammals, one jaw joint is formed by the squared bone of the skull and the dentary bone of the lower jaw. In other tetrapods, the location of this joint is determined by the intersection of the quadrate bone above and the articular bone below. In *Diarthrognathus*, both configurations are preserved, and both the quadrate and articular bones are reduced. These bones evolved to become two of the middle-ear bones in mammals.

Gryphaea

An extinct molluskan genus, *Gryphaea* fossils occur in rocks from the Jurassic period to the Eocene epoch (that is, between about 200 million and 34 million years ago). Related to the oysters, *Gryphaea* is characterized by its distinctively convoluted shape. The left valve, or shell, was much larger and more convoluted than the flattish right valve. Fine markings extended across the shell at right angles to the direction of growth. In some mature specimens, the coiling of the shell became so pronounced that it is unlikely that the shell could be opened at all, at which point the animal must have died.

Holectypus

Holectypus is a genus of extinct echinoids, animals much like the modern sea urchins and sand dollars. *Holectypus* fossils appear exclusively in marine rocks of Jurassic to Cretaceous age (that is, between roughly 200 million and 66 million years ago). *Holectypus* was bun shaped with a flat bottom and arched back.

Inoceramus

Fossils of the extinct pelecypod (clam) genus *Inoceramus* appear as fossils in Jurassic to Cretaceous rocks. Especially important and widespread in Cretaceous rocks, *Inoceramus* had a distinctive shell. It is large, thick, and wrinkled in a concentric fashion, making identification relatively simple. The many pits at the dorsal region were the anchoring points for the ligaments that closed the shell.

Multituberculate

A multituberculate is any member of an extinct group of small, superficially rodentlike mammals that existed from about 178 million to 50 million years ago (that is, from the middle of the Jurassic Period until the early Eocene Epoch). During most of this span, they were the most common mammals. Adult multituberculates were usually the size of mice, though the largest species approached the size of beavers. They were dominantly herbivorous and granivorous. The distinguishing characteristic of multituberculates is the construction of their molars, with two or three longitudinal rows of cusps. In fossils of more primitive forms, there are five or six cusps, whereas up to 30 cusps are present in advanced genera. Multituberculates had a single pair of long lower incisors and possibly one to three pairs of upper incisors. In most genera, the anterior lower premolars were large shearing teeth.

The relationship of multituberculates to living mammals is controversial. Some authorities argue that they branched off before the emergence of the last common ancestor of monotremes, marsupials, and placentals. Other authorities argue that multituberculates are more closely related to the latter two groups.

Pliosaurs

These large carnivorous marine reptiles are characterized by their massive heads, short necks, and streamlined, tear-shaped bodies. Pliosaurs have been found as fossils from the Jurassic and Cretaceous periods. They are classified in Order Plesiosauria, along with their long-necked relatives, the plesiosaurs. Pliosaurs possessed powerful jaws and large teeth, and they used four large fins to swim through Mesozoic seas.

One notable pliosaur is *Liopleurodon*, a genus found in Middle Jurassic deposits in England and northern France. *Liopleurodon* is significant in that several fossils of variable quality that range in length from 5 to 25 metres (16 to 85 feet) have been placed in this genus, leading many authorities to question whether such specimens should be reclassified into other genera.

On the other hand, some groups did indeed grow quite large. For example, *Kronosaurus*, an Early Cretaceous pliosaur from Australia, grew to about 12 metres (about 40 feet) long. The skull alone measured about 3.7 metres (12.1 feet) long. An even larger pliosaur from the Jurassic, dubbed "Predator X," was unearthed in Svalbard in 2009. Although it remains unclassified at present, some details are known. Its length and weight are estimated at 15 metres (about 50 feet) long and 45 tonnes (almost 100,000 pounds), respectively. The jaws of this creature are thought to have produced a bite force of 33,000 pounds per square inch, perhaps the highest bite force of any known animal.

Pycnodontiformes

Pycnodontiformes is an order of extinct fishes of the class Actinopterygii, containing the genus *Pycnodus*, common in Jurassic seas. *Pycnodus* is typical of pycnodonts, which were characterized by deep, narrow bodies that were very circular in outline in side view. The pycnodonts had a downturned beak and small mouth with an abundance of bulblike, rounded teeth with thick enamel surfaces. These

Illustrated Liopleurodon catching its prey. DEA Picture Library/Getty Images.

structures enabled pycnodonts to crush their prey, such as the shelled invertebrates of coral reefs.

Spalacotherium

An extinct genus of primitive, probably predaceous, mammals, *Spalacotherium* is known from fossils found in European deposits dating from the Late Jurassic and Early Cretaceous periods (some 160 million to 100 million years ago). The genus *Spalacotherium* has a symmetrodont dentition, characterized by molar teeth with three cusps arranged in a triangle. The symmetrodonts are among the oldest known mammals and also among the most common European faunas of the time.

Triconodon

Triconodon is a genus of extinct mammals found in European deposits of the Late Jurassic Period. The genus is representative of the triconodonts, known from fossils throughout North America, Europe, Africa, and China. *Triconodon* was about the size of a domestic cat. *Triconodon* was relatively large for its time, since most early mammals were very small. However, its brain was smaller than that of most living mammals. The canine teeth were large and strongly developed, so it is probable that *Triconodon* was an active predator. The premolars are simple, but the molars—for which the genus is named—have three distinctive cone-shaped cusps.

Trigonia

A genus of mollusks that first appeared during the Jurassic period, *Trigonia* still exists today. It has a triangular shell with distinctive concentric ridges on its surface as well as nodular outgrowths. A different ornamental pattern is present in the posterior parts of the shell.

JURASSIC GEOLOGY

The Jurassic Period was characterized by its high level of tectonic activity. The supercontinent Pangea broke apart into several pieces as a result of the processes of continental rifting and seafloor spreading. Igneous rocks laid down during the Jurassic were largely the result of such processes, whereas the production of sedimentary rock was influenced by rising sea levels. In contrast, the production of metamorphic rocks resulted from the subduction of tectonic plates and mountain-building processes.

The Economic Significance of Jurassic Deposits

Jurassic igneous rocks have yielded uranium and gold in the Sierra Nevada range of North America, including placer deposits that were mined during the California Gold Rush of the mid-1800s. Some of the diamonds in Siberia were emplaced during Jurassic times. The shallow seas inundating Jurassic continents allowed for extensive deposition of sedimentary rocks that have provided important resources in many regions. For example, clay and limestone have been used for brick, cement, and other building materials in various areas of Europe; iron ore is prevalent in western Europe and England; and Jurassic salt is mined in both the United States and Germany.

Energy resources have also been derived from Jurassic deposits. Jurassic coals are found throughout Eurasia. One significant example is from the Late and Middle Jurassic Yan'an Formation in the Ordos Desert of China. A significant amount of American petroleum production comes from deposits trapped against salt domes of Jurassic age in the Gulf Coast of the United States. The North Sea and Arabian oil fields can also be traced back to organic-rich deposition in restricted Jurassic marine basins. Oil also is found in northern Germany and Russia.

The Occurrence and Distribution of Jurassic Rocks

Jurassic rocks are widely distributed and include sedimentary, igneous, and metamorphic rocks. Because of continuous subduction and destruction of ocean crust in trenches, Middle Jurassic oceanic crust and sediments are generally the oldest sediments remaining in the deep sea. The Jurassic was a time marked by a high level of plate tectonic activity, and igneous rocks of Jurassic age are concentrated in the areas of activity, such as spreading centres (rifts and oceanic ridges) and mountain-building areas near subduction zones. In the areas where the Atlantic Ocean was opening and other continents were splitting apart, basalts that make up oceanic crust today accumulated in the basins. Notably, basalts are found along the east coast of North America and in southern Africa where it was connected to Antarctica. Volcanic ash can also be found near active margins. For example, many ash beds occur in the Late Jurassic Morrison Formation in western North America. Granite batholiths (igneous rocks that were emplaced at depth) can be found along the western margin of North and South America where subduction was occurring during the Jurassic.

Jurassic sedimentary rocks can be found on all modern continents and include marine, marginal marine, and terrestrial deposits. Jurassic marine sediments are also found on the modern seafloor. Because sea levels were high enough to cover large portions of continents, seaways formed on landmasses throughout the Jurassic. Thus, marine sandstones, mudstones, and shales often alternate with terrestrial conglomerates, sandstones, and mudstones. Marine carbonate limestones are mostly found in the tropics and the midlatitudes, where waters were warm and faunal productivity high. In Europe, black shales are common where restricted circulation in shallow marine basins caused bottom waters to become oxygen-deficient. Red beds, windblown sands, lake deposits, and coals can be found in terrestrial systems. Deltaic sands and salt deposits are found in what were once marginal marine environments.

North America

The geologic profile of Jurassic North America is best separated into three different zones: the east coast, where rifting opened the Atlantic Ocean; the western interior, where continental sediments and epicontinental seaway sediments accumulated; and the west coast, where deformation occurred because of the presence of offshore subduction trenches.

In eastern North America, Late Triassic–Early Jurassic extensional basins were filled with red beds and other continental sediments, and pillow lavas were extruded into lake basins. The basaltic Watchung Flows of the Newark Basin are Early Jurassic in age, based on potassium-argon dating techniques that show them to be 185 to 194 million years old. More than 150 metres (500 feet) of Lower Jurassic lake beds were deposited in various basins on the east coast. Some of these bedded sediments may reflect orbital cycles. Middle Jurassic volcanoclastic rocks have been found beneath sediments on the continental shelf of New England. Upper Jurassic marine sediments include clastics interfingering with carbonates in the Atlantic and Gulf Coast basins. Middle Jurassic strata include evaporites, red beds, carbonates, and shelf-margin reefs. The Smackover Formation of the Gulf Coast sequences is a sedimentary unit typical of the Middle Jurassic.

In the western interior of North America, the Middle Jurassic is characterized by a series of six marine incursions. These epicontinental seaways are referred to collectively as the Carmel and Sundance seas. The Carmel Sea is older and not as deep as the Sundance. In these epicontinental seaways, marine sandstones, mudstones, limestones, and shales were deposited—some with marine fossils. Fully marine sequences interfinger with terrestrial sediments deposited during times of low sea levels and with marginal marine sediments that accumulated in environments bordering the seaways.

In the Late Jurassic, sea levels dropped in North America, and terrestrial sedimentation occurred across much of the continent. The Morrison Formation, a clastic deposit of lacustrine and fluvial mudstone, siltstone, sandstone, and conglomerate, is famous for fossil-rich beds that contain abundant plant and dinosaur remains. Uplift of the continental interior occurred between central Arizona and southern California from the Late Triassic until the Middle Jurassic.

Throughout the Jurassic the western margin of North America was bounded by an active subduction zone. This led to very complex geology and much plate tectonic activity, including collisions between terranes and North America, creation of volcanoes, and mountain-building episodes. Accretion of microcontinents and volcanic island arcs to the continent occurred along the entire coast of North America. More than 50 Jurassic terranes have been incorporated onto the continent. Some of the terranes may have originated from tropical areas and traveled far before colliding into North America. During the Nevadan orogeny, volcanic island arcs, including the Sierra Nevada, collided with the continent from northern California to British Columbia, and this resulted in the development of faults and emplacement of igneous intrusions. Deformation of the Foothills Terrane in the Sierra Nevada occurred 160 to 150 million years ago. Jurassic deep-sea rocks now uplifted and exposed in California are between 150 million and 200 million years old, as are intrusive igneous bodies such as the granite batholiths of Yosemite and the High Sierra. During the Jurassic, sediments accumulating off the continental margin were accreted along with the terranes. Many formations in the region are composed of ophiolites (oceanic crust), basalts, and deepwater marine sediments such as cherts, slates, and carbonates. Such a variety of rock types, deposited in a number of different environments, makes this region a geologic patchwork.

Eurasia and Gondwana

Similar to those in North America, Jurassic rocks in the rest of the world can be divided into three types: igneous rocks associated with continental rifting and seafloor spreading, sedimentary rocks associated with epicontinental seaways and terrestrial systems, and deformed deposits associated with subduction and mountain-building (orogenic) zones. Continental rifting between the regions of the Gondwana continent resulted in vast outpourings of basalts similar to those in the Newark Basin (although not as large in extent). These flood basalts are most notable in southern Africa, though thick volcanic sequences are also found on other landmasses that were breaking up at the time—Australia, South America, and India. Other rift-related sedimentary rocks also accumulated in these spreading centres.

The warm, shallow trough of the Tethys Sea between Eurasia and Gondwana accumulated thick sequences of Jurassic sediments. Carbonates are predominant and include fossiliferous shallow-water marls, limestones, and reefs. Siliceous limestones are fairly common, suggesting that an abundance of sponges were available to provide the silica. Evaporites formed along marginal environments around the seaway, while fine sandstones and mudstones are present mainly in nearshore environments near highlands. Deformation of these sediments began in the Late Jurassic, but most of the folding and faulting occurred after the Jurassic. The deformed sediments are exposed today in the Alps.

As seafloor spreading continued, Tethys widened further. Deeper-water sediments present within the Tethyan realm suggest that deepening basins developed during this time. The interiors of continents experienced different levels of marine inundation. As sea levels rose, Tethys expanded and at times covered large parts of the continental interior of Eurasia, allowing for the deposition of the sediments discussed above. Jurassic carbonates can be found in the Jura Mountains and southern France and in England. Fossiliferous, fine-grained lithographic limestones of Germany were deposited in lagoonal and marginal marine environments adjacent to the seaway. Clastic facies include the Early Jurassic shales of western Europe, the Late Jurassic clays of England and Germany, and the clays of the Russian Platform. The Arctic region was primarily a clastic province dominated by clay-rich rocks, shale, siltstone, sandstone, and conglomerate.

There are many examples of Jurassic black shales in Europe that represent intervals of low oxygen conditions at the seafloor. These conditions may have been developed because of restricted circulation and high levels of productivity. Some of the black shales contain exceptionally preserved vertebrate and invertebrate fossils that provide much of the paleontological information about the Jurassic.

On most of the southern landmasses (India, Antarctica, Africa, Australia, and New Zealand), marine deposits are generally restricted to the edges of continents because the continents were mainly above sea level for much of the Jurassic. Continental deposits consist mainly of red beds, sandstones, and mudstones that were deposited under fluvial, lacustrine, and eolian (wind-dominated) environments. Many parts of Eurasia also were dominated by terrestrial environments, accumulating coal beds and other continental sediments.

The Pacific margin of Asia, which was surrounded by subduction zones such as those along the west coast of North America, developed volcanic island arcs and associated basins from Japan to Indonesia. As the Pacific plate subducted under New Zealand during the Late Jurassic, terrane accretion, volcanic activity, and deformation occurred. Subduction zones off the west margin of South America resulted in igneous activity, deformation, and mountain building similar to that occurring in North America.

Ocean Basins

The oldest oceanic evidence for seafloor spreading (and magnetic anomalies) dates from about 147 million years ago, and the oldest oceanic sediments date from the Middle Jurassic. The Indian Ocean began to open at this time as India separated from Australia and Antarctica. The oldest crust of the Pacific basin dates from the Late Jurassic.

By the Early Jurassic, much of the flood basalts associated with the opening of the Atlantic Ocean had already been formed, and some significant basalts are found in the Newark Basin. In the early stages of formation of the Atlantic, nonmarine deposits such as fluvial (river), deltaic, and lacustrine (lake) sediments accumulated within the basin. In other cases, as on the Gulf Coast, marginal marine deposits such as evaporites (salt deposits) accumulated. The Jurassic Gulf Coast salt domes are huge (200 metres, or 660 feet, tall and 2 km, or 1.2 miles, in diameter), suggesting prolonged intervals of seawater evaporation. As the basins grew larger, connections were made with the open ocean, and the basins filled with marine waters and normal marine sediments. However, because these new oceans were still restricted and did not have vigorous circulation, oxygen content was low, allowing for the deposition of organic-rich shales. The source of North Sea oil comes from organic material buried during the Jurassic.

The Major Subdivisions of the Jurassic System

The Jurassic Period is divided into three epochs: Early Jurassic (about 200 million to 176 million years ago), Middle Jurassic (175.6 million to 161.2 million years ago), and Late Jurassic (about 161 million to 145.5 million years ago). (These intervals are sometimes referred to as the Lias, Dogger, and Malm, respectively.) Rocks that originated during the Jurassic period compose the Jurassic System. This system in turn is subdivided into stages, which are often established by using ammonites, bivalves, and protozoans (single-celled organisms) as index fossils. Some controversy exists among researchers as to where the boundaries between the stages should be drawn and what the dates of the boundaries should be. Difficulties arise because many Jurassic ammonites have only a limited geographic distribution. Regional ammonite zones have been established for many areas, but their exact placement in relationship to global correlations is unclear.

The Stages of the Jurassic Period

The Jurassic Period is divided into 11 stages. The Early Jurassic rock system has four stages—the Hettangian,

Sinemurian, Pliensbachian, and Toarcian. The Middle Jurassic also has four stages—the Aalenian, Bajocian, Bathonian, and Callovian, whereas the Late Jurassic has three stages—the Oxfordian, Kimmeridgian, and Tithonian. The stages of the Jurassic Period are described in detail below.

Hettangian Stage

This stage is the lowest of the four divisions of the Lower Jurassic Series. It is the interval that represents all rocks formed worldwide during the Hettangian Age, which occurred between 199.6 million and 196.5 million years ago. The Hettangian Stage underlies the Jurassic Sinemurian Stage, and it overlies the Rhaetian Stage of the Triassic Period.

The name of this stage refers to its type district, located at the village of Hettange-Grande, near Thionville in the Lorraine region of France. The type district consists of a thick succession (57 to 70 metres, or 187 to 230 feet) of basal sandstones overlain by limestones and marls. The limestones bear the bivalve *Gryphaea arcuata* and other fossils that correlate to the biozone of the ammonite *Psiloceras planorbis*. Other species of this genus occur throughout eastern Siberia, North America, and South America, but the definitions of and relationships between Hettangian ammonites are not well established, making correlations difficult. In northwestern Europe the Lower Hettangian is referred to as the Planorbis Zone, the Middle Hettangian as the Liasicus Zone, and the Upper Hettangian as the Angulata Zone.

Sinemurian Stage

The Sinemurian Stage is the second of the four divisions of the Lower Jurassic Series. It is the interval that contains all rocks formed worldwide during the Sinemurian Age, which occurred between 196.5 million and 189.6 million years ago. The Sinemurian Stage overlies the Hettangian Stage and underlies the Pliensbachian Stage.

The Sinemurian Stage was named for exposures at Semur (the ancient Roman town of Sinemurum) in northeastern France, where a condensed sequence of limestones contains fossils of ammonites that lived during this time interval. In northwestern Europe, six major ammonite biozones have been recognized for the Lower and Upper Sinemurian. Because Sinemurian ammonites are less geographically differentiated than earlier Jurassic forms, theoretically there should be more possibilities for large-scale regional stratigraphic correlations. However, many of the ammonite species are rare outside of northwestern Europe, and detailed fine-scale correlations and temporal divisions have not yet been developed for most regions around the world.

Pliensbachian Stage

The third of the four divisions of the Lower Jurassic Series, the Pliensbachian Stage represents all rocks formed worldwide during the Pliensbachian Age, which occurred between 189.6 million and 183 million years ago. The Pliensbachian Stage overlies the Sinemurian Stage and underlies the Toarcian Stage.

The stage's name is derived from the village of Pliensbach, Germany, which is near Boll in the Swabian Alps. The Pliensbachian Stage is represented by up to 195 metres (640 feet) of deposits, mostly marls, in Germany, Belgium, and Luxembourg. Five ammonite biozones, beginning with *Uptonia jamesoni* and ending with *Pleuroceras spinatum*, are recognized for the Lower and Upper Pliensbachian of northwestern Europe. The ammonites of this age worldwide exhibit a high level of regional differentiation, making global correlation difficult.

Toarcian Stage

The fourth and uppermost division of the Lower Jurassic Series, the Toarcian Stage represents all rocks formed worldwide during the Toarcian Age, which occurred between 183 million and 175.6 million years ago. The Toarcian Stage overlies the Lower Jurassic Pliensbachian Stage and underlies the Aalenian Stage of the Middle Jurassic Series.

The stage's name is derived from the village of Thouars (known as Toarcium in ancient Roman times) in western France. The standard succession is better known from the Lorraine region of northeastern France, where about 100 metres (330 feet) of marls and shales with nodular limestones are represented. In northwestern Europe there are two ammonite zones each in the Lower, Middle, and Upper Toarcian, ranging from the Tenuicostatum Zone to the Levesquei Zone. Many Toarcian ammonites are distributed widely around the world, which allows for better global correlations of Toarcian rocks than for those of some other Jurassic stages. However, some differences in species' longevities and their definitions in various regions complicate correlation efforts.

Aalenian Stage

The first and lowest division of the Middle Jurassic Series, this interval corresponds to all rocks formed worldwide during the Aalenian Age, which occurred between 175.6 million and 171.6 million years ago. The Aalenian Stage underlies the Bajocian Stage and overlies the Toarcian Stage of the Lower Jurassic Series.

The name for this stage is derived from the town of Aalen, located 80 km (50 miles) east of Stuttgart in the Swabian Alps of Germany. The Aalenian Stage is divided into the Lower Aalenian and the Upper Aalenian, each of which in Europe is subdivided into two standard ammonite biozones: the Opalinum and Scissum zones for the Lower Aalenian and the Murchisonae and Concavum zones for the Upper Aalenian. In other parts of the world there is an almost complete absence of the ammonite group upon which the standard European zonation is based, so that several different zonation sequences have been recognized in different parts of Asia and North America. Some of these zones are approximately coeval and equivalent to the standard European zonations.

Bajocian Stage

The Bajocian Stage is the second of the four divisions of the Middle Jurassic Series, representing all rocks formed worldwide during the Bajocian Age, which occurred between 171.6 million and 167.7 million years ago. (Some researchers have proposed a longer time span for this stage that extends into more recent time.) The Bajocian Stage overlies the Aalenian Stage and underlies the Bathonian Stage.

The name for this stage is derived from the town of Bayeux in northwestern France. Bajocian rocks exhibit great variation and include coral reef limestones, oolitic deposits, and crinoidal limestones. Eight standard ammonite biozones have been recognized in the majority of European strata—five zones in the Lower Bajocian and three in the Upper Bajocian. However, because of significant differentiation of ammonites in various parts of the world, it is impossible to use these ammonite chronologies outside of Europe. Other regions employ zonation schemes for Bajocian strata that recognize different numbers of zones based on alternative species.

Bathonian Stage

The Bathonian Stage is the third division of the Middle Jurassic Series. It encompasses all rocks formed worldwide during the Bathonian Age, which occurred between 167.7 million and 164.7 million years ago. (Some researchers have proposed a longer time span for this stage that extends into more recent time intervals.) The Bathonian Stage overlies the Bajocian Stage and underlies the Callovian Stage.

The stage's name is derived from the city of Bath in the historic county of Somerset, England. The rock units that make up this stage include about 130 metres (430 feet) of strata, including parts of the Great Oolite and the Cornbrash Beds.

The Bathonian Age is divided into Early, Middle, and Late Bathonian, which are subdivided into various ammonite biozones. Many Bathonian ammonites have only a regional occurrence, so that different zonation schemes came to be established for various parts of the world. For example, unlike the Aalenian and Bajocian stages, two different ammonite sequences are used for the sub-Mediterranean region and northwestern Europe. Several distinct zonations have been developed for separate regions of the circum-Pacific belt. Some of these can be well correlated to the standard European ammonite biozones. However, many stratigraphic sequences in Asia and North America are difficult to correlate globally.

Callovian Stage

This interval is the uppermost of the four divisions of the Middle Jurassic Series, corresponding to all rocks formed worldwide during the Callovian Age, which occurred between 164.7 million and 161.2 million years ago. (Some researchers have proposed a longer time span, from 160 million to 154 million years ago, with concomitant changes in the dates of other Jurassic stages.) The Callovian Stage overlies the Bathonian Stage and underlies the Oxfordian, the lowest stage of the Upper Jurassic Series.

The name for this stage is derived from the Kellaways area in Wiltshire, England, which was known as Callovium during Roman times. In England the Callovian includes strata from the Cornbrash Beds, Kellaways Beds, and Oxford Clay. The Callovian is subdivided into the Lower, Middle, and Upper Callovian, and throughout Europe each of these intervals is further subdivided into two standard ammonite biozones. Outside of Europe the Callovian sequences are not well developed, because of gaps in marine strata, small geographic ranges among the ammonites, and the presence of long-lived species that are unsuitable for correlation. In some regions ammonite associations are present but cannot easily be correlated to European forms. However, in certain other regions and time intervals in the circum-Pacific belt (such as the Lower Callovian of Mexico), a large number of European species can be found, permitting global correlations.

Oxfordian Stage

The Oxfordian Stage is the first and lowest of the three divisions of the Upper Jurassic Series. The interval encompasses all rocks formed worldwide during the Oxfordian Age, which occurred between 161.2 million and 155.6 million years ago. (Some researchers have proposed a longer span for this stage that extends into more recent time.) The Oxfordian Stage underlies the Kimmeridgian Stage and overlies the Callovian Stage of the Middle Jurassic Series.

The name for this stage is derived from Oxford, Oxfordshire, England. The stage includes up to 90 metres (295 feet) of strata, including portions of the Oxford Clay and the Corallian Beds. The Oxfordian is divided into the Lower, Middle, and Upper Oxfordian, each of which is further subdivided into zones. In Europe there are seven standard ammonite biozones, with two (the Mariae and

Cordatum) in the Lower Oxfordian, two (the Plicatilis and Transversarium) in the Middle Oxfordian, and three (the Bifurcatum, Bimammatum, and Planula) in the Upper Oxfordian. Outside of Europe the distribution of ammonites and other fossils used in correlations is often patchy because of unsuitable habitats during the Oxfordian and deformation of the strata after deposition. In addition, because of the limited geographic range of many species, it is difficult to correlate strata between regions of the world. In North America a number of different zones have been established for different areas, but gaps within the sequences prevent the zones from spanning the entire Oxfordian. In Asia and the southern Pacific there are fewer established zones, and their exact placement in relationship to global correlations is unclear.

Kimmeridgian Stage

The Kimmeridgian Stage is the second of the three divisions of the Upper Jurassic Series, encompassing all rocks formed worldwide during the Kimmeridgian Age, which occurred between 155.6 million and 150.8 million years ago. (Some researchers have proposed a more recent endpoint for this stage.) The Kimmeridgian Stage overlies the Oxfordian Stage and underlies the Tithonian Stage.

The name for this stage is derived from the Kimmeridge area in Dorset, southern England. In England the Kimmeridgian includes the Kimmeridge Clay. The Kimmeridgian Stage is divided into the Lower Kimmeridgian and the Upper Kimmeridgian, each of which contains three standard ammonite biozones—the Platynota, Hypselocyclum, and Divisum in the Lower Kimmeridgian and the Acanthicum, Eudoxus, and Beckeri in the Upper Kimmeridgian. In North America only Mexico has a detailed ammonite stratigraphic zonation developed for much of the Kimmeridgian. In other regions the presence of ammonites that are useful for correlation is sparse, and often these species cover a wide range of time or are not easily correlated to other areas. There are large regions where no ammonites have been found, making the development of stratigraphic zones and global correlations very difficult. Bivalves such as *Buchia* and *Retroceramus* have been used to correlate strata from the circum-Pacific region.

Tithonian Stage

This interval is the uppermost of the three divisions of the Upper Jurassic Series. It corresponds to all rocks formed worldwide during the Tithonian Age, which occurred between 150.8 million and 145.5 million years ago. The Tithonian Stage overlies the Kimmeridgian Stage and underlies the Berriasian, the lowest stage of the Cretaceous Period.

The name of this stage is derived not from a geographic source but from the Greek mythological figure Tithonus, who was the consort of Eos (Aurora), goddess of the dawn. The Tithonian Stage has replaced the Volgian and Purbeckian Stages, which were previously locally recognized in Russia and England, respectively.

In Europe the Tithonian is divided into the Lower, Middle, and Upper Tithonian. Each of these intervals is further divided into numerous standard European ammonite biozones: the Lower Tithonian includes the Hybonotum and Darwini zones; the Middle Tithonian includes the Semiforme, Fallauxi, and Ponti zones; and the Upper Tithonian includes the Micracanthum and Durangites zones.

In other parts of the world, Mexico is one of the few regions where an extensive, detailed ammonite stratigraphic zonation has been developed. Elsewhere only a few zones have been recognized, and in some areas the exact timing and correlations of these zones have not been finalized. As with the other Upper Jurassic stages, the lack of well-developed global correlations is due to patchy distribution of ammonites and tightly constrained geographic distributions for individual species.

SIGNIFICANT JURASSIC FORMATIONS AND DISCOVERIES

Certain geologic structures have greatly increased the scientific understanding of Jurassic time. Three of the four items described below are units of rocks that contain examples of some of the fossil life-forms described above. Although the rock formations are useful for preserving the harder and more durable parts of dinosaurs and other forms of Jurassic life, the fourth structure, the coprolite, possessed the ability to protect the less-durable remains of other organisms. Without coprolites, the remains of several species would have been completely destroyed and thus unknown to science.

Coprolites

A coprolite is defined as the fossilized excrement of animals. The English geologist William Buckland coined the term in 1835 after he and fossilist Mary Anning recognized that certain convoluted masses occurring in the Lias rock strata of Gloucestershire and dating from the Early Jurassic Period had a form that would have been produced by their passage in the soft state through the intestines of reptiles or fishes. These bodies had long been known as fossil fir cones and bezoar stones (hardened undigestible contents of the intestines). Buckland's conjecture that they were of fecal origin and similar to the excrement of hyenas was confirmed upon analysis. They were found to consist essentially of calcium phosphate and carbonate, and they not infrequently contained fragments of unaltered bone. The name coprolites, from the Greek *kopros* ("dung") and *lithos* ("stone"), was accordingly given them by Buckland. Coprolites often preserve the remains of plants and small animals that would otherwise be destroyed or lost. They are therefore important sources of concentrated information about ancient biota and environments.

The Morrison Formation

The Morrison Formation is a series of sedimentary rocks deposited during the Jurassic Period in western North America, from Montana to New Mexico. The Morrison Formation is famous for its dinosaur fossils, which have been collected for more than a century, beginning with a find near the town of Morrison, Colorado, in 1877. Radiometric dating indicates that the Morrison Formation is between 148 million and 155 million years old. Correlation of fossils indicates that it was deposited during the Kimmeridgian and early Tithonian ages and possibly during the latest Oxfordian Age.

The sediments in the Morrison Formation include multicoloured mudstones, sandstones, and conglomerates, as well as minor amounts of marls, limestone, and claystones. The sediments were derived from western mountains, such as the Sierra Nevada range, that were uplifted during Late Jurassic time. There are also numerous volcanic ash beds within the formation that have been used to date the deposits through radiometric techniques. Some sediments in the lowest portion of the Morrison Formation are marine in origin, but the majority of the sediments were deposited along rivers, streams, lakes, mudflats, swamps, and alluvial plains that covered the western interior of North America during the Late Jurassic.

The nonmarine sediments contain abundant fossils—plants as well as the famous invertebrate and vertebrate animals. Dinosaur National Monument in eastern Utah was established to preserve and exhibit fossils from the Morrison Formation. Many of the dinosaur fossils are found as jumbled accumulations consisting of dozens of partially disarticulated skeletons. These probably resulted from the transportation of dinosaur carcasses along streams and their subsequent burial on sandbars. The dinosaurs are quite diverse and represent a number of different habitats. Mollusks, fishes, insects, crocodiles, turtles, and other fossils suggest that some lakes in the area were freshwater but that saline, alkaline lakes were also present.

The Purbeck Beds

This unit of exposed sedimentary rocks occurs in southern England and spans the boundary between the Jurassic and Cretaceous periods, approximately 145.5 million years ago. The highly varied Purbeck Beds, which overlie rocks of the Portland Beds, record a marked change in sedimentary facies, indicating major alterations in environmental conditions. Limestones, marls, clays, and old soil horizons are present in thicknesses of up to 170 metres (560 feet).

The type section is at Durlston Bay near Swanage, Dorset. Each of the Lower, Middle, and Upper Purbeck beds contains distinctive units. The Lower Purbeck is completely Jurassic in age, having been deposited during the Tithonian Age, and the Upper Purbeck is entirely Cretaceous in age, having been deposited during the

Berriasian Age. The boundary between the two geologic time periods appears to occur in the Cinder Bed unit of the Middle Purbeck.

The varied rock types of the Purbeck Beds were deposited in marine, marginal marine (such as brackish lagoons), and freshwater settings. Ancient land soils in the Lower Purbeck include the fossilized stumps of coniferous trees and primitive palmlike cycads. In addition, shales and clays occasionally contain fossil insects. The Middle and Upper Purbeck consist of freshwater limestones that are quarried for use as building stone. Marls and shales are interbedded with the limestones.

The lowest unit of the Middle Purbeck, the Marly Freshwater Beds, has a Mammal Bed containing about 20 mammalian species. The Cinder Bed, located within the Middle Purbeck, is a marine unit containing varied fauna, including large quantities of oysters, trigonids (a type of Mesozoic clam), and fragments of echinoids (sea urchins). The Upper Building Stones unit of the Middle Purbeck contains fossils of turtles and fish that probably lived in brackish water. The Upper Purbeck contains freshwater fossils and is the source of "Purbeck Marble" building stones.

The Solnhofen Limestone

This famous Jurassic Period limestone unit located near the town of Solnhofen, southern Germany, contains exceptionally preserved fossils from the Tithonian Age. The Solnhofen Limestone is composed of thin beds of fine-grained limestones interbedded with thin shaley layers. They were originally deposited in small, stagnant marine basins (possibly with a very high salt content and low oxygen content) surrounded by reefs. The limestones have been quarried for hundreds of years for buildings and for lithographic printmaking. The Solnhofen Limestone is also known as Solnhofen Plattenkalk.

More than 750 plant and animal species have been described from the Solnhofen Limestone. The most common fossils are crinoids, ammonites, fishes, and crustaceans. The most famous fossil from Solnhofen is *Archaeopteryx*, an ancient bird that left impressions of its feathers preserved in the rock. It is the oldest bird fossil to have been found by paleontologists.

The Solnhofen is well known for the exceptional preservation of soft-bodied organisms such as jellyfish, squid, and insects that are not usually incorporated into the fossil record. The burial of such organisms in the fine-grained sediments of stagnant marine basins allowed even the impressions of internal organs to be preserved.

CHAPTER 4

The Cretaceous Period

This interval of geologic time was the last of the three periods of the Mesozoic Era. The Cretaceous began 145.5 million years ago and ended 65.5 million years ago. It followed the Jurassic Period and was succeeded by the Paleogene Period of the Cenozoic Era. The Cretaceous is the longest period of the Phanerozoic Eon. Spanning 80 million years, it represents more time than has elapsed since the extinction of the dinosaurs, which occurred at the end of the period.

The name Cretaceous is derived from *creta*, Latin for "chalk," and was first proposed by J.B.J. Omalius d'Halloy in 1822. D'Halloy had been commissioned to make a geologic map of France, and part of his task was to decide upon the geologic units to be represented by it. One of his units, the Terrain Crétacé, included chalks and underlying sands. Chalk is a soft, fine-grained type of limestone composed predominantly of the armourlike plates of coccolithophores, tiny floating algae that flourished during the Late Cretaceous (about 100 million to 65.5 million years ago). Most Cretaceous rocks are not chalks, but most chalks were deposited during the Cretaceous. Many of these rocks provide clear and easily accessed details of the period because they have not been deformed or eroded and are relatively close to the surface—as can be seen in the white cliffs bordering the Strait of Dover between France and England.

The Cretaceous Period began with the Earth's land assembled essentially into two continents, Laurasia in the north and Gondwana in the south. These were almost completely separated by the equatorial Tethys seaway, and the various segments of Laurasia and Gondwana had already started to rift apart. North America had just begun pulling away from Eurasia during the Jurassic, and South America had started to split off from Africa, from which India, Australia, and Antarctica were also separating. When the Cretaceous Period ended, most of the present-day continents were separated from each other by expanses of water such as the North and South Atlantic Ocean. At the end of the period, India was adrift in the Indian Ocean, and Australia was still connected to Antarctica.

The climate was generally warmer and more humid than today, probably because of very active volcanism associated with unusually high rates of seafloor spreading. The polar regions were free of continental ice sheets, their land instead covered by forest. Dinosaurs roamed Antarctica, even with its long winter night.

The lengthy Cretaceous Period constitutes a major portion of the interval between ancient life-forms and those that dominate Earth today. Dinosaurs were the dominant group of land animals, especially "duck-billed" dinosaurs (hadrosaurs), such as *Shantungosaurus*, and horned forms, such as *Triceratops*. Giant marine reptiles such as ichthyosaurs, mosasaurs, and plesiosaurs were common in the seas, and flying reptiles (pterosaurs) dominated the sky. Flowering plants (angiosperms) arose close to the beginning of the Cretaceous and became more abundant as the period progressed. The Late Cretaceous was a time of great productivity in the world's oceans, as borne out by the deposition of thick beds of chalk in western Europe, eastern Russia, southern Scandinavia, the Gulf Coast of North America, and western Australia. The Cretaceous ended with one of the greatest mass extinctions in the history of Earth, exterminating the dinosaurs, marine and flying reptiles, and many marine invertebrates.

THE CRETACEOUS ENVIRONMENT

When the Cretaceous Period began, Earth's continents were joined into two large, continuous blocks. By the end of the period, these blocks had separated into multiple smaller pieces. Although sea level crested during the Cretaceous, producing vast areas of shallow seas, the close proximity of the landmasses inhibited ocean circulation. In addition, by the middle of the period, average temperatures had climbed to their highest level in Earth's history. Reduced ocean circulation combined with warm temperatures stripped the oxygen from equatorial seas, enabling the development of black shale deposits.

Paleogeography

The position of Earth's landmasses changed significantly during the Cretaceous Period—not unexpected, given its long duration. At the onset of the period there existed two supercontinents, Gondwana in the south and Laurasia in the north. South America, Africa (including the adjoining pieces of what are now the Arabian Peninsula and the Middle East), Antarctica, Australia, India, Madagascar, and several smaller landmasses were joined in Gondwana in the south, while North America, Greenland, and Eurasia (including Southeast Asia) formed Laurasia. Africa had split from South America, the last land connection being between Brazil and Nigeria. As a result, the South Atlantic Ocean joined with the widening North Atlantic. In the region of the Indian Ocean, Africa and Madagascar separated from India, Australia, and Antarctica in Late Jurassic to Early Cretaceous times (145.5 million to 99.6 million years ago). Once separated from Australia and Antarctica, India began its journey northward, which culminated in a later collision with Asia during the Cenozoic Era. Madagascar broke away from Africa during the Late Cretaceous, and Greenland separated from North America. Australia was still joined to Antarctica. These were barely attached at the junction of what are now North and South America.

Sea level was higher during most of the Cretaceous than at any other time in Earth history, and it was a major factor influencing the paleogeography of the period. In general, world oceans were about 100 to 200 metres (330 to 660 feet) higher in the Early Cretaceous and roughly 200 to 250 metres (660 to 820 feet) higher in the Late Cretaceous than at present. The high Cretaceous sea level is thought to have been primarily the result of water in the ocean basins being displaced by the enlargement of mid-oceanic ridges.

As a result of higher sea levels during the Late Cretaceous, marine waters inundated the continents, creating relatively shallow epicontinental seas in North America, South America, Europe, Russia, Africa, and Australia. In addition, all continents shrank somewhat as their margins flooded. At its maximum, land covered only about 18 percent of the Earth's surface, compared with approximately 28 percent today. At times, Arctic waters were connected to the Tethys seaway through the middle of North America and the central portion of Russia. On several occasions during the Cretaceous, marine animals living in the South Atlantic had a seaway for migration to Tethys via what is presently Nigeria, Niger, Chad, and Libya. Most of western Europe, eastern Australia, parts of

Africa, South America, India, Madagascar, Borneo, and other areas that are now land were entirely covered by marine waters for some interval of Cretaceous time.

Detailed study indicates 5 to 15 different episodes of rises and falls in sea level. The patterns of changes for the stable areas throughout history are quite similar, although several differences are notable. During most of the Early Cretaceous, parts of Arctic Canada, Russia, and western Australia were underwater, but most of the other areas were not. During the Middle Cretaceous, east-central Australia experienced major inundations called transgressions. In the Late Cretaceous, most continental landmasses were transgressed but not always at the same time. One explanation for the lack of a synchronous record is the concept of geoidal eustacy, in which, it is suggested, as the Earth's continents move about, the oceans bulge at some places to compensate. Eustacy would result in sea level being different from ocean basin to ocean basin.

Water circulation and mixing were not as great as they are today, because most of the oceans (e.g., the developing North Atlantic) were constricted, and the temperature differences between the poles and the Equator were minimal. Thus, the oceans experienced frequent periods of anoxic (oxygenless) conditions in the bottom waters that reveal themselves today as black shales. Sometimes, particularly during the mid-Cretaceous, conditions extended to epicontinental seas, as attested by deposits of black shales in the western interior of North America.

The Cretaceous world had three distinct geographic subdivisions: the northern boreal, the southern boreal, and the Tethyan region. The Tethyan region separated the two boreal regions and is recognized by the presence of fossilized reef-forming rudist bivalves, corals, larger foraminiferans, and certain ammonites that inhabited only the warmer Tethyan waters. Early in the Cretaceous, North and South America separated sufficiently for the marine connection between the Tethys Sea and the Pacific to deepen substantially. The Tethys-to-Pacific marine connection allowed for a strong westward-flowing current, which is inferred from faunal patterns. For example, as the Cretaceous progressed, the similarity between rudist bivalves of the Caribbean and western Europe decreased, while some Caribbean forms have been found on Pacific seamounts, in Southeast Asia, and possibly in the Balkans.

The remnants of the northern boreal realm in North America, Europe, Russia, and Japan have been extensively studied. It is known, for instance, that sediments in the southwestern Netherlands indicate several changes of temperature during the Late Cretaceous. These temperature swings imply that the boundary between the northern boreal areas and the Tethys region was not constant with time. Russian workers recognize six paleobiogeographic zones: boreal, which in this context is equivalent to Arctic; European; Mediterranean, including the central Asian province; Pacific; and two paleofloristic zonations of land. Southern boreal areas and the rocks representing the southern Tethys margin lack this level of detail.

Magnetically, the Cretaceous was quiet relative to the subsequent Paleogene Period. In fact, magnetic reversals are not noted for a period of some 42 million years, from the early Aptian to the late Santonian ages. The lengths of Earth's months have changed regularly for at least the past 600 million years because of tidal friction and other forces that slow the Earth's rotation. The rate of change in the synodic month was minimal for most of the Cretaceous but has accelerated since. The reasons for these two anomalies are not well understood.

Paleoclimate

In general, the climate of the Cretaceous Period was much warmer than at present, perhaps the warmest on a worldwide basis than at any other time during the Phanerozoic Eon. The climate was also more equable in that the temperature difference between the poles and the Equator was about one-half that of the present. Floral evidence suggests that tropical to subtropical conditions existed as far as 45° N, and temperate conditions extended to the poles. Evaporites are plentiful in Early Cretaceous rocks—a fact that seems to indicate an arid climate, though it may have resulted more from constricted ocean basins than from climatic effects. The occurrence of evaporites mainly between latitudes 10° and 30° N suggests arid subtropics, but the presence of coals poleward of 30° indicates humid midlatitudes. Occurrences of Early Cretaceous bauxite and laterite, which are products of deep weathering in warm climates with seasonal rainfall, support the notion of humid midlatitudes.

Temperatures were lower at the beginning of the period, rising to a maximum in the mid-Cretaceous and then declining slightly with time until a more accentuated cooling during the last two ages of the period. Ice sheets and glaciers were almost entirely absent except in the high mountains, so, although the end of the Cretaceous was coolest, it was still much warmer than it is today.

Models of the Earth's climate for the mid-Cretaceous based on the positions of the continents, location of water bodies, and topography suggest that winds were weaker than at present. Westerly winds were dominant in the lower to midlatitudes of the Pacific for the entire year. In the North Atlantic, however, winds blew from the west during winter but from the east during summer. Surface water temperatures were about 30 °C (86 °F) at the Equator year-round, but at the poles they were 14 °C (57 °F) in winter and 17 °C (63 °F) in summer. A temperature of 17 °C is suggested for the ocean bottom during the Albian Age, but it may have declined to 10 °C (50 °F) by the Maastrichtian. These temperature values have been calculated from oxygen isotope measurements of the calcitic remains of marine organisms. The data support models that suggest diminished ocean circulation both vertically and latitudinally. As stated in the section Paleogeography, above, low circulation could account for the periods of black shale deposition during the Cretaceous.

Other paleontological indicators suggest details of ocean circulation. The occurrence of early and mid-Cretaceous rudists and larger Tethyan foraminiferans in Japan may very well mean that there was a warm and northward-flowing current in the region. A similar occurrence of these organisms in Aptian-Albian sediments as far south as southern Tanzania seems to indicate a southward-flowing current along the east coast of Africa. The fact that certain warm-water life-forms found in the area of present-day Argentina are absent from the west coast of Africa suggests a counterclockwise gyre in the South Atlantic. In addition, the presence of larger foraminiferans in Newfoundland and Ireland indicates the development of a "proto-Gulf Stream" by the mid-Cretaceous.

CRETACEOUS LIFE

The Cretaceous Period is biologically significant because it is a major part of the transition from the early life-forms of the Paleozoic Era to the advanced diversity of the current Cenozoic Era. For example, most if not all of the flowering plants (angiosperms) made their first appearance during the Cretaceous. Although dinosaurs were the dominant animals of the period, many modern animals, including the placental mammals, made their debut during the Cretaceous. Other groups—such as clams and snails, snakes and lizards, and most fishes—developed distinctively modern characteristics before the mass extinction marking the end of the period.

Marine Life

The marine realm can be divided into two paleobiogeographic regions, the Tethyan and the boreal. This division is based on the occurrence of rudist-dominated organic reeflike structures. Rudists were large, rather unusual bivalves that had one valve shaped like a cylindrical vase and another that resembled a flattened cap. The rudists were generally dominant over the corals as framework builders. They rarely existed outside the Tethyan region, and the few varieties found elsewhere did not create reeflike structures. Rudist reeflike structures of Cretaceous age serve as reservoir rocks for petroleum in Mexico, Venezuela, and the Middle East.

Other organisms almost entirely restricted to the Tethys region were actaeonellid and nerineid snails, colonial corals, calcareous algae, larger bottom-dwelling (benthic) foraminiferans, and certain kinds of ammonites and echinoids. In contrast, belemnites were apparently confined to the colder boreal waters. Important bivalves of the boreal realm were the reclining forms (e.g., *Exogyra* and *Gryphaea*) and the inoceramids, which were particularly widespread and are now useful for distinguishing among biostratigraphic zones.

Marine plankton took on a distinctly modern appearance by the end of the Cretaceous. The coccolithophores became so abundant in the Late Cretaceous that vast quantities accumulated to form the substance for which the Cretaceous Period was named—chalk. The planktonic foraminiferans also contributed greatly to fine-grained calcareous sediments. Less-abundant but important single-celled animals and plants of the Cretaceous include the diatoms, radiolarians, and dinoflagellates. Other significant marine forms of minute size were the ostracods and calpionellids.

Ammonites were numerous and were represented by a variety of forms ranging from the more-usual coiled types to straight forms. Some of the more-unusual ammonites, called heteromorphs, were shaped like fat corkscrews and hairpins. Such aberrant forms most certainly had difficulty moving about. Ammonites preyed on other free-swimming or benthic invertebrates and were themselves prey to many larger animals, including the marine reptiles called mosasaurs.

Other marine reptiles were the long-necked plesiosaurs and the more fishlike ichthyosaurs. Sharks and rays

Fossils of coiled ammonites. Ross Rappaport/Photonica/Getty Images

(chondrichthians) also were marine predators, as were the teleost (ray-finned) fishes. One Cretaceous fish, *Xiphactinus*, grew to more than 4.5 metres (15 feet) and is the largest known teleost.

Terrestrial Life

Although the fossil record is irregular in quality and quantity for the Early Cretaceous, it is obvious that dinosaurs continued their lengthy dominance of the land. The Late Cretaceous record is much more complete, particularly in the case of North America and Asia. It is known, for instance, that during the Late Cretaceous many dinosaur types lived in relationships not unlike the present-day terrestrial mammal communities. Although the larger dinosaurs, such as the carnivorous *Tyrannosaurus* and the herbivorous *Iguanodon*, are the best-known, many smaller forms also lived in Cretaceous times. *Triceratops* , a large three-horned dinosaur, inhabited western North America during the Maastrichtian age.

Various types of small mammals that are now extinct existed during the Triassic and Jurassic, but two important groups of modern mammals evolved during the Cretaceous. Placental mammals, which include most modern mammals (e.g., rodents, cats, whales, cows, and primates), evolved during the Late Cretaceous. Although almost all were smaller than present-day rabbits, the Cretaceous placentals were poised to take over terrestrial environments as soon as the dinosaurs vanished. Another mammal group, the marsupials, evolved during the Cretaceous as well. This group includes the native species of Australia, such as kangaroos and koalas, and the North American opossum.

In the air, the flying reptiles called pterosaurs dominated. One pterosaur, *Quetzalcoatlus*, from the latest

Cretaceous of what is now Texas (U.S.), had a wingspan of about 15 metres (49 feet). Birds developed from a reptilian ancestor during the Jurassic and Cretaceous. *Hesperornis* was a Cretaceous genus of flightless diving bird that had large feet and sharp backward-directed teeth adapted for preying on fish.

The land plants of the Early Cretaceous were similar to those of the Jurassic. They included the cycads, ginkgoes, conifers, and ferns. The angiosperms appeared in the Early Cretaceous, became common by the beginning of the middle of the Cretaceous, and came to represent the major component of the landscape by the mid-Late Cretaceous. This flora included figs, magnolias, poplars, willows, sycamores, and herbaceous plants. With the advent of many new plant types, insects also diversified.

The End-Cretaceous Mass Extinction

As mentioned in chapter 1, at or very close to the end of the Cretaceous Period, many animals that were important elements of the Mesozoic world became extinct. On land the dinosaurs perished, but plant life was less affected. Of the planktonic marine flora and fauna, only about 13 percent of the coccolithophore and planktonic foraminiferan genera survived the extinction. Ammonites and belemnites became extinct, as did such marine reptiles as ichthyosaurs, mosasaurs, and plesiosaurs. Among the marine benthos, the larger foraminiferans (orbitoids) died out, and the hermatypic corals were reduced to about one-fifth of their genera. Rudist bivalves disappeared, as did bivalves with a reclining life habit, such as *Exogyra* and *Gryphaea*. The stratigraphically important inoceramids also died out. Overall, approximately 80 percent of animal species disappeared, making this one of the largest mass extinctions in Earth's history.

Many theories have been proposed to explain the Late Cretaceous mass extinction. Since the early 1980s, much attention has been focused on the asteroid theory formulated by American scientists Walter and Luis Alvarez. This theory states that the impact of an asteroid on the Earth may have triggered the extinction event by ejecting a huge quantity of rock debris into the atmosphere, enshrouding the Earth in darkness for several months or longer. With no sunlight able to penetrate this global dust cloud, photosynthesis ceased, resulting in the death of green plants and the disruption of the food chain. There is much evidence in the rock record that supports this hypothesis. A huge crater 180 km (112 miles) in diameter dating to the latest Cretaceous has been discovered buried beneath sediments of the Yucatán Peninsula near Chicxulub, Mexico. In addition, tektites (fractured sand grains characteristic of meteorite impacts) and the rare-earth element iridium, which is common only deep within the Earth's mantle and in extraterrestrial rocks, have been found in deposits associated with the extinction. There is also evidence for some spectacular side effects of this impact, including an enormous tsunami that washed up on the shores of the Gulf of Mexico and widespread wildfires triggered by a fireball from the impact.

The asteroid theory has met with skepticism among paleontologists who prefer to look to terrestrial factors as the cause of the extinction. A huge outpouring of lava, known as the Deccan Traps, occurred in India during the latest Cretaceous. Some paleontologists believe that the carbon dioxide that accompanied these flows created a global greenhouse effect that greatly warmed the planet. Others note that tectonic plate movements caused a major rearrangement of the world's landmasses, particularly during the latter part of the Cretaceous. The climatic changes resulting from such continental drift could have caused a gradual deterioration of habitats favourable to the dinosaurs and other animal groups that suffered extinction. It is, of course, possible that sudden catastrophic phenomena such as an asteroid impact contributed to an environmental deterioration already brought about by terrestrial causes.

Significant Dinosaurs of the Cretaceous Period

Dinosaurs continued to evolve throughout the Cretaceous time. Several feathered, horned, and armoured types lived during the period, some with very specialized features. Fossils of several predatory genera, including *Albertosaurus* and *Velociraptor* also appear in Cretaceous rocks. During the second half of the period, the hadrosaurs (duck-billed dinosaurs), such as *Anatosaurus*, *Lambeosaurus*, and *Maiasaura*, became the most abundant dinosaurs in North America.

Albertosaurus

Albertosaurus, formerly known as *Gorgosaurus*, is a genus of large carnivorous dinosaurs of the Late Cretaceous Period found as fossils in North America and eastern Asia. Albertosaurs are an early subgroup of tyrannosaurs, which appear to have evolved from them.

In structure and presumed habits, *Albertosaurus* was similar to *Tyrannosaurus* in many respects. Both had reduced forelimbs and a large skull and jaws, although *Albertosaurus* was somewhat smaller. *Albertosaurus* was about 9 metres (30 feet) long, and the head was held 3.5 metres (11.5 feet) off the ground. The hands were similar to those of tyrannosaurs in being reduced to the first two fingers and a mere rudiment of the third. The jaws of

Albertosaurus possessed numerous large, sharp teeth, which were recurved and serrated As in tyrannosaurs, the teeth were larger and fewer than in other carnivorous dinosaurs, and, rather than being flattened and bladelike in cross-section, the teeth were nearly round—an efficient shape for puncturing flesh and bone. Like nearly all large carnivores, it is possible that *Albertosaurus* was at least in part a scavenger, feeding upon dead or dying carcasses of other reptiles or scaring other predators away from their kills.

Albertosaurus fossils occur in rocks that are slightly older than those containing *Tyrannosaurus* fossils. It is thought that albertosaurs and tyrannosaurs evolved in eastern Asia because the oldest fossils are found in China and Mongolia. According to this view, albertosaurs migrated from Asia to North America, where they became the dominant carnivores of the Late Cretaceous.

Anatosaurus

Formerly known as *Trachodon*, this genus of bipedal duck-billed dinosaurs (hadrosaurs) of the Late Cretaceous Period is commonly found as fossils in North American rocks 70 million to about 66 million years old. Related forms such as *Edmontosaurus* and *Shantungosaurus* have been found elsewhere in the Northern Hemisphere.

Anatosaurus grew to a length of 9–12 metres (30–40 feet) and was heavily built. The skull was long and the beak broad and flat, much like a duck's bill. As in all iguanodontids and hadrosaurs, there were no teeth in the beak itself, which was covered by a horny sheath. However, several hundred rather blunt teeth were arranged in rows along the sides of the cheeks at any given time. There were dozens of teeth along each row, and several rows of exposed and partially worn replacement teeth were present behind the outer teeth. Not all were functional simultaneously, but, as teeth became worn or lost, they were replaced continually by new ones.

Some *Anatosaurus* specimens have been found desiccated and remarkably well preserved, with skin and internal structures remaining. Such evidence indicates that the outer hide was leathery and rough. *Anatosaurus* may have fed mostly on twigs, seeds, fruits, and pine needles, judging from fossilized stomach remains. No digested remains of aquatic plants have been found. The flat, blunt, hooflike claw bones of *Anatosaurus* and other duckbills suggest that they were much like today's browsing mammals in their habits, probably traveling in herds and feeding on a variety of land vegetation.

Anatosaurus was a member of the duckbill lineage called hadrosaurines, which, unlike lambeosaurine hadrosaurs, did not evolve elaborate crests on the skull. *Trachodon* was a name assigned to hadrosaur remains that consisted only of isolated teeth.

Ankylosaurus

This genus of armoured ornithischian dinosaurs lived 70 million to roughly 66 million years ago in North America during the Late Cretaceous Period. *Ankylosaurus* is a genus belonging to a larger group (infraorder Ankylosauria) of related four-legged, herbivorous, heavily armoured dinosaurs that flourished throughout the Cretaceous Period.

Ankylosaurus was one of the largest ankylosaurs, with a total length of about 10 metres (33 feet) and a probable weight of about four tons. Its head was square, flat, and broader than it was long. Its teeth, like those of the related stegosaurs, consisted of a simple curved row of irregularly edged (crenulated) leaf-shaped teeth. The body was short and squat, with massive legs to support its weight. Like other ankylosaurs, its back and flanks were protected from attack by thick bands of armour consisting of flat bony plates. These plates were supplemented by rows of bony spikes projecting from the animal's flanks and by bony knobs on its back. The skull was also heavily armoured and spiked. *Ankylosaurus*'s long tail terminated in a thick "club" of bone, which it probably swung as a defense against predators. This club was formed by the last tail vertebrae, which were nested tightly against each other and a sheath of several bony plates. The armour schemes of other ankylosaurs varied somewhat, but all were well protected against attack by carnivorous dinosaurs. The earliest ankylosaurs, called nodosaurs, lacked the tail club and had rather different armour patterns.

Caudipteryx

This genus of small feathered theropod dinosaurs is known from rock deposits of western Liaoning province, China, that date from about 125 million years ago, during the Early Cretaceous. *Caudipteryx* was one of the first-known feathered dinosaurs. Fossil specimens have impressions of long feathers on the forearms and tail. These feathers were symmetrical and similar to those of living flightless birds. However, they differed from those of living and fossil flying birds, such as

Caudipteryx, *an early Cretaceous dinosaur thought to be one of the first known dinosaurs with feathers.* Encyclopædia Britannica, Inc.

Archaeopteryx. Furthermore, the forelimbs of *Caudipteryx* were too short to have functioned as wings, suggesting that complex feathers originally evolved in nonflying animals for purposes other than flight.

With its small head, long neck, compact body, and fan of tail feathers, *Caudipteryx* probably resembled a small pheasant or turkey, and it may have occupied a similar ecological niche. In members of this genus, teeth were present on the premaxillae (the bones at the front of the upper jaw). However, the maxillae and the lower jaws were toothless and presumably beaked. Furthermore, numerous gastroliths (stomach stones) were found in the rib cages of some specimens. These probably functioned as a gastric mill for grinding up tough forage, such as plant material and the chitinous exoskeletons of insects, as in the muscular gizzards of many birds.

Caudipteryx was a primitive member of Oviraptorosauria, a group of theropods that were closely related to birds. Oviraptorosaurs differed from most other theropods in having a deep belly and a short, stiff tail. In addition, many forms had few, if any, teeth. According to some authorities, the reduced dentition and deep abdomen may have been adaptations for herbivory. Some oviraptorosaurs, however, possessed significant numbers of teeth, and these forms may have been omnivorous or insectivorous.

Deinonychus

This long-clawed carnivorous dinosaur flourished in western North America during the Early Cretaceous Period. A member of the dromaeosaur group, *Deinonychus* was bipedal, walking on two legs, as did all theropod dinosaurs. Its principal killing devices were large sicklelike talons 13 cm (5 inches) long on the second toe of each foot. The slender, outstretched tail was enclosed in bundles of bony rods. These extensions of the tail vertebrae were ideal for helping the animal maintain balance as it ran or attacked prey.

Deinonychus was the model for the "raptor" dinosaurs of the motion picture *Jurassic Park* (1993). The name raptor has come to apply to dromaeosaurs in general as a contraction for *Velociraptor*, a genus of dromaeosaur that was considerably smaller than *Deinonychus*. However, the term *raptor* (from the Greek word for "seize" or "grab") is more correctly applied to birds such as hawks and eagles, which grasp prey with their talons. *Deinonychus* measured about 2.5 metres (8 feet) or perhaps more in length and weighed 45–68 kg (100–150 pounds). It was evidently a fast, agile predator whose large brain enabled it to perform relatively complex movements during the chase and kill.

Dromaeosaurs and troodontids are the closest known relatives of *Archaeopteryx* and existing birds. These dinosaurs share with birds a number of features, including unusually long arms and hands and a wrist that is able to flex sideways. Such adaptations apparently helped these dinosaurs to grasp prey and later enabled birds to generate an effective flight stroke.

Dilong

A genus of small feathered theropod dinosaurs, *Dilong* is known from rock deposits of western Liaoning province, China, that date from 128 million to 127 million years ago, during the Early Cretaceous. *Dilong* was one of the most primitive known tyrannosaurs, a group that includes *Tyrannosaurus* and other similar dinosaurs, and the first tyrannosauroid discovered with feathers. *Dilong* was comparatively small, with a total length of 1.6 metres (about 5 feet) and an estimated mass of 5 kg (about 11 pounds). *Dilong* differs from *Tyrannosaurus* in having proportionally larger forelimbs and three-fingered, grasping hands. It also shared many advanced features of the skull with later tyrannosaurs—such as fused nasal bones, extensive sinuses, and a rounded snout with anterior teeth that are D-shaped in cross section. This pattern of anterior teeth gave the animal a "cookie-cutter" bite when hunting or consuming prey. In most other aspects of its anatomy, *Dilong* resembled juveniles of larger and later tyrannosaurs. The existence of *Dilong* demonstrates that tyrannosaurs were anatomically distinctive before they evolved into gigantic predators.

Dilong was the first primitive tyrannosaur known from reasonably complete remains. One of the fossil specimens includes impressions of protofeathers. This is the first evidence that, like many other coelurosaurs (that is, theropod dinosaurs closely related to birds), tyrannosaurs were feathered. The protofeathers were made up of branched filaments that extended to 2 cm (0.8 inch) long,

Dilong paradoxus, *an early Cretaceous dinosaur that is one of the more primitive tyrannosaurs.* Encyclopædia Britannica, Inc.

but these filaments would have resembled a coat of hair rather than the contour feathers of birds. *Dilong* and most other feathered coelurosaurs could not fly and were not descended from flying animals. This evidence suggests that feathers first evolved as insulation and only later were co-opted for flight.

Dromaeosaurs

The dromaeosaurs (family Dromaeosauridae) are a group of small to medium-sized carnivorous dinosaurs that flourished in Asia and North America during the Cretaceous Period. Agile, lightly built, and fast-running, these theropods were among the most effective predators of their time.

All dromaeosaurs were bipedal, and the second toe of each foot was extremely flexible and bore a specialized killing claw, or talon, that was not used in walking. Instead, it was always held off the ground because it was much larger and was jointed differently from the other claws. The largest killing claw belonged to *Deinonychus* and measured up to 13 cm (5 inches) in length.

Dromaeosaurs had large heads equipped with many sharp serrated teeth, and their long arms ended in slender three-clawed hands that were used for grasping. Like troodontids and birds, dromaeosaurs had a unique wrist joint that allowed the hands to flex sideways. This evidently helped them seize their prey. In birds the same motion produces the flight stroke. The tails of dromaeosaurs were also unusually long and were somewhat stiffened by bundles of slim bony rods that were extensions of the arches of the tail vertebrae.

Dromaeosaurs apparently ran down their prey (probably small- to medium-sized herbivores), seizing it with the front claws while delivering slashing kicks from one of the taloned hind legs. In doing so, dromaeosaurs may have been able to hold this one-footed pose by using the rigidly outstretched tail as a counterbalance, or they may have attacked by using both feet in a single leaping action. The relatively large brains of dromaeosaurs enabled them to carry out these complex movements with a degree of coordination unusual among reptiles but quite expected in these closest relatives of birds.

Fossil evidence supporting the prediction of grasping arms and slashing foot claws was borne out by the discovery in the 1970s of a *Velociraptor* preserved in a death position with a small ceratopsian dinosaur, *Protoceratops.* The hands of *Velociraptor* were clutching the frill of *Protoceratops*, and the large foot claw was found embedded in its throat.

Utahraptor was considerably larger than Deinonychus but is incompletely known. *Dromaeosaurus* and *Velociraptor* both reached a length of about 1.8 metres (6 feet). There is debate as to whether *Microraptor*, the smallest and most birdlike dinosaur known, is a dromaeosaur or a troodontid. Only about the size of a crow, *Microraptor* appears to have possessed feathers. The single specimen was discovered in China in 2000 from deposits dating to the Early Cretaceous.

Euoplocephalus

This armoured dinosaur inhabited North America during the Late Cretaceous Period. Like its close relative *Ankylosaurus* and the more distantly related *Nodosaurus*, *Euoplocephalus* was a massive animal that likely weighed more than two tons. *Euoplocephalus* differed from these and most other ankylosaurs in having a bone that protected the eyelid. The teeth, as in all ankylosaurs, were limited to a single curved row and were used to eat plants.

Hesperornis

Hesperornis is a genus of extinct birds found as fossils in Late Cretaceous Period deposits dating from about 120 million to 66 million years ago. This bird is known mostly from the Great Plains region of the United States, but some remains have been found as far north as Alaska. *Hesperornis* was primitive in that teeth were present in the lower jaw. The rear portion of the upper jaw also had teeth. This evidence suggests that the horny beak characteristic of today's birds had not yet evolved in *Hesperornis*.

Hesperornis was clearly an actively swimming bird that probably chased and caught fish. Although unrelated to today's loons (order Gaviiformes), many of *Hesperornis*'s skeletal features resembled those of loons, and, like loons, *Hesperornis* is thought to have been a good diver. The wings were small and useless for flight, and the wing bones were splintlike. The breastbone lacked the prominent keel that serves as an anchor for powering flight muscles. The legs, however, were powerfully developed and clearly adapted for rapid diving and swimming through water. The neck was slender and the head long and tapered. Both were probably capable of rapid side-to-side movement

Hypsilophodon

A genus of small to medium-sized herbivorous dinosaurs that flourished about 115 million to 110 million years ago during the Early Cretaceous Period, *Hypsilophodon* was up to 2 metres (6.5 feet) long and weighed about 60 kg (130 pounds). It had short arms with five fingers on each hand and was equipped with much longer four-toed hind feet. In its mouth was a set of high, grooved, self-sharpening cheek teeth adapted for grinding up plant matter. In its horny beak were several incisor-like teeth used to nip off vegetation.

For many decades paleontologists thought that *Hypsilophodon*'s long fingers and toes enabled it to live in trees, but this inference was based on an incorrect reconstruction of its hind foot, which suggested it could grasp and perch. The dinosaur is now recognized to have been a ground dweller with a conventional ornithopod foot. *Hypsilophodon* is typical of a lineage of ornithopods known as Hypsilophodontidae. Two other major groups of ornithopods—the hadrosaurs, or duck-billed dinosaurs, and the iguanodontids—are closely related. Hypsilophodontids survived into the Late Cretaceous, when they lived alongside the iguanodontids and hadrosaurs that probably arose from early members of the lineage.

Ichthyornis

Ichthyornis, a genus of extinct seabirds from the Late Cretaceous, occur as fossils in the U.S. states of Wyoming, Kansas, and Texas. *Ichthyornis* somewhat resembled present-day gulls and terns and may even have had webbed feet. The resemblance, however, is superficial, because *Ichthyornis* and its relatives lacked many features that all the living groups of birds have.

Ichthyornis was about the size of a domestic pigeon and had strongly developed wings. The breastbone was large, with a strong keel, and the wing bones were long and well developed. The shoulder girdle was similar to that of strong-flying birds of the present. The legs were strong, with short shanks, long front toes, and a small, slightly elevated hind toe. The tail had a well-developed terminal knob made of several fused vertebrae (pygostyle), as did the tails of all but the most primitive birds such as *Archaeopteryx*. Indications are that *Ichthyornis*, like its modern relatives, lacked teeth. The brain of *Ichthyornis* showed greater development than that of another Cretaceous seabird, *Hesperornis*, but its brain was still smaller than that of modern birds. Other traits of *Ichthyornis* are not known for certain, as the known fossil material is fragmentary and the association of some of the bones is in question. Some portions may turn out to belong to other kinds of Cretaceous birds.

Because it was once thought to have had teeth, *Ichthyornis* was formerly grouped with *Hesperornis*, but it is now classified as the sole genus of the order Ichthyornithiformes. *Ichthyornis* was one of the notable discoveries of the American paleontologist Othniel Charles Marsh.

Lambeosaurus

This duck-billed dinosaur (hadrosaur) is notable for the hatchet-shaped hollow bony crest on top of its skull. Fossils of this herbivore date to the Late Cretaceous Period of North America. *Lambeosaurus* was first discovered in 1914 in the Oldman Formation, Alberta, Canada. These specimens measured about 9 metres (30 feet) long, but larger specimens up to 16.5 metres (54 feet) in length have been found recently in Baja California, Mexico. *Lambeosaurus* and related genera are members of the hadrosaur subgroup, Lambeosaurinae.

Several lambeosaurines possessed a range of bizarre cranial crests, and various functions for these crests have been proposed. For example, it has been suggested that the complex chamber extensions of the breathing passage between the nostrils and the trachea contained in the crest served as resonating chambers for producing sound or as expanded olfactory membranes to improve the sense of smell. Other proposed functions such as air storage, snorkeling, or combat have been dismissed for various reasons. No single function or suite of functions appears to fit all lambeosaurine crests, and it is possible that their strange shapes were mainly features by which members of different species recognized each other from members of other species. As in all other duck-billed dinosaurs, the dentition was expanded and adapted for chewing large quantities of harsh plant tissues.

Lambeosaurinae and Hadrosaurinae are the two major lineages of the duck-billed dinosaur family, Hadrosauridae. Members of the two subgroups are distinguished by the presence or absence of cranial crests and ornamentation and by the shape of the pelvic bones.

Maiasaura

Maiasaura, a genus of duck-billed dinosaurs (hadrosaurs), appear as fossils from the Late Cretaceous of North America. The discovery of *Maiasaura* fossils led to the theory that this group of bipedal herbivores cared for their young.

In 1978 a *Maiasaura* nesting site was discovered in the Two Medicine Formation near Choteau, Montana, U.S. The remains of an adult *Maiasaura* were found in close association with a nest of juvenile dinosaurs, each about 1 metre (3.3 feet) long. Hatchlings that were too large (about

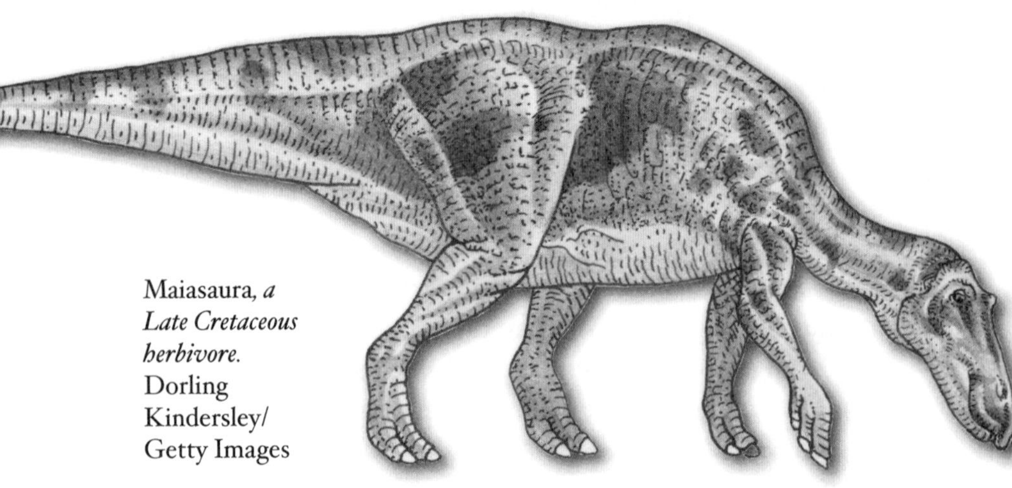

Maiasaura, *a Late Cretaceous herbivore.* Dorling Kindersley/ Getty Images

0.5 metre long) to fit into eggs, and nests with clutches of eggs, as well as many broken eggshells, were found nearby. The bones of the embryos, however, were not fully ossified, which means the young could not have walked immediately upon hatching and would have required some degree of parental care. Hundreds of skeletons preserved in one specific ashbed in Montana, as well as those preserved in nesting sites, suggest that *Maiasaura* was migratory. Such evidence also demonstrates that these dinosaurs were social animals that nested in groups. They probably returned to the same nesting site year after year. Studies of bone structure indicate that it would have taken about seven or eight years for *Maiasaura* to reach an adult size of 8 metres (26 feet).

Nodosaurus

Nodosaurus is a genus of armoured dinosaurs found as fossils in North America dating from 95 million to 90 million years ago during the Late Cretaceous Period. A heavy animal about 5.5 metres (18 feet) long, *Nodosaurus* had a long tail but a very small head and a minuscule brain. For protection against predators, it relied upon a heavy coat of thick bony plates and knobs that covered its back. The front legs were much smaller than the hind legs, and the back was strongly arched.

Nodosaurids (family Nodosauridae) and ankylosaurids (family Ankylosauridae) are the two commonly recognized groups within Ankylosauria, the armoured dinosaurs. Of the two subgroups, nodosaurids are generally regarded as more primitive, having generally lived before the ankylosaurids (nearly all of which date from the Late Cretaceous). Nodosaurid ancestors of *Nodosaurus* are first found in Middle Jurassic deposits of Europe, though they are mostly known from the Early Cretaceous, and some survived to the end of the period. Nodosaurids lacked the tail club of ankylosaurids, and their skulls were generally not as short or broad, nor was the skull covered with protective plates (scutes).

Ornithomimus

This genus of ostrichlike dinosaurs is known from fossils in Mongolian, European, and North American deposits dating from 125 million to 66 million years ago.

Ornithomimus was about 3.5 metres (11.5 feet) long, and, although it was a theropod dinosaur, it was likely omnivorous. Its name means "bird mimic," and, like most other members of its subgroup (Ornithomimidae), it was toothless and had beaklike jaws. The small, thin-boned skull had a large brain cavity. Its three fingers were unusual among dinosaurs in that they were all approximately the same length. *Ornithomimus*'s legs were very long, especially its foot bones (metatarsals). The legs and feet, along with its toothless beak and long neck, provide a superficial resemblance to the living ostrich. A related ornithomimid is so ostrichlike that its name means "ostrich-mimic " Ornithomimidae also includes small forms such as *Pelecanimimus*, larger ones such as *Garudimimus* and *Harpymimus*, and the giant *Deinocheirus*, known only from a 2.5-metre (8-foot) shoulder girdle and forelimb from the Late Cretaceous of Mongolia.

Oviraptor

This group of small, lightly built predatory or omnivorous dinosaurs brooded its eggs in a manner similar to birds. Found as fossils in deposits from the Late Cretaceous Period of eastern Asia and North America, *Oviraptor* was about 1.8 metres (6 feet) long and walked on two long, well-developed hind limbs. The forelimbs were long and

Oviraptor philoceratops, *from Djadochta Cretaceous beds, Shabarkh Uso, Mongolia.* Courtesy of the American Museum of Natural History, New York

slender, with three long clawed fingers clearly suited for grasping, ripping, and tearing. *Oviraptor* had a short skull with very large eyes surrounded by a bony ring, and it was possibly capable of stereoscopic vision. The skull also had strange cranial crests, and the jaws lacked teeth but were probably sheathed with a horny, beaklike covering.

Oviraptor is named from the Latin terms for "egg" and "robber," because it was first found with the remains of eggs that were thought to belong to *Protoceratops*, an early horned dinosaur. However, microscopic studies of the eggshells have shown that they were not ceratopsian but theropod. Later, several other *Oviraptor* skeletons were found atop nests of eggs in a brooding position exactly like that of living birds.

PACHYCEPHALOSAURUS

This genus of large and unusual dinosaurs are known from fossils in North American deposits dating to the Late Cretaceous Epoch. *Pachycephalosaurus,* which grew to be about 5 metres (16 feet) long, was a biped with strong hind limbs and much less developed forelimbs. The unusual and distinctive feature of *Pachycephalosaurus* is the high, domelike skull formed by a thick mass of solid bone grown over the tiny brain. This bone growth covered the temporal openings that were characteristic of the skulls of related forms. Abundant bony knobs in front and at the sides of the skull further added to the unusual appearance. *Pachycephalosaurus* and closely related forms are known as the bone-headed, or dome-headed, dinosaurs. These dinosaurs, which are also found in Mongolia, had a variety of skull shapes. In the most basal forms, the dome was not thick but flat. Late forms had thick domes shaped like kneecaps, or a large sagittal crest with spikes and knobs pointing down and back from the sides of the skull. It has been suggested that these animals were head butters like living rams, but the configuration of the domes does not support this hypothesis. Flank-butting remains a possibility in some species, but a more likely function in most was species recognition or display.

PACHYRHINOSAURUS

Pachyrhinosaurus is a genus of horned ceratopsid dinosaurs that roamed northwestern North America from 71 million to 67 million years ago. It is closely related to *Styracosaurus* and *Centrosaurus* and more distantly related to *Triceratops*. Like other ceratopsids, it possessed a prominent skull characterized by a narrow but massive beak and a bony frill. The Greek name *Pachyrhinosaurus* means "reptile with a thick nose."

Pachyrhinosaurus was both large and quadrupedal. It grew to 6 metres (20 feet) in length and weighed about 1,800 kg (almost 2 tons). A herbivore, *Pachyrhinosaurus* used the batteries of teeth in its jaws to slice open and consume plants. Some of its horns grew in unicorn fashion between and slightly behind the eyes, whereas others decorated the top edge of the frill. *Pachyrhinosaurus* also sported thickened knobs of bone. The largest of these knobs covered the top of the nose. The function of these knobs, horns, and frill is unknown, but they may have been used for species recognition, competition between males, or defense against predators.

Specimens of *Pachyrhinosaurus* are known from bone beds in southern Alberta, Can., and the North Slope of Alaska, U.S. In both locations, the bone beds contain juveniles and adults, which suggests that this dinosaur may have provided parental care by herding. Although average global temperatures were much warmer during the Cretaceous Period than they are today, *Pachyrhinosaurus* populations in Alaska and northern Canada did have to contend with months of winter darkness. It remains unknown whether they migrated south during the Alaskan winter.

Pentaceratops

Specimens of this five-horned herbivorous dinosaur have been found as fossils in North America and possibly eastern Asia dating from the Late Cretaceous Period. *Pentaceratops* was about 6 metres (20 feet) long and had one horn on its snout, one above each eye, and one on each side of the large bony neck frill. It was a ceratopsian related to the more familiar *Triceratops* and is especially well known from the Kirtland Shale of New Mexico, U.S.

Protoceratops

Fossils of this ceratopsian dinosaur were discovered in the Gobi Desert from 80-million-year-old deposits of the Late Cretaceous Period. *Protoceratops* was a predecessor of the more familiar horned dinosaurs such as *Triceratops*. Like other ceratopsians, it had a rostral bone on the upper beak and a small frill around the neck, but *Protoceratops* lacked the large nose and eye horns of more derived ceratopsians.

Protoceratops evolved from small bipedal ceratopsians such as *Psittacosaurus*, but *Protoceratops* was larger and moved about on all four limbs. The hind limbs, however, were more strongly developed than the forelimbs (as expected in an animal that evolved from bipedal ancestors), which gave the back a pronounced arch. Although small for a ceratopsian, *Protoceratops* was still a relatively large animal. Adults were about 1.8 metres (6 feet) long and would have weighed about 180 kg (400 pounds). The skull was very long, about one-fifth the total body length. Bones in the skull grew backward into a perforated frill. The jaws were beaklike, and teeth were present in both the upper and lower jaws. An area on top of the snout just in front of the eyes may mark the position of a small hornlike structure in adults.

The remains of hundreds of individuals have been found in all stages of growth. This unusually complete series of fossils has made it possible to work out the rates and manner of growth of *Protoceratops* and to study the range of variation evident within the genus. Included among *Protoceratops* remains are newly hatched young. Ellipsoidal eggs laid in circular clusters and measuring about 15 cm (6 inches) long were once attributed to

Protoceratops, but they are now known to belong to the small carnivorous dinosaur *Oviraptor.*

Psittacosaurus

Psittacosaurus is a primitive member of the horned dinosaurs (Ceratopsia) found as fossils dating from 122 million to 100 million years ago in Early Cretaceous deposits of Mongolia and China.

Psittacosaurus measured about 2 metres (6.5 feet) long and was probably bipedal most of the time. The skull was high and narrow and is characterized by a small bone (rostral) that forms the upper beak. The anterior region of the skull was shaped very much like a parrot's beak in that the upper jaw curved over the lower, hence the dinosaur's name ("psittac" being derived from the Latin term for "parrot"). Apart from these unusual features, *Psittacosaurus* appears likely to have evolved from bipedal ornithopod dinosaurs sometime in the Late Jurassic or very Early Cretaceous.

Spinosaurus

This genus of theropod dinosaurs is known from incomplete North African fossils that date to Cenomanian times (roughly 100 to 94 million years ago). *Spinosaurus*, or "spined reptile," was named for its "sail-back" feature, created by tall vertebral spines. It was named by German paleontologist Ernst Stromer in 1915 on the basis of the discovery of a partial skeleton from Bahariya Oasis in western Egypt by his assistant Richard Markgraf. These fossils were destroyed in April 1944 when British aircraft inadvertently bombed the museum in Munich in which they were housed. For several decades *Spinosaurus* was known only from Stromer's monographic descriptions. However, additional fragmentary remains were discovered during the 1990s and 2000s in Algeria, Morocco, and

A specialist retouches the reconstructed head of a Spinosaurus, which resembles that of a crocodile. Vanderlei Almeida/AFP/Getty Images

Tunisia. Related taxa in the family Spinosauridae include *Baryonyx* from England, *Irritator* from Brazil, and *Suchomimus* from Niger.

Spinosaurus, which was longer and heavier than *Tyrannosaurus*, is the largest known carnivorous dinosaur. It possessed a skull 1.75 metres (roughly 6 feet) long, a body length of 14–18 metres (46–59 feet), and an estimated mass of 12,000–20,000 kg (13–22 tons).

Like other spinosaurids, *Spinosaurus* possessed a long, narrow skull resembling that of a crocodile and nostrils near the eyes instead of the end of the snout. Its teeth were straight and conical instead of curved and bladelike as in other theropods. All of these features are adaptations for piscivory (that is, the consumption of fish). Other spinosaurids have been found with partially digested fish scales and the bones of other dinosaurs in their stomach regions, and spinosaurid teeth have been found embedded in pterosaur bones. The sail over the animal's back was probably used for social displays or species recognition rather than for temperature regulation. Some authorities maintain that the sail was actually a hump used to store water and lipids.

Struthiomimus

Struthiomimus is a genus of ostrichlike dinosaurs found as fossils from the Late Cretaceous Period in North America. *Struthiomimus* (meaning "ostrich mimic") was about 2.5 metres (8 feet) long and was obviously adapted for rapid movement on strong, well-developed hind limbs. The three-toed feet were especially birdlike in that they had exceedingly long metatarsals (foot bones), which, as in birds (and some other dinosaurs), did not touch the ground. *Struthiomimus* had a small, light, and toothless skull perched atop a slender and very flexible neck. The jaws were probably covered by a rather birdlike horny beak. The forelimbs were also long and slender, terminating in three-fingered hands with sharp claws adapted for grasping. The hand, as in all members of the theropod subgroup Ornithomimidae, is diagnostic in that all three fingers are nearly the same length.

Therizinosaurs

This group of theropod dinosaurs lived during the Late Cretaceous in Asia and North America and were characterized by their relatively small skulls, leaf-shaped teeth, and extended fingers with extremely long and robust claws. Therizinosaurs also lacked teeth in the front half of their upper jaws, and they had long necks, wrist bones similar to those of birds, widely spaced hips, a backward-pointing pubis bone, and four widely spread toes similar to those of sauropod dinosaurs. Fossil specimens have been known since the 1950s, but their unusual combination of skeletal features (especially their teeth, hips, and toes) made their relationships to other dinosaur groups contentious. By the mid-1990s, the discovery of new, more complete specimens had confirmed their theropod ancestry. Therizinosaurs are divided into five genera (*Beipiaosaurus*, *Falcarius*, *Alxasaurus*, *Erlikosaurus*, and *Therizinosaurus*).

Unlike most other theropods, therizinosaurs were most likely herbivorous. It is likely that the transition from carnivory to herbivory occurred early in the evolution of the group. The transition involved changes in dentition and changes to the hips and hind limbs—which allowed more room and better support for the larger gut needed to digest plants. The most primitive therizinosaur, *Falcarius*, has been described as a transitional species because it has herbivorous dentition and wider hips. However, it also possessed a pubis bone and legs that resembled those of its running, carnivorous ancestors.

Some therizinosaur fossils show remarkable preservation. For example, *Beipiaosaurus* specimens show large patches of featherlike integument on the chest, forelimbs, and hind limbs. Several embryonic therizinosaur skeletons have been found inside fossilized eggs. These embryos show several unambiguous theropod characteristics that are lost by adulthood. They provide insight into the order of bone formation in dinosaurs.

Triceratops

Triceratops is a genus of large plant-eating dinosaurs characterized by a great bony head frill and three horns. Its fossils date to only the last 5 million years of the Late Cretaceous Period, which makes *Triceratops* one of the last of the dinosaurs to have evolved.

Triceratops, restoration by C. Lang. Courtesy of the American Museum of Natural History, New York

The massive body measured nearly 9 metres (30 feet) long and must have weighed four to five tons, and the skull alone was sometimes more than 2 metres (6.5 feet) long. Each of the two horns above the eyes was longer than 1 metre (3.3 feet). The frill, unlike that of other ceratopsians, was made completely of solid bone, without the large openings typically seen in ceratopsian frills. The front of the mouth was beaklike and probably effective for nipping off vegetation. The cheek teeth were arranged in powerful groups that could effectively grind plant matter. The hind limbs were larger than the forelimbs, but both sets were very stout. The feet ended in stubby toes probably covered by small hooves. *Triceratops* was an upland, browsing animal that may have traveled in groups or small herds.

Velociraptor

A sickle-clawed dinosaur that flourished in central and eastern Asia during the Late Cretaceous Period, *Velociraptor* is closely related to the North American *Deinonychus* of the Early Cretaceous. Both reptiles were dromaeosaurs, and both possessed an unusually large claw on each foot, as well as ossified tendon reinforcements in the tail that enabled them to maintain balance while striking and slashing at prey with one foot upraised. *Velociraptor* was smaller than *Deinonychus*, reaching a length of only 1.8 metres (6 feet) and perhaps weighing no more than 45 kg (100 pounds). *Velociraptor* appears to have been a swift, agile predator of small herbivores.

Other Significant Life-Forms of the Cretaceous Period

Several notable molluscan and mammalian groups lived during the Cretaceous Period.

Anchura

This genus of extinct marine gastropods (snails) appears as fossils only in marine deposits of Cretaceous age. It is thus a useful guide or index fossil because it is easily recognizable. The shell whorls are globular and ornamented with raised crenulations; the spire is sharply pointed; the body whorl, the final and largest whorl, has a prominently extended outer lip.

Archelon

An extinct genus of giant sea turtle known from fossilized remains found in North American rocks of the Late Cretaceous epoch, *Archelon* was protected by a shell similar to that found in modern sea turtles, and reached a length of about 3.5 metres (12 feet). The front feet evolved into powerful structures that could efficiently propel the great bulk of *Archelon* through the water.

Baculites

This genus of extinct cephalopods (animals related to the modern squid, octopus, and nautilus) found as fossils in

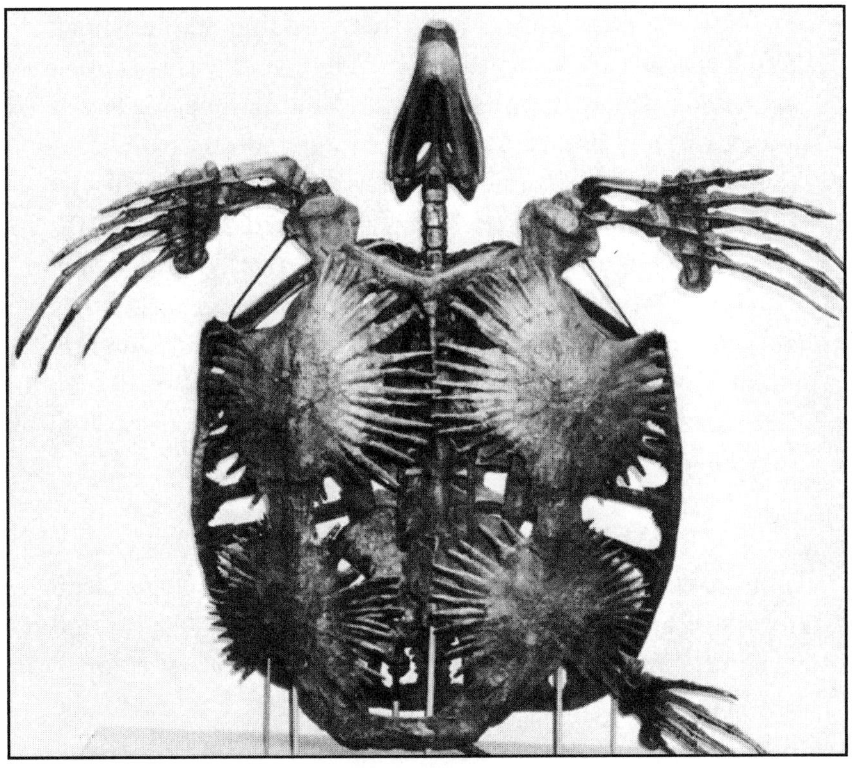

Skeleton of the Cretaceous marine turtle Archelon, length 3.25 metres (10.7 feet). Courtesy of the Peabody Museum of Natural History, Yale University

Late Cretaceous marine rocks. *Baculites,* restricted to a narrow time range, is an excellent guide or index fossil for Late Cretaceous time and rocks. The distinctive shell begins with a tightly coiled portion that becomes straight in form, with a complex, ammonite sutural pattern.

Clidastes

Clidastes is an extinct genus of ancient marine lizards belonging to a family of reptiles called mosasaurs. *Clidastes* fossils are found in marine rocks from the Late Cretaceous Period in North America. Excellent specimens have been found in the chalk deposits of Kansas.

Clidastes was 4 metres (13 feet) or longer. The head alone was about 60 cm (24 inches) long and was equipped with many sharply pointed curved teeth. The neck was short, but the body and tail were long and relatively slender. This aquatic lizard probably swam by undulating its body in the same way that terrestrial lizards do. The limbs terminated in broad appendages that provided directional control as it moved through the water. *Clidastes* was clearly an efficiently swimming predator and probably fed mostly on fish as well as on ammonoids (a cephalopod similar to the present-day nautilus). *Clidastes* and other mosasaurs may have gone ashore to reproduce.

Condylarthra

This extinct group of mammals includes the ancestral forms of later, more advanced ungulates (that is, hoofed placental mammals). The name *Condylarthra* was once applied to a formal taxonomic order, but it is now used informally to refer to ungulates of Late Cretaceous and Early Paleogene times. Their greatest diversity occurred during the Paleocene Epoch (65.5 million to 55.8 million years ago), but similar forms persisted into the middle of Oligocene Epoch and died out about 30 million years ago.

Condylarths appear to have originated in Asia during the Cretaceous Period. The earliest condylarths were the zhelestids, rodent-sized ungulates from the Late Cretaceous of Uzbekistan. A somewhat later North American form is the genus *Protungulatum* that lived near the end of Cretaceous or early in the Paleocene.

The condylarths were a diverse group that developed many traits of adaptive significance. They are thought to be the ancestors of the perissodactyls and perhaps even the cetaceans. Some forms remained relatively small, whereas others attained large size. *Phenacodus*, a

Phenacodus, *restoration painting by Charles R. Knight, 1898* Courtesy of the American Museum of Natural History, New York

well-known condylarth from the Eocene Epoch (55.8 million to 33.9 million years ago), grew to be as large as a modern tapir. In addition, the teeth of some condylarths appear almost carnivore-like. *Arctocyon*, for example, has long canines and triangular premolars.

Dawn Redwood

This genus of conifers represented by a single living species, *Metasequoia glyptostroboides*, from central China. Fossil representatives, such as *M. occidentalis*, dated to about 90 million years ago during the Late Cretaceous Period, are known throughout the middle and high latitudes of the

Northern Hemisphere. Climatic cooling and drying that began about 65.5 million years ago and continued throughout the Cenozoic Era caused the geographic range of the dawn redwood to contract to its present relic distribution. The leaves are arranged in pairs on deciduous branchlets, and this deciduous character probably accounts for the tree's abundance in the fossil record. *Metasequoia* is closely related to the redwood genera of North America, *Sequoia* and *Sequoiadendron*.

The dawn redwood holds an interesting place in the history of paleobotany as one of the few living plants known first as a fossil. Its fossil foliage and cones were originally described under the name *Sequoia*. In 1941, Japanese botanist Miki Shigeru of Osaka University coined the name *Metasequoia* for fossil foliage with opposite, rather than spirally arranged, leaves. The first living *Metasequoia* trees were discovered in 1944 by Chinese botanist Wang Zhan in Sichuan province, China. Today, *M. glyptostroboides* is a common ornamental tree that grows well in temperate climates worldwide.

Deltatheridium

A genus of extinct mammals found as fossils in rocks from Late Cretaceous times of Asia and, questionably, North America, *Deltatheridium* was a small insectivorous mammal about the size of a small rat. It is now recognized to be a metatherian, a member of the group of mammals related to marsupials. *Deltatheridium* has figured prominently in debates about mammalian evolution because it also has some features that are similar to early placental mammals.

Exogyra

This extinct molluscan genus is common in shallow-water marine deposits of the Jurassic and Cretaceous periods.

Exogyra is characterized by its very thick shell, which attained massive proportions. The left valve, or shell, is spirally twisted, whereas the right valve is flattish and much smaller. A distinctive longitudinal pattern of ribbing is well developed in the left valve, and pitting is common.

Monopleura

A genus of extinct and unusual bivalves (clams) found as fossils in Cretaceous rocks, *Monopleura* is representative of a group of aberrant clams known as the pachyodonts. The animal's thick, triangular shell is capped by a much smaller dome-shaped shell. In some of the pachyodonts, there were open passageways through the shell that allowed for the passage of fluids. *Monopleura* and other pachyodonts were sedentary in habit. The animal apparently grew upright with the pointed end anchored in the substrate.

Mosasaurs

These extinct aquatic lizards from family Mosasauridae attained a high degree of adaptation to the marine environment and were distributed worldwide during the Cretaceous Period. The mosasaurs competed with other marine reptiles—the plesiosaurs and ichthyosaurs—for food, which consisted largely of ammonoids, fish, and cuttlefish. Many mosasaurs of the Late Cretaceous were large, exceeding 9 metres (30 feet) in length, but the most common forms were no larger than modern porpoises.

Mosasaurs had snakelike bodies with large skulls and long snouts. Their limbs were modified into paddles having shorter limb bones and more numerous finger and toe bones than those of their ancestors. The tail region of the body was long, and its end was slightly downcurved in a manner similar to that of the early ichthyosaurs. The backbone consisted of more than 100 vertebrae. The structure of the skull was very similar to that of the modern monitor lizards, to which mosasaurs are related. The jaws bore many conical, slightly recurved teeth set in individual sockets. The jawbones are notable in that they were jointed near mid-length (as in some of the advanced monitors) and connected in front by ligaments only. This arrangement enabled the animals not only to open the mouth by lowering the mandible but also to extend the lower jaws sideways while feeding on large prey.

Plesiosaurs

This group of long-necked marine reptiles are known from fossils that date from the Late Triassic Period into the Late Cretaceous Period (215 million to 80 million years ago). Plesiosaurs had a wide distribution in European seas and around the Pacific Ocean, including Australia, North America, and Asia. Some forms known from North America and elsewhere persisted until near the end of the Cretaceous Period.

Plesiosaurus , an early plesiosaur, was about 4.5 metres (15 feet) long, with a broad, flat body and a relatively short tail. It swam by flapping its fins in the water, much as sea lions do today, in a modified style of underwater "flight." The nostrils were located far back on the head near the eyes. The neck was long and flexible, and the animal may have fed by swinging its head from side to side through schools of fish, capturing prey by using the long, sharp teeth present in the jaws.

Early in their evolutionary history, the plesiosaurs split into two main lineages: the pliosaurs, in which the neck was short and the head elongated; and the plesiosaurids, in which the head remained relatively small and the neck assumed snakelike proportions and became very flexible. The late evolution of plesiosaurs was marked by a great increase in size. For example, *Elasmosaurus*, a plesiosaurid, had as many as 76 vertebrae in its neck alone and reached a length of about 13 metres (43 feet), fully half of which consisted of the head and neck.

Pteranodon

These flying reptiles (pterosaurs) are known from fossils in North American deposits that date from about 100 million to 90 million years ago during the Late Cretaceous Period. *Pteranodon* had a wingspan of 7 metres (23 feet) or more, and its toothless jaws were very long and pelican-like.

A crest at the back of the skull (a common feature among pterosaurs) may have functioned in species recognition. The crest of males was larger. The crest is often thought to have counterbalanced the jaws or have been necessary for steering in flight, but several pterosaurs had no crests at all. As compared with the size of the wings, the body was small (about as large as a turkey), but the hind limbs were relatively large compared with the torso. Although the limbs appear robust, the bones were completely hollow, and their walls were no thicker than about one millimetre. The shape of the bones, however, made them resistant to the aerodynamic forces of flight

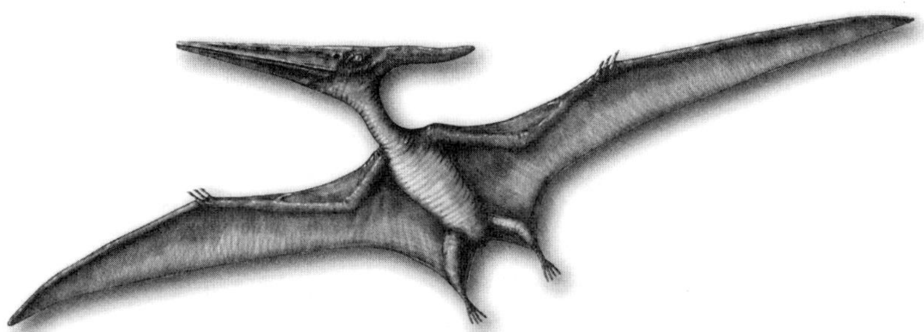

Drawing of a Pteranodon. Encyclopædia Britannica, Inc.

Pteranodon, like other pterosaurs, was a strong flier with a large breastbone, reinforced shoulder girdles, and muscular attachments on the arm bones—all evidence of power and maneuverability. However, as in the largest present-day birds, *Pteranodon*'s large size precluded sustained beating of the wings, so it most likely soared more than it flapped. The eyes were relatively large, and the animal may have relied heavily upon sight as it searched for food above the sea.

Fossils of *Pteranodon* and related forms are found in Europe, South America, and Asia in rocks formed from substances found in marine environments, which supports the inference of a pelican-like lifestyle. It is probable that *Pteranodon* took off from the water by facing into sea breezes that provided enough force to lift the reptile into the air when the wings were spread.

Scaphites

Scaphites is an extinct genus of cephalopods (animals related to the modern octopus, squid, and nautilus) found as fossils in marine deposits. Because *Scaphites* is restricted to certain divisions of Cretaceous time, it is a useful index, or guide, fossil. Its shell form and manner of growth are quite unusual. At first, the shell in *Scaphites* is tightly coiled. Later, it grows in a straight fashion but then coils again at its terminus, and the mature shell takes the form of a double loop linked by a straight segment.

Turritellids

Turritellids include any of several species of gastropods (snails) abundantly belonging to the genus *Turritella* and represented in fossil and living form from the Cretaceous Period up to the present. Many forms or species of turritellids are known. All are characterized by a high, pointed shell that narrows greatly at the apex. The shell is frequently ornamented by lines, ridges, or grooves.

CRETACEOUS GEOLOGY

As plant and animal life continued to evolve during the Cretaceous, so to did the landscape. Although the Cretaceous Period was known for its tectonic activity, the interval was also characterized by the deposition of chalks, marine limestones, carbon-rich shales, coal, and petroleum. In addition, the Sierra Nevada mountain range emerged during the Cretaceous, and the eruptions of the Deccan Traps in India branded the end of the period as a time of intense volcanism.

THE ECONOMIC SIGNIFICANCE OF CRETACEOUS DEPOSITS

In the course of approximately 30 million years during the middle of the Cretaceous Period, more than 50 percent of the world's known petroleum reserves were formed. Almost three-fourths of this mid-Cretaceous petroleum accumulated in a relatively small region around what is now the Persian Gulf. Much of the remainder accumulated in another limited region, of the Americas between the Gulf of Mexico and Venezuela. Evidently the low-latitude Tethys seaway collected along its margins large amounts of organic matter, which today are found as petroleum in the Gulf Coast of the United States and Mexico, the Maracaibo Basin in Venezuela, the Sirte (or Surt) Basin in Libya, and the Persian Gulf region. Other mineral deposits of commercial value occur in the circum-Pacific mountain systems and chain of island arcs. Such metals as gold, silver, copper, lead, zinc, molybdenum, tungsten, tin, iron, and manganese were concentrated into ore deposits of various dimensions during episodes of igneous activity in the late Mesozoic.

The Occurrence and Distribution of Cretaceous Rocks

The occurrence and distribution of Cretaceous rocks resulted from the interplay of many forces. The most important of these were the position of the continental landmasses, level of the sea relative to these landmasses, local tectonic and orogenic (mountain-building) activity, climatic conditions, availability of source material (for example, sands, clays, and even the remains of marine animals and plants), volcanic activity, and the history of rocks and sediments after intrusion or deposition. The plate tectonics of some regions were especially active during the Cretaceous. Japan, for example, has a sedimentary record that varies in time from island to island, north to south. The Pacific margin of Canada shows evidence of an Early Cretaceous inundation, but by the Late Cretaceous much of the region had been uplifted 800 to 2,000 metres (2,600 to 6,600 feet). Chalks and limestones, on the other hand, were deposited underwater in the western interior of North America when sea levels were at their highest. Many Cretaceous sedimentary rocks have been eroded since their deposition, while others are merely covered by younger sediments or are presently underwater or both.

A comparison of the rock record for the North American western interior with that for eastern England reveals chalk deposition in eastern England from Cenomanian to Maastrichtian time, whereas chalks and marine limestone are limited to late Cenomanian through early Santonian time in North America. Yet the two areas have nearly identical histories of inundation. It has been noted that the only land areas of western Europe during the Late Cretaceous were a few stable regions representing low-lying islands within a chalk sea. Sedimentary evidence indicates an arid climate that would have minimized erosion of these islands and limited the deposition of sands and clays in the basin. In contrast, the North American interior sea received abundant clastic sediments, eroded from the new mountains along its western margin.

In North America the Nevadan orogeny took place in the Sierra Nevada and the Klamath Mountains from Late Jurassic to Early Cretaceous times; the Sevier orogeny produced mountains in Utah and Idaho in the mid-Cretaceous; and the Laramide orogeny, with its thrust faulting, gave rise to the Rocky Mountains and Mexico's Sierra Madre Oriental during the Late Cretaceous to Early Paleogene. In the South American Andean system, mountain building reached its climax in the mid-Late Cretaceous. In Japan the Sakawa orogeny proceeded through a number of phases during the Cretaceous.

In addition to the areas that have been mentioned above, Cretaceous rocks crop out in the Arctic, Greenland, central California, the Gulf and Atlantic coastal plains of the United States, central and southern Mexico, and the Caribbean islands of Jamaica, Puerto Rico, Cuba, and Hispaniola. In Central and South America, Cretaceous rocks are found in Panama, Venezuela, Colombia, Ecuador, Peru, eastern and northeastern Brazil, and central and southern Argentina. Most European countries have Cretaceous rocks exposed at the surface. North Africa, West Africa, coastal South Africa, Madagascar, Arabia, Iran, and the Caucasus all have extensive Cretaceous outcrops, as do eastern Siberia, Tibet, India, China, Japan, Southeast Asia, New Guinea, Borneo, Australia, New Zealand, and Antarctica.

Types of Cretaceous Rocks

The rocks and sediments of the Cretaceous System show considerable variation in their lithologic character and the thickness of their sequences. Mountain-building episodes accompanied by volcanism and plutonic intrusion took place in the circum-Pacific region and in the area of the present-day Alps. The erosion of these mountains produced clastic sediments—such as conglomerates, sandstones, and shales—on their flanks. The igneous rocks of Cretaceous age in the circum-Pacific area are widely exposed.

The Cretaceous Period was a time of great inundation by shallow seas that created swamp conditions favourable for the accumulation of fossil fuels at the margin of land areas. Coal-bearing strata are found in some parts of Cretaceous sequences in Siberia, Australia, New Zealand, Mexico, and the western United States.

Farther offshore, chalks are widely distributed in the Late Cretaceous. Another rock type, called the Urgonian limestone, is similarly widespread in the Upper Barremian–Lower Aptian. This massive limestone facies, whose name is commonly associated with rudists, is found in Mexico, Spain, southern France, Switzerland, Bulgaria, Central Asia, and North Africa.

The mid-Cretaceous was a time of extensive deposition of carbon-rich shale. These so-called black shales result when there is severe deficiency of oxygen in the bottom waters of the oceans. Some authorities believe that this oxygen deficiency, which also resulted in the extinction of many forms of marine life, was caused by extensive undersea volcanism about 93 million years ago. Others believe that oxygen declined as a consequence of poor ocean circulation, which is thought to have resulted from the generally warmer climate that prevailed during the

Cretaceous, the temperature difference between the poles and the Equator being much smaller than at present, and the restriction of the North Atlantic, South Atlantic, and Tethys. Cretaceous black shales are extensively distributed on various continental areas, such as the western interior of North America, the Alps, the Apennines of Italy, western South America, western Australia, western Africa, and southern Greenland. They also occur in the Atlantic Ocean, as revealed by the Deep Sea Drilling Program (a scientific program initiated in 1968 to study the ocean bottom), and in the Pacific, as noted on several seamounts.

In typical examples of circum-Pacific orogenic systems, regional metamorphism of the high-temperature type and large-scale granitic emplacement occurred on the inner, continental side, whereas sinking, rapid sedimentation, and regional metamorphism predominated on the outer, oceanic side. The intrusion of granitic rocks, accompanied in some areas by extrusion of volcanic rocks, had a profound effect on geologic history. This is exemplified by the upheaval of the Sierra Nevada, with the intermittent emplacement of granitic bodies and the deposition of thick units of Cretaceous shales and sandstones with many conglomerate tongues in the Central Valley of California.

Volcanic seamounts of basaltic rock with summit depths of 1,300 to 2,100 metres (4,300 to 6,900 feet) are found in the central and western Pacific. Some of them are flat-topped, with shelves on their flanks on which reef deposits or gravels accumulated, indicating a shallow-water environment. Some of the deposits contain recognizable Cretaceous fossils Although the seamounts were formed at various times during the late Mesozoic and Cenozoic eras, a large number of them were submarine volcanoes that built up to the sea surface during the Cretaceous. They sank to their present deep levels some time after the age indicated by their youngest shallow-water fossils.

In west-central India the Deccan Traps consist of more than 1,200 metres (4,000 feet) of lava flows that erupted from the Late Cretaceous to the Eocene Epoch (some 50 million years ago) over an area of some 500,000 square km (190,000 square miles). Volcanic activity on the western margin of the North American epicontinental sea frequently produced ashfalls over much of the western interior seaways. One of these, the "X" bentonite near the end of the Cenomanian, can be traced more than 2,000 km (1,200 miles) from central Manitoba to northern Texas.

The Correlation of Cretaceous Strata

Correlation of Cretaceous rocks is usually accomplished using fossils. Ammonites are the most widely employed fossils because of their frequency of occurrence and geographic extent, but no single fossil group is capable of worldwide correlation of all sedimentary rocks. Most ammonites, for example, did not occur in all latitudes, because some preferred the warmer waters of the Tethys seaway while others resided in cooler boreal waters. Furthermore, ammonites are rarely found in sediments deposited in nonmarine and brackish environments, and they are seldom retrieved from boreholes sufficiently intact for confident identification.

Many ammonites are very good index fossils, but they are not perfect. For instance, when Cretaceous stage boundaries were proposed by an international group of geologists in 1983, the problems of correlating the boundary between the Campanian Stage and the underlying Santonian were examined. Other ammonite species were considered for selection as the boundary's index fossil, including belemnites, crinoids, coccolithophores, and foraminiferans. It was generally agreed that a boundary level close to the currently used appearance of the belemnite species *Gonioteuthis granulataquadrata* from the boreal realm—i.e., the temperate paleobiogeographic region—would be desirable because this boundary could be correlated with a number of other events. It is desirable to have a reference section for the boundaries of all Cretaceous stages, and the Campanian example serves to illustrate the variety of fossil groups used to define boundaries and the complexity of the definition problem. The boundaries of the other stages have similar problems of restricted distribution for fossils in the classic type areas. Other fossil types useful for defining Cretaceous stage boundaries are inoceramid bivalves, echinoids, larger foraminiferans, and calpionellids.

On a more local scale, correlation can be achieved using a variety of fossil groups. Rudist, inoceramid, and exogyrid bivalves have been used in many areas to subdivide (zone) the Cretaceous Period for the purpose of correlation. Rudist bivalves, for example, have been employed in conjunction with larger foraminiferans to zone sediments of the Tethyan regions in parts of Europe. Echinoids and belemnites have been used together to zone the Late Cretaceous of eastern England. Angiosperm pollen provides for recognition of zones for the Late Cretaceous of the North American Atlantic Coastal Plain.

Some fossil groups are useful for correlation between several regions because of their nektonic or planktonic life habit. Principal among these are ammonites, belemnites, planktonic foraminiferans, calcareous nannofossils, and radiolarians. In North America, for instance, Late Cretaceous strata in Texas, Arkansas, Mexico, and the Caribbean have been correlated using planktonic foraminiferans. Occasionally ostracods (small bivalved crustaceans) are useful; e.g., they have been used to correlate Early Cretaceous strata of northwestern Europe with those of the Russian Platform.

The epicontinental sea of the North American western interior has been particularly well studied, primarily because it can be zoned to great precision. Sixty ammonite zones, to cite a case in point, are recognized in rocks deposited between the late Albian and the late Maastrichtian. In addition, frequent bentonite beds resulting from the volcanic ash of the Sevier orogenic events provide radiometric dates with which to verify independently the synchronicity of the ammonite zones. This detailed resolution of about a half-million years per zone is unusual for the Cretaceous Period. Interestingly, the youngest Cretaceous biozone of the North American western interior is recognized regionally by the occurrence of the dinosaur genus *Triceratops*, because the last approximately one million years in that area are characterized by nonmarine sediments.

For some of the geologic record, more-detailed subdivisions within zones can be developed on the basis of magnetic reversals. The Cretaceous Period, however, has a dearth of magnetic reversals. Specifically, only 16 reversals are noted for latest Jurassic to Aptian time, none for Aptian to late Santonian time, and just nine from the late Santonian to the Cenozoic boundary. Magnetic reversals occur far more frequently in Cenozoic rocks.

The Major Subdivisions of the Cretaceous System

The rocks that were either deposited or formed during the Cretaceous Period make up the Cretaceous System. The Cretaceous System is divided into two rock series, Lower and Upper, which correspond to units of time known as the Early Cretaceous Epoch (145.5 million to 99.6 million years ago) and the Late Cretaceous Epoch (about 100 million to 65.5 million years ago).

Both the Early and the Late Cretaceous epochs in turn are divided into six ages of variable length. Their definition was initiated during the mid- to late 1800s, when geologists working in France, Belgium, The Netherlands, and Switzerland recognized and named the 12 corresponding rock stages. Each of the stages is defined by rocks, sediments, and fossils found at a particular locality called the type area. For example, A.D. d'Orbigny defined and described the Cenomanian Stage in 1847, based on some 847 fossil species characteristic of the strata, and confirmed Le Mans, France, as the type area. The Cenomanian Age is thus defined on the basis of the rocks, sediments, and fossils in the type area for the Cenomanian Stage. For the Lower Cretaceous Series the stages are the Berriasian, Valanginian, Hauterivian, Barremian, Aptian, and Albian. For the Upper Cretaceous they are the Cenomanian, Turonian, Coniacian, Santonian, Campanian, and Maastrichtian. The longest is the Aptian, lasting about 13 million years; the Santonian is the shortest at just over 2 million years.

A type area is not always the best place to define a stage. The type area for the Coniacian Stage, for example, is in Cognac, France, but there the boundary with the underlying Turonian is marked by a discontinuity, and one stratigraphically important fossil group, the inoceramid bivalves, is poorly represented. These conditions make correlation of the base of the Coniacian Stage difficult at sites away from the type area.

Since the inception of the 12 Cretaceous stages, geologists have worked to solve such problems caused by incompleteness of the stratigraphic record and fossils of poor utility in type areas. It is now customary to define the base of one stage and to consider that stage as continuing until the beginning of the next younger stage. Researchers meet periodically to discuss problems of stage boundaries and to suggest solutions. In 1983 a group of geologists from around the world met in Copenhagen, Denmark, and suggested that alternative type areas be designated for all the stage boundaries discussed. Further, they suggested that the long Albian Stage be divided into three substages: the Lower, Middle, and Upper Albian. It is agreed that stages are "packages of zones" and that the most sensible way to define a stage is by the base of the earliest biozone at a boundary type area. Traditionally, ammonites have been used to define biozones within the type area of Cretaceous stages, but other animals, such as inoceramid bivalves, belemnites, and even calpionellids, are sometimes used (*see* the section Correlation below). The number of usable biozones for the Cretaceous varies from area to area. For example, about 25 ammonite zones are employed in the type areas of western Europe for the whole of the Cretaceous, but at least 55 are recognized in the Upper Cretaceous alone for the western interior of North America.

The Stages of the Cretaceous Period

The 80-million-year-long Cretaceous Period is divided into two long epochs and 12 stages. Each of these stages is described in detail below.

Berriasian Stage

The Berriasian is the first of six main divisions (in ascending order) of the Lower Cretaceous Series. It corresponds to all rocks deposited worldwide during the Berriasian Age, which occurred between 145.5 million and 140.2

million years ago. Rocks of the Berriasian overlie those of the Jurassic System's Tithonian Stage and underlie rocks of the Valanginian Stage.

The name for this stage is derived from Barrias, in southeastern France, for which the surrounding area serves as the classic type district for rocks of this age. In Great Britain and elsewhere in northern Europe, the Berriasian is represented by the lower portions of the Wealden Series. The Berriasian Stage is characterized by a distinct ammonite genus used as an index fossil.

Valanginian Stage

The second of six main divisions in the Lower Cretaceous Series, the Valanginian Stage encompasses those rocks deposited worldwide during the Valanginian Age, which occurred 140.2 million to 133.9 million years ago. Rocks of the Valanginian Stage overlie those of the Berriasian Stage and underlie rocks of the Hauterivian Stage.

The name for this stage is derived from the type district near Valangin, Switzerland. In Great Britain and elsewhere in northern Europe, the Valanginian is represented by portions of the Wealden Beds. Limestones dominate the Valanginian of the Swiss Alps and the Middle East. The Valanginian is characterized by sandstones in India, Australia, Japan, Mongolia, and northern Siberia. Shales occur in New Zealand, parts of Mongolia, and North Africa. The Valanginian has been divided into three biozones representing shorter spans of time and characterized by certain ammonites that are used as index fossils.

Hauterivian Stage

The third of six main divisions in the Lower Cretaceous Series, the Hauterivian Stage represents rocks deposited worldwide during the Hauterivian Age, which occurred

133.9 million to 130 million years ago. Rocks of the Hauterivian Stage overlie those of the Valanginian Stage and underlie rocks of the Barremian Stage.

The name of the stage is derived from the village of Hauterive in Switzerland, the surrounding area of which serves as the classic type district for rocks of this age. The Hauterivian Stage is represented in northern Continental Europe by part of the thick Hils clay, whereas in Britain it includes the middle part of the Wealden sandstones and clays. The base of the stage is defined by the first appearance of the ammonite *Acanthodiscus radiatus* and related species, which are used as index fossils. The Hauterivian has been divided into several shorter spans of time called biozones. One of these is characterized by the planktonic foraminiferan *Caucasella hoterivica*, which is another index fossil for rocks of this age.

Barremian Stage

The Barremian Stage is the fourth division of the Lower Cretaceous Series and encompasses rocks deposited worldwide during the Barremian Age, which occurred 130 million to 125 million years ago. Rocks of the Barremian Stage overlie those of the Hauterivian Stage and underlie rocks of the Aptian Stage.

The classic type district for rocks of this age is located at Angles, in Alpes-de-Hautes-Provence département in southeastern France, but the stage's name is derived from localities at nearby Barrême. In northern Continental Europe the Barremian Stage is represented by portions of the thick Hils clay, while in England it includes the upper portions of the Wealden sandstones and clays. The base of the stage is generally taken at a point containing the ammonite genus *Pseudothurmannia* as an index fossil. The Barremian has been divided into several biozones representing shorter spans of time, one of which is characterized by the calcareous nannofossil *Nannoconus steinmanni*. The planktonic foraminiferan *Hedbergella sigali* is also an index fossil for rocks of this age.

Aptian Stage

The fifth stage of the Lower Cretaceous Series, the Aptian Stage corresponds to all rocks deposited worldwide during the Aptian Age, which occurred 125 million to 112 million years ago. Rocks of the Aptian Stage overlie those of the Barremian Stage and underlie rocks of the Albian Stage.

The name of the stage is derived from the town of Apt in Vaucluse département in southeastern France, for which the surrounding area serves as the classic type district for rocks of this age. In Britain the Aptian Stage is represented by part of the Lower Greensand formation. Elsewhere in northern Europe it consists of portions of the thick Hils clay, while in the United States it includes the Dakota Sandstone. The ammonite genus *Prodeshayesites* is used as an index fossil to mark the base of the Aptian Stage in Britain, Germany, and France. The Aptian has been divided into several shorter spans of time called biozones, some of which are characterized by calcareous nannofossils of *Nannoconus bucheri* and *N. wassalli*. The planktonic foraminiferans *Globigerinelloides algerianus* and *G. blowi* are also considered index fossils for rocks of this stage.

Albian Stage

The Albian Stage is uppermost of six main divisions of the Lower Cretaceous Series. It represents all rocks deposited worldwide during the Albian Age, which occurred between 112 million and 99.6 million years ago. Albian rocks overlie rocks of the Aptian Stage and underlie rocks of the Cenomanian Stage.

The name for this stage is derived from the Alba, the Roman name for Aube, France, for which the surrounding area serves as the classic type district for rocks of this age. In Britain the Albian is represented by the Upper Greensand–Gault Clay sequence of rocks. Elsewhere in northern Europe it consists of the upper portions of the thick Hils clay. Sandstones and shaley limestones dominate the Albian of the Middle East and North Africa, and sandstones, shales, and basaltic lavas occur in East Asia. The Albian is divided into several biozones representing shorter spans of time that are characterized by various distinctive ammonite genera.

Cenomanian Stage

The Upper Cretaceous Series begins with the Cenomanian Stage, a division representing rocks deposited worldwide during the Cenomanian Age, which occurred 99.6 million to 93.6 million years ago. Rocks of the Cenomanian Stage overlie those of the Albian Stage and underlie rocks of the Turonian Stage.

The name for this stage is derived from Cenomanum, the Roman name for Le Mans in northwestern France. The Cenomanian has been divided into several biozones representing shorter spans of time and characterized by fossil ammonite genera that are used as index fossils.

Turonian Stage

The Turonian Stage is the second of six main divisions in the Upper Cretaceous Series and encompasses all rocks deposited worldwide during the Turonian Age, which occurred 93.6 million to 88.6 million years ago. Rocks of the Turonian Stage overlie those of the Cenomanian Stage and underlie rocks of the Coniacian Stage.

The name of the stage is derived from Turonia, the Roman name for Touraine, France. In Great Britain the Turonian is represented by the calcareous Middle Chalk, whereas elsewhere in Europe limestones predominate. In

North America a complete Turonian record exists in the western interior region of the United States. Numerous biozones representing smaller divisions of Turonian rocks are recognized by index fossils such as certain ammonites and a Cretaceous clam (*Inoceramus labiatus*).

Coniacian Stage

The third division of the Upper Cretaceous Series is the Coniacian Stage. It corresponds to all rocks deposited worldwide during the Coniacian Age, which occurred 88.6 million to 85.8 million years ago. Rocks of the Coniacian Stage overlie those of the Turonian Stage and underlie rocks of the Santonian Stage.

The name for this stage is derived from the town of Cognac in western France. The Coniacian Stage is represented in Britain by part of the Upper Chalk and in the United States by part of the Niobrara Limestone. Conventionally, the base of the stage is defined by the first appearance of the ammonite *Barroisiceras haberfellneri*, which is used as an index fossil. The Coniacian has been divided into several shorter spans of time called biozones, one of which is characterized by the planktonic foraminiferan *Whiteinella inornata*.

Santonian Stage

The Santonian Stage is the fourth division of the Upper Cretaceous Series. It corresponds to rocks deposited worldwide during the Santonian Age, which occurred 85.8 million to 83.5 million years ago. Rocks of the Santonian overlie those of the Coniacian Stage and underlie rocks of the Campanian Stage.

The stage's name derives from the town of Saintes in western France, the area surrounding which is the classic type district for rocks of this age. The Santonian Stage is represented in northern Continental Europe by the

Granulaten Chalk, in Britain by part of the Upper Chalk, and in the United States by part of the Niobrara Limestone. Though it does not occur in the type district, the ammonite *Texanites texanum* is widely used as an index fossil to mark the base of the stage in regions as distant as Texas, Japan, southern Africa, Madagascar, and the Middle East. The Santonian has been divided into several shorter spans of time called biozones, some of which are characterized by the calcareous nannofossils *Marthasterites furcatus* and *Lithastrinus grilli*. The planktonic foraminiferans *Marginotruncana carinata* and *M. concavata* are also used as index fossils for rocks of this stage.

Campanian Stage

The fifth division of the Upper Cretaceous Series is the Campanian Stage, which represents rocks deposited worldwide during the Campanian Age, which occurred 83.5 million to 70.6 million years ago. Rocks of the Campanian Stage overlie those of the Santonian Stage and underlie rocks of the Maastrichtian Stage.

The name for this stage is derived from a hillside called La Grande Champagne at Aubeterre-sur-Dronne in northern France. Chalk deposits dominate the Maastrichtian record in much of northern Continental Europe and in Great Britain, where it is represented by the Upper Chalk. Several biozones representing shorter spans of time within the Campanian are characterized by ammonites of the genus *Baculites*, which are used as index fossils.

Maastrichtian Stage

The Maastrichtian Stage (also spelled Maestrichtian) is the uppermost division of the Upper Cretaceous Series, encompassing all rocks deposited worldwide during the Maastrichtian Age, which occurred 70.6 million to 65.5 million years ago. Rocks of the Maastrichtian Stage overlie those of the Campanian Stage and underlie rocks of the Danian Stage of the Paleogene System.

The stage's name is derived from the city of Maastricht in the southeastern Netherlands, whose surrounding area serves as the classic type district for rocks of this age. The Maastrichtian Stage is extensively represented by chalk formations in northern Continental Europe and in England—for example, the Trimingham Chalk and part of the Norwich Chalk. The first appearance of the fossil ammonite *Hoploscaphites constrictus* is often taken as the base of this stage. The Maastrichtian has been divided into several shorter spans of time called biozones, some of which are characterized by the calcareous microfossils of *Micula mura*, *Lithraphidites quadratus*, and *Broinsonia parca.* The planktonic foraminiferans *Abathomphasus mayaroensis* and *Racemigulembelina fructicosa* are also index fossils of the stage.

Significant Cretaceous Formations and Discoveries

Many fossils that date from Cretaceous times were discovered in the Lance Formation, the Hell Creek Formation, and the Niobrara Limestone of North America. All three formations occur over wide areas that span several U.S. states. These formations have provided paleontologists with a range of specimens from several groups of Cretaceous plants and animals, and several recovered specimens belong to some of the more familiar groups of dinosaurs, such as *Triceratops* and *Tyrannosaurus*.

The Hell Creek Formation

The Hell Creek Formation is a division of rocks in North America that date to the end of the Cretaceous. Named for exposures studied on Hell Creek, near Jordan,

Montana. The formation occurs in eastern Montana and portions of North Dakota, South Dakota, and Wyoming. The Hell Creek Formation is about 175 metres (575 feet) thick and consists of grayish sandstones and shales with interbedded lignites. It was deposited as coastal-plain sediments during the withdrawal of the shallow Cretaceous seas that covered much of the interior of western North America.

Fossils in the formation include the remains of plants, dinosaurs, and many small Cretaceous mammals, including some early primates. The rich dinosaur fauna includes theropods (such as *Tyrannosaurus*), pachycephalosaurs, ornithopods, ankylosaurs, and ceratopsians (such as

John Scannella, left, and Sonya Scarff excavate dinosaur fossils from the Hell Creek Formation in Montana. Montana State University, Mountains and Minds

Triceratops). Some outcrops in the Hell Creek Formation straddle the Cretaceous-Tertiary boundary and contain high concentrations of iridium, possible evidence of an asteroid impact at the end of the Cretaceous Period.

The Lance Formation

A division of rocks in the western United States dating to the end of the Cretaceous Period, this formation was named for exposures studied near Lance Creek, Niobrara county, Wyoming. Varying in thickness from about 90 metres (300 feet) in North Dakota to almost 600 metres (2,000 feet) in parts of Wyoming, the Lance Formation consists of grayish sandy shales, light-coloured sandstones, and thin lignite beds. This formation is well known for its Late Cretaceous fossils, which include plants, dinosaurs, and mammals. The duck-billed dinosaur *Trachodon*, the great carnivore *Tyrannosaurus*, the herbivores *Triceratops* and *Ankylosaurus*, pterosaurs, birds, and mammals (including marsupials) have been found in the Lance. The formation also contains examples of spectacular fossil preservation, including a so-called dinosaur "mummy," a complete duck-billed dinosaur skeleton surrounded by skin impressions.

The Niobrara Limestone

The Niobrara Limestone is a division of rocks in the central United States that also dates back to the Late Cretaceous. Named for exposures studied along the Missouri River near the mouth of the Niobrara River, Knox county, Nebraska, the Niobrara Limestone occurs over a wide area including Nebraska, Kansas, North and South Dakota, Minnesota, Montana, Wyoming, Colorado, and New Mexico. The Niobrara varies in thickness from about 60 metres (200 feet) to more than 270 metres (890 feet) and consists of chalks, shales, limestones, and many thin layers of bentonite (altered volcanic ash deposits that appear like soapy clays).

The Niobrara marks the withdrawal of the Cretaceous seas from the region of the Rocky Mountain geosyncline. Fossils of aquatic reptiles such as the mosasaur *Clidastes*, which was about 4.5 metres (15 feet) long, and flying reptiles such as *Pteranodon*, which possessed a 7.5-metre (25-foot) wingspread, have been found in the Niobrara.

EARTH AT THE END OF THE MESOZOIC

The Mesozoic Era was a time of transition in Earth's history. At the beginning of the era, the continents were joined into a single sprawling landmass called Pangea. However, by the end of the era, Pangea had split into seven or more large pieces that were well on their way to assuming their present arrangement.

Life during the Mesozoic Era also made significant advances. Substantially depleted by the Permian extinction, the greatest mass extinction of all time, Early Mesozoic habitats provided opportunities for enterprising forms of life. First appearing during the Late Triassic, dinosaurs quickly diversified to become masters of terrestrial, aquatic, and aerial environments. While these animals and other large reptiles reigned, the first true birds emerged from one of the many dinosaur lines during the Late Jurassic. Although mammal-like reptiles also appeared during the Early Triassic, the first true mammals did not evolve until the end of the period. Since many of the ecological niches were occupied by the dinosaurs, mammals would have to wait for the extinction of nearly all of the dinosaurs at the K-T boundary for their turn at world domination.

Glossary

aberrant Deviating from the natural or usual type.

angiosperms A vascular plant, or plant with channels that carry fluids, characterized by seeds in a closed ovary.

batholiths A great mass of intruded igneous rock that for the most part has been stopped in its rise a considerable distance from the surface.

bivalve A type of animal that has a shell made up of two valves.

continental rifting The division of the large plates that make up Earth's crust along a normal fault.

diatom Any of a class of minute, planktonic, unicellular or colonial algae with silicified skeletons.

echinoid A type of animal having spiny skin, such as a sea urchin.

emplacement The putting into position of something.

epicontinental Lying upon a continent or continental shelf.

facies A part of a rock or group of rocks that differs from the whole formation in regard to age, composition, or fossil content.

filament Threads or thin flexible threadlike objects, processes, or appendages.

gymnosperm Any of a class of woody vascular plants that produces naked seeds not enclosed in an ovary.

histological Having to do with a branch of anatomy that deals with the minute structure of animal and plant tissues as discernible with the microscope.

integumentary Having to do with a covering or enclosure, such as skin, or membrane.

isotope Any of two or more species of atoms of a chemical element with the same atomic number on the periodic table but differing in atomic mass or mass number.

orogeny The process of mountain formation, especially through the folding of Earth's crust.

phanerozoic Relating to a period of geologic time that comprises the Paleozoic, Mesozoic, and Cenozoic Eras.

phylogenetic Relating to the evolution of a genetically related group of organisms from their common ancestors.

placer deposit Alluvial, marine, or glacial deposit containing particles of valuable minerals, such as gold.

pluton Rock formed by the solidification of magma within Earth's crust.

recurved Curved backward or inward.

siliceous Relating to or containing silica or silicate, a chemical compound containing silicon and oxygen.

stratigraphic Having to do with the origin, composition, distribution, and succession of geologic layers (strata).

strut A structural support that resists pressure in the direction of its length.

sutural Having to do with the line of union in an immovable articulation, such as between the bones of the skull.

taxonomic Having to do with the orderly classification of plants and animals based on their presumed natural relationships.

terrane Area or surface over which particular rocks or groups of rocks are prevalent.

zenith Culminating point.

For Further Reading

Chiappe, Luis M., and Lawrence M. Witmer. *Mesozoic Birds: Above the Heads of Dinosaurs.* Berkeley, CA: University of California Press, 2002.

Erwin, Douglas H. *Extinction: How Life on Earth Nearly Ended 250 Million Years Ago*. Princeton, NJ: Princeton University Press, 2006.

Everhart, Michael. *Sea Monsters: Prehistoric Creatures of the Deep*. Washington, DC: National Geographic, 2007.

Fastovsky, David E., and David B. Weishampel. *The Evolution and Extinction of the Dinosaurs. 2nd ed.* New York, NY: Cambridge University Press, 2005.

Fraser, Nicholas. *Dawn of the Dinosaurs: Life in the Triassic*. Bloomington, IN: Indiana University Press, 2006.

Haines, Tim, and Paul Chambers. *The Complete Guide to Prehistoric Life*. Ontario, CAN: Firefly Books, 2006.

Larson, Peter, and Kenneth Carpenter, eds. *Tyrannosaurus Rex: The Tyrant King*. Bloomington, IN: Indiana University Press, 2008.

Long, John, and Peter Schouten. *Feathered Dinosaurs: The Origin of Birds*. New York, NY: Oxford University Press, 2008.

McGowan, Christopher. *The Dragon Seekers: How an Extraordinary Circle of Fossilists Discovered the Dinosaurs and Paved the Way for Darwin.* New York, NY: Perseus Books, 2001.

Novacek, Michael. *Time Traveler: In Search of Dinosaurs and Ancient Mammals from Montana to Mongolia*. New York, NY: Farrar, Straus, and Giroux, 2002.

Paul, Gregory S. *Dinosaurs of the Air: The Evolution and Loss of Flight in Dinosaurs and Birds.* Baltimore, MD: The Johns Hopkins University Press, 2002.

Paul, Gregory, ed. *The Scientific American Book of Dinosaurs: The Best Minds in Paleonotology Create a Portrait of the Prehistoric Era*. New York, NY: St. Martin's Griffin, 2003.

Poinar, Jr., George, and Roberta Poinar. *What Bugged the Dinosaurs?: Insects, Disease, and Death in the Cretaceous*. Princeton, NJ: Princeton University Press, 2008.

Sampson, Scott P. *Dinosaur Odyssey: Fossil Threads in the Web of Life.* Berkeley, CA: University of California Press, 2009.

Rogers, Kristina A. Curry, and Jeffrey A. Wilson. *The Sauropods: Evolution and Paleobiology.* Berkeley, CA: University of California Press, 2005.

Stinchcomb, Bruce. *Mesozoic Fossils I: Triassic and Jurassic*. Atglen, PA: Schiffer Publishing, 2008.

Tanke, Darren, and Kenneth Carpenter, eds. *Mesozoic Vertebrate Life*. Bloomington, IN: Indiana University Press, 2001.

Thompson, J. L. Cloudsley. *Ecology and Behavior of Mesozoic Reptiles*. Berlin, DE: Springer-Verlag, 2005.

Weishampel, David B., Peter Dodson, and Halszka Osmólska, eds. *The Dinosauria.* Rev. ed. Berkeley, CA: University of California Press, 2007.

Woodburne, Michael O., ed. *Late Cretaceous and Cenozoic Mammals of North America: Biostratigraphy and Geochronology.* New York, NY: Columbia University Press, 2004.

Index

A

Aalenian Stage, 196, 198–199, 200
Alberti, Friedrich August von, 103
Albertosaurus, 71, 222–223
Albian Stage, 216, 262, 263, 264, 267–268
Allosaurus, 42, 51, 70, 72, 73, 152, 155–156, 162, 163
Alpine-Himalayan ranges, 29
Alvarez, Walter, 96, 97, 221
American Journal of Science and Arts, 37
ammonites, 30, 31, 32, 33, 96, 98, 113, 146, 148, 195, 197, 198, 199, 200, 201, 202, 203, 204, 218, 220, 260–261, 262, 264, 266, 267, 269, 270
Anatosaurus (*Trachodon*), 41, 222, 223–224
Anchisaurus, 37
Anchura, 246
Anisian Stage, 135, 136, 137
ankylosaurs, 50, 88, 89, 91–92, 94, 171, 224, 225, 230, 235, 236, 272
Ankylosaurus, 224–225, 230, 273
Apatosaurus (*Brontosaurus*), 42, 49, 59, 63, 65, 152, 155, 156–158, 161, 166
Aptian Stage, 216, 258, 262, 263, 266, 267
Archaeopteryx, 71, 74, 99, 100, 153, 155, 158–159, 164, 208, 226, 227, 232
Archelon, 246
archosaurs, 44, 45, 69, 78, 79, 116, 152
asteroid theory of extinction, 33, 96, 97–99, 110, 221, 222, 273
Atlantosaurus, 42
Aucella, 182

B

Baculites, 246–247
Bajocian Stage, 196, 198, 199, 200
Barosaurus, 59
Barremian Stage, 258, 263, 266–267
Bathonian Stage, 196, 199–200
Bauria, 121–122
Bavarisaurus, 50
Bernissart excavation site, 51, 168
Berriasian Stage, 203, 207, 263, 264–265
Bird, Roland T., 51, 52
body temperature regulation in dinosaurs, 55–57, 59, 60, 67
Bothriospondylus, 39

brachiosaurs, 159–160
Brachiosaurus, 42, 59, 65, 67, 158, 159
Buckland, William, 37, 38, 204, 205

C

caenagnathids, 75
Callovian Stage, 196, 200–201
camarasaurs, 160–161
Camarasaurus, 42, 67
Campanian Stage, 260, 261, 263, 269, 270, 271
Camptosaurus, 42, 161–162
Canon City excavation site, 42
Cardioceras, 182–183
Carnian Stage, 135, 137, 138
carnivorous dinosaurs, overview of, 50–51
carnosaurs, 73, 162
Caudipteryx, 21, 100, 225–226
Cenomanian Stage, 256, 260, 263, 267, 268
Cenozoic Era, 22, 23, 24, 29, 209, 212, 216, 250, 259, 262
Central Atlantic Magmatic Province, 26
Cerapoda, 76–88
ceratopsians, 46, 49, 50, 51, 58, 76–77, 83–88, 94, 177, 181, 182, 237, 239, 240, 241, 245, 272
ceratopsids, 85, 86, 238
Ceratosauria, 71–72, 73
Ceratosaurus, 71, 72, 155, 162–163
cetiosaurs, 67, 71
Cetiosaurus, 38, 40
Chicxulub crater, 32, 33, 98, 221
Chondrosteiformes, 122
Cimmerian continent, 27, 28
Cladeiodon, 38
cladistics, 46
Clidastes, 247
coccolithophores, 32–33, 96, 98, 209, 217, 220, 261
Coelophysis, 43, 50–51, 70, 71, 72, 116, 118, 119
coelurosaurs, 73–74, 162, 180, 228, 229
Coelurus, 42, 70, 169
Como Bluff excavation site, 42
Compsognathus, 39, 40, 50, 70, 74, 163
Condylartha, 248–249
Confuciusornis, 163–165
Coniacian Stage, 263, 268, 269
continental rifting, 24–25, 28, 29, 33, 47, 48, 102, 105–106, 134, 141, 142, 188, 189, 192, 210
Cope, E.D., 42, 43, 83
coprolites, 51, 176, 204–205
Corythosaurus, 81
Cretaceous Period, 23, 25, 26, 28, 31, 32, 33, 34, 43, 48, 49, 51, 52, 66, 69, 71, 73, 74, 75, 79, 82, 83, 89, 91, 93, 94, 95, 99, 100, 101, 103, 109, 117, 125, 129, 140, 145, 155, 156–157, 159, 163, 167, 169, 174, 179, 184, 185, 187, 203, 206, 209–274
  climate, 215–216
  geography, 211–215
  geology, 255–274
  invertebrates, 217–218, 246–247, 250–251, 254–255
  marine life, 217–219, 246–248, 250–253, 254–255
  plants, 220, 249–250
  vertebrates, 219–220, 222–249, 250–254
Cynognathus, 122–123

D

Daonella, 123
dawn redwood, 249–250
Deccan Traps, 26, 221, 255, 260
Deinodon, 41
Deinonychus, 51, 59, 76, 99, 226–227, 229, 245–246
Deltatheridium, 250
Diarthrognathus, 182, 183
Dilong, 180, 227–229
Dilophosaurus, 72, 73
Dimorphodon, 165–166
Diplodocus, 42, 49, 59, 65, 67, 166–167
Docodon, 167
Dollo, Louis, 40
dromaeosaurs, 75–76, 99, 181, 226, 227, 229–230, 245
Dromaesaurus, 59

E

Egg Mountain excavation site, 55
Ellsworth, Solomon, Jr., 37
Eoraptor, 44
Euoplocephalus, 91, 92, 230
Euparkeria, 44, 123
eurypterids, 111
Exogyra, 250–251
extinction, 26, 30, 32–34, 83, 93–99, 102, 103, 104, 109–112, 115, 145–146, 210, 211, 220–222, 274

F

fabrosaurids, 76, 79
foraminifera, 33–34, 96, 98, 111, 113, 114, 148, 213, 216, 217, 218, 220, 261, 269, 271

G

geoidal eustacy, 213
Gondwana, 24, 25, 27, 28, 29, 104, 105, 141, 142, 154, 192, 210, 211
Great Exhibition of 1851, 39, 168
Gryphaea, 183, 217, 220

H

hadrosaurs, 49, 53, 58, 77, 78, 80, 81, 87, 177, 210, 222, 223, 224, 232, 233, 234
Hadrosaurus, 41
Hatcher, J.B, 42, 43
Hauterivian Stage, 263, 265–266
Hell Creek Formation, 177, 178, 271–272
herbivorous dinosaurs, overview of, 48–50
herding behavior, 51–52
Herrerasaurus, 44, 69, 118, 119–120
Hesperornis, 220, 231, 233
heterodontosaurs, 77, 79, 181
Hettangian Stage, 139, 195, 196, 197
Hitchcock, Edward, 37
Holectypus, 184
Horner, John R., 53–54
Huxley, T.H., 39, 43
Hylaeosaurus, 38, 39
Hypacrosaurus, 53
Hypsilophodon, 231–232
hypsilophodontids, 77, 79–80, 82

I

Icarosaurus, 117
Ichthyornis, 232–233

ichthyosaurs, 34, 39, 95, 115, 124–125, 150, 210, 218, 220, 251
Iguanodon, 37–38, 39, 40, 51, 161, 167–169, 219
iguanodontids, 77, 78, 80, 81, 223, 232
Induan Stage, 135, 136
Inoceramus, 184

J

Jurassic Period, 23, 24, 25, 26, 27, 28, 31, 32, 42, 63, 64, 66, 72, 73, 76, 88, 89, 90, 91, 93, 95, 103, 115, 116, 117, 121, 124, 125, 129, 134, 139, 140, 208, 209, 210, 212, 219, 220, 241, 250, 257, 262, 265, 274
  climate, 144–145
  geography, 141–144
  geology, 188–204
  invertebrates, 148–150, 151, 182–184, 187
  marine life, 146–151, 182–184, 185–187
  plants, 154–155
  vertebrates, 150–154, 155–182, 183, 184–187

K

Kentrosaurus, 89, 90–91
Kimmeridgian Stage, 196, 201, 202–203, 205
K–T boundary event, 95–99, 274
Kunlun Mountains, 28

L

Ladinian Stage, 135, 136–137
Lagerpeton, 44
Lagosuchus, 44, 116
Lambeosaurus, 81, 222, 233–234
Lance Creek Formation, 42–43, 271, 273
Laosaurus, 42
Laurasia, 24, 27, 28, 104, 105, 134, 141, 142, 209–210, 211
Leidy, Joseph, 40, 41
Leptolepis, 126
Lesothosaurus, 76
Lewis and Clark, 37
Lewisuchus, 44

M

Maastrichtian Stage, 216, 256, 262, 263, 270–271
Maiasaura, 53, 222, 234–235
maniraptorans, 75–76
Mantell, Gideon, 37–38, 168
Marasuchus, 126–127
Marsh, O.C., 42–43, 100, 233
marsupials, 32, 185, 219, 250, 273
Massospondylus, 38, 64
Megalosaurus, 37, 39, 40, 70, 72, 168
Mesozoic Marine Revolution, 31
metabolism in dinosaurs, 56, 57–60
Microraptor, 69, 230
Monoclonius, 43
Monopleura, 251
Moody, Pliny, 37
Morrison Formation, 42, 89, 140, 189, 191, 205–206
mosasaurs, 95, 210, 220, 251–252
multituberculates, 184–185

Muschelkalk Sea, 25, 115
Myophoria, 127

N

Niobrara Limestone, 269, 270, 271, 273–274
Nodosaurus, 91, 230, 235–236
Norian Stage, 135, 137–138, 139
Nothosaurus, 127–128

O

Olenekian Stage, 135–136
Omosaurus, 39
ophiolite sequences, 29
ornithischians, 40, 45, 60, 61, 62, 71, 76–93, 116, 152, 153, 156, 170, 171, 181, 224
ornithomimids, 74–75, 180–181
Ornitholestes, 70, 169
Ornithomimus, 236–237
ornithopods, 39, 49, 50, 52, 76, 77–82, 85, 93, 94, 153, 162, 181, 232, 241, 272
Ornithoscelida, 39
orogeny, 25, 26, 27–28, 134, 140, 141, 142, 189, 191–192, 257, 259, 262
Oviraptor, 53, 86, 99, 236–238, 241
oviraptorids, 75
Owen, Richard, 34, 36, 38, 39, 67
Oxfordian Stage, 196, 200, 201–202, 205

P

pachycephalosaurs, 76–77, 82–83, 94, 181, 182, 272
Pachycephalosaurus, 82, 181, 238
Pachyrhinosaurus, 21, 238–239
Palaeosaurus, 38
Palaeoscincus, 40, 91
paleontology, history of, 34–43, 45–46, 103–104
Paleozoic Era, 23, 24, 27, 30, 109, 115, 155, 216
Pamirs, 27
Pangea, 24, 26, 27, 28, 47, 48, 102, 104, 105, 106, 107, 133, 140, 141, 142, 144, 188, 274
Panthalassa, 104, 105, 106, 107–108
Parasaurolophus, 81
Pentaceratops, 21, 239–240
Permian extinction, 30, 102, 109, 110–111, 115, 274
phytosaurs, 128
Pisanosaurus, 76
placental mammals, 32, 185, 217, 219, 248, 250
Plateosaurus, 38, 64, 116, 120–121
plesiosaurs, 34, 39, 95, 127, 210, 218, 220, 251, 252–253
Plesiosaurus, 252
Pleuromeia, 128–129
Pliensbachian Stage, 196, 197, 198
pliosaurs, 185, 252
prosauropods, 52, 63–65, 93, 120, 121
Protoceratops, 46, 50, 53, 75, 83, 85–86, 230, 237, 240–241
protoceratopsids, 76, 84, 85, 87
Pseudolagosuchus, 44
psittacosaurids, 85
Psittacosaurus, 83, 85, 87, 240, 241
Pteranodon, 253–254
pterodactyloids, 131, 169–170
pterosaurs, 95, 129–131, 141, 152, 210, 219–220, 253, 254

Purbeck Beds, 206–207
pycnodontiformes, 186–187

Q

Quetzalcoatlus, 170, 219–220

R

reproduction in dinosaurs, 53–55
Rhaetian Stage, 135, 138–139, 196
Rhamphorhynchus, 130, 170
Ricqlès, Armand de, 52, 53
Rocky Mountains, 25, 54, 141, 142–143, 257, 274

S

Santonian Stage, 256, 260, 262, 263, 269–270
saurischians, 39, 40, 45, 60, 61, 62, 63–76, 116, 120, 152, 153
Sauropodomorpha, 62, 63, 71
sauropods, 40, 49, 50, 52, 53, 59, 63, 64, 65–68, 69, 90, 93, 94, 121, 152, 157, 159, 160, 166, 177
Scaphites, 254
Scelidosaurus, 38–39, 88, 173
Scutellosaurus, 88, 170–172, 173
Seeley, H.G., 39, 60
Seismosaurus, 50, 65, 153
shales, 28
Sierra Nevada range, 25, 143, 192, 205, 255, 257, 259
siliciclastic rocks, 28
Sinemurian Stage, 196–197
Sinosauropteryx, 163
Smith, Nathan, 37
Solnhofen Limestone Formation, 140, 158, 207–208
Spalacotherium, 182, 187
Spinosaurus, 241–243
Stegoceras, 82
stegosaurs, 50, 88, 89–91, 93, 94, 224
Stegosaurus, 42, 89, 90, 91, 153, 155, 172–173
Steneosaurus, 174
Sternberg, Charles H., 43
Struthiomimus, 70, 74, 75, 243
Suess, Eduard, 27

T

Tenontosaurus, 51
Tetanurae, 72–76, 86
Tethys Sea, 27–29, 105, 108, 134, 142, 144, 145, 192–193, 210, 212, 213–214, 217, 259, 260, 261
Tetractinella, 131–132
thecodonts, 30, 115, 116
therapsids, 30, 115, 122, 132
therizinosaurids, 75, 99, 243–244
theropods, 62, 63, 68–76, 78, 79, 86, 93, 94, 99, 119, 120, 152, 153, 156, 158, 162, 163, 164, 176, 180, 225, 226, 227, 228, 229, 236, 237, 241, 242, 243, 244
Thrinaxodon, 132
thyreophors, 88–89
Tithonian Stage, 196, 202, 203–204, 205, 206, 207, 265
Toarcian Stage, 196, 197, 198
Torosaurus, 43, 84, 85, 86

Triassic Period, 23, 24, 25, 26, 30, 34, 35–36, 44, 48, 52, 63–64, 66, 69, 76, 78, 93, 95, 102–139, 140, 190, 191, 196, 252, 272, 274
climate, 106–109
geography, 104–106
geology, 133–139
invertebrates, 112–114, 123, 127, 131–132, 133
marine life, 18, 122, 123, 124–126, 127–128, 131–132, 133
plants, 117–118, 128–129, 133
vertebrates, 114–117, 118–122, 123–128, 129–131, 132
Triceratops, 43, 45, 46, 49, 83–85, 210, 219, 238, 240, 244–245, 262, 273
Triconodon, 182, 187
Trigonia, 187
trilobites, 111
Tritylodon, 132–133
Troodon, 99
troodontids, 41, 71, 227, 229, 230
Tropites, 133
turbidites, 28
Turonian Stage, 263, 268–269
Turritellids, 254–255
tyrannosaurs, 69, 70, 71, 73, 74, 83, 174–181, 223, 227, 228, 229, 272
Tyrannosaurus rex, 51, 83, 151, 174–175, 176–179, 180, 219, 222, 227, 229, 242, 272, 273

V

Valanginian Stage, 263, 265, 266
Velociraptor, 50, 59, 76, 99, 222, 227, 230, 245–246
Voltzia, 133

Y

Yinlong, 181–182